# CLEOPATRA

## AND THE
## UNDOING OF
## HOLLYWOOD

# CLEOPATRA

## AND THE
## UNDOING OF
## HOLLYWOOD

## HOW ONE FILM ALMOST
## SUNK THE STUDIOS

### PATRICK HUMPHRIES

The
History
Press

**Jacket illustrations**
*Front:* Richard Burton and Elizabeth Taylor in *Cleopatra* (20th Century Fox/Alamy)
*Back & Embellishments:* Houston, M.G. and Hornblower, F.S., *Ancient Egyptian,
Assyrian, and Persian Costumes and Decorations*, London: A.&C. Black, 1920.

All internal images from the collection of Andrew Batt.

First published 2023

The History Press
97 St George's Place, Cheltenham,
Gloucestershire, GL50 3QB
www.thehistorypress.co.uk

British Library Cataloguing in Publication Data.
A catalogue record for this book is available from the British Library.

ISBN 978 1 80399 018 7

Typesetting and origination by The History Press
Printed and bound in Great Britain by TJ Books Limited, Padstow, Cornwall.

Trees for Life

# Contents

Introduction    7

1  'Place called Hollywood ...'    23
2  National Velvet    32
3  Elizabeth's Place in the Sun    38
4  Queens of the Nile    52
5  Rain Stops Play    60
6  'No Liz, No Cleo!'    65
7  The Three Lives of Richard Burton    75
8  The Once and Future King    87
9  Pandora's Box Opens    92
10  *Le Scandale*    103
11  The Burtons    117
12  'Fasten Your Seat Belts'    127
13  *La Dolce Vita*    137
14  'Czar of All the Rushes'    142
15  'The Cost is Staggering'    152
16  Rex Harrison, Rake's Progress    157
17  Caesar Reigns    165
18  The Times, They Are A-Changin'    180
19  'You Must Know Something I Don't'    186
20  Finally, The World is Ready    197

21 'Infamy, infamy ...'                          206
22 'I Should Have Known Better'                  212

Afterword: *The V.I.P.s*                         222
Bibliography                                     230
Acknowledgements                                 233
Index                                            235

# Introduction

That weekday evening in 1964 was much like any other in suburban south-east London for a boy on the edge of his teenage years. Following my mum's well intentioned, but calorically catastrophic high tea, homework had to be tackled: incomprehensible Latin, bewildering geography, baffling physics, hopeless French translation. Whole exercise books had to be filled, by hand, with the Christmas present Parker fountain pen regularly refilled. Impenetrable maths had to be tackled without the benefit of a calculator. The Repeal of the Corn Laws to be done by recall and research with no access to the yet-to-be-invented Internet.

On the whole, I would really rather have been watching one of the two television channels, even if they were scratchy black and white. Or listening to the pop music which had infused the British Isles with a ubiquitous passion. School exercise books which, the year before, had been covered with doodles of Second World War Tiger tanks and Spitfires, were now replaced with painstakingly drawn electric guitars and drum kits. Boys' hair was tantalisingly creeping over the collar. Would Santa bring a pair of those fabulous Beatle boots? Or perhaps one of their 32s 6d long players? Or even – unimaginably – a ticket to see them perform in nearby Lewisham or Croydon?

I knew that somewhere out there, bobbing on the North Sea, the pirate radio station Radio Caroline was playing the pop music that the

BBC Light Programme wouldn't let you hear. At night in bed, with my homework at best half done, by pressing my ear to the crackle of my birthday transistor, I could pick up the coming-and-going tunes. They came from far, far away, on the white-wave, pirate-ship, static-bobbing distance. Listening to pirate radio was the nearest a public schoolboy got to danger during 1964.

I was an only child. It was just me and my mum and dad. So, it was a welcome distraction when my Uncle Leslie chose to drop in. He wasn't really my uncle but actually a close family friend. Leslie often stopped at the pub, then came to us for a chat and a drink on his way home from work. That would be the drink he had before driving off and popping into the pub for a drink. The drink tended to make him absent-minded. But never enough to make him forget having a cigarette. He smoked a lot; everybody did then.

Leslie passed the time of day with us – the events at the office; the problems he was having with his racy, new sports car; the price of cigarettes, the foul perversion of the new Labour government. It's funny to think that he was demonstrably younger than I am as I write this. Adults seemed so much more adult, more grown up then.

Mind you, my father and Leslie were old school friends. They had served their king and country in the RAF. They had seen friends and relatives killed and they lost their youth to that conflict. They had survived a world war; that entitled them, then in their mid-forties, to smoke. And to drink – a lot.

Then Leslie dropped his bombshell. He had just popped into the Grove Tavern for a quick drink, prior to his arrival to dropping in to *us* for a quick drink. (There was no breathalyser to interrupt this sort of social drinking then.) Anyway, that actress was there, Leslie informed us, in his absent-minded, cigarette-waving, 'don't-mind-if-I-do-old-boy, oh-one-for-the-road' way.

'Actress? What actress?' asked my mother, moderately curious. This was long before the current obsession with celebrity. But it was a time when stars, *real* stars, held a vivid sway over the general public. Actors and actresses were personalities, larger-than-life figures who you never saw off screen and who rarely ventured from their Mayfair mansions or

Hollywood villas. No camera phone interrupted their remote unattainability. They would never have come south of the river, and certainly never patronised pubs near us in Dulwich.

'That actress,' said Leslie. 'You know …'

A top-up distracted him further. The usual 'just a quick one then' routine that owed more to the Drones Club than 1960s discotheques. My father poured his usual mahogany dark whisky for his old school friend, while chiding him gently about his meanness. Cigarettes were matched, held in fingers as mahogany-stained as the whisky they swigged like the water that rarely troubled it. As the fags flared, they both settled down for their usual strident denunciation of the latest perniciousness of Harold Wilson's Labour administration.

'But *which* actress?' my mother persisted. She would have had a smouldering Nelson on the go. I think she was knitting, the sort of activity which allowed her to keep busy in a wifely way but also keep a keen ear open.

'That one they're always writing about,' Leslie conceded vaguely.

Was it someone from *Coronation Street*? she wondered.

Leslie didn't know, he rarely watched the television.

Was she a film actress?

Leslie was pretty certain on this point that she was. But when pushed, could not bring to mind any of the films in which she had appeared. It had, after all, been some time since Leslie had actually been to the cinema. That Jean Kent, now *she* was a cracker … And didn't Joan Greenwood have a marvellously sexy voice? And didn't Ida Lupino come from Herne Hill?

This led to further they-don't-make-'em-like-that-anymore ruminations on film stars; names I had never heard of. And films that had once been screened at the crumbling old flea pit down the road in Herne Hill, which is long gone now. Funny, stilted, jerky black-and-white silent films. Not like the glorious, strictly reserved for school holiday treats in Technicolor and Cinerama such as *The Alamo*, *The Great Escape*, *The Fall of the Roman Empire* and *Zulu* that I loved.

Mum resumed her knitting, helping herself to another gin from the Bentley-green Gordon's bottle and probably treating herself to another

Nelson while the men puffed at their Senior Service. Matches flared, glasses were topped. Then Leslie remembered. She had that chap with her. He was an actor as well. They were always writing about him too. While he naturally could not remember the chap's name, Leslie's confidence grew when he remembered that he was not only an actor, but that he was … *Welsh*!

'Welsh?' my mother's interest was definitely piqued now.

'Yes,' Leslie confirmed. 'They're always together in the papers.'

Alarm bells were now ringing in our household.

'Elizabeth Taylor!' announced Leslie emphatically. That's who she was. 'Elizabeth Taylor!'

The ash was still on his cigarette by the time my mother had hauled my father out of the house and into his beloved blue Jaguar Mk 2. A terse instruction ordered him to drive to the Grove Tavern. In a time before trattoria, bistros or Harvesters, the Grove was where we dined as a family to commemorate big occasions: wedding anniversaries, birthdays, my getting into Dulwich College, my first report from Dulwich College at Christmas 1963 (bottom of the class, just out of academic interest).

Of course, by the time my parents got there, like the elusive myth she was, Elizabeth Taylor – and 'the Welsh chap' – had gone. My mother's frustration was evident. They stayed for a drink but had missed the moment.

They *had* been there. Leslie had not been wrong. It was not a dream. The *South London Press* reported it prominently the next day. In its picture, Taylor is giving the photographer the snake eye, while Burton was plainly in high spirits (the paper reported they had already popped into Camberwell's Fox On The Hill). This was south London *news*. The most famous woman in the world, on a local pub crawl.

I never did find out quite what drew Elizabeth Taylor to the Grove that evening for that drink. It was probably the fact that Richard Burton could barely pass a pub without popping in for a top-up. She did claim, 'Even at the height of our notoriety, we could go into an ordinary pub in London and nobody looked around, except maybe to say, "Hello luv" – and that's very precious to us.'

What I do remember is the galvanising effect the news had on my mother. For all of her life, Elizabeth Taylor had been front-page news, her every marriage, indiscretion and illness as well documented as the assassination in Dallas, not long before.

Like most of the Western world, my mum had been mesmerised by Elizabeth Taylor. The very thought that this unattainable screen goddess had been quaffing at the pub we used to go to as a family to commemorate big occasions was unimaginable – literally unimaginable – inconceivable – my mum simply could not conceive of the glamorous, glorious Elizabeth Taylor sitting perhaps where she had once sat.

Elizabeth Taylor was beyond famous. She had transcended mere film stardom; she glowed in her own inimitable firmament. Elizabeth Taylor was not simply a legend; she was the personification of fame, sexual allure, legend, myth. She had been famous since she was 12 years old. By 1964, then only 32, Elizabeth Taylor had gone stratospheric. And for all the scandal, illness and tragedy, that notoriety was all down to one film.

☥

*Cleopatra* remains, quite simply, one of the most fabled films of all time. While others have won more Oscars, attracted better reviews and taken more money at the box office, the 1963 Elizabeth Taylor film stands alone in cinema legend.

It began life in 1958 as a vehicle for studio contract player Joan Collins. In his search for a guaranteed box office hit, following a suggestion from producer Walter Wanger, Twentieth Century Fox president Spyros Skouras found a script in their vaults of a 1917 silent version of *Cleopatra* and remarked, 'All this needs is a little rewriting.' The film was awarded a modest $2 million budget, and a sixty-four-day shoot was scheduled. When *Cleopatra* eventually opened in 1963 – nearly three years after the project was green-lighted – it ended up costing more than twenty times the amount originally envisaged.

This is a story of superlatives. Taylor was the first star to demand – and get – a million-dollar fee. The lavish extravagance of *Cleopatra*, spread over its turbulent five-year history, has entered movie history legend. That single production saw venomous boardrooms battles rage; it all but bankrupted Twentieth Century Fox, and in doing so, *Cleopatra* almost singlehandedly set in motion the decline of the Hollywood studio system. The film drew a line in the sand – before *Cleopatra*, the Hollywood studios, by and large, pulled the strings. Post-*Cleo*, the independent mavericks inveigled their way into the studio system. They proved that films could turn a profit on what one scene of *Cleopatra* had cost. They could produce successful films for what Twentieth Century Fox spent on Elizabeth Taylor's hairstyles.

It was during the making of *Cleopatra* that Taylor fell in love with her co-star, Richard Burton, and the ensuing romance on location in Italy virtually invented the concept of celebrity journalism as the world's best-known lovers fled from the paparazzi. There had been infamous liaisons beforehand, but Taylor's reputation as a proven husband rustler was at its height. The media portrayed her as a siren, who had only recently snatched husband number four – crooner Eddie Fisher – from the arms of his wife, the saintly Debbie Reynolds.

Burton, meanwhile, had blitzkrieged the London theatre scene during the 1950s, then took the thirty pieces of silver Hollywood offered and became a film actor. Running parallel was his reputation as a hellraiser. However, it was the white-hot fusion with Taylor in *Cleopatra* which turned Burton into a film star.

The rumours percolated, the denials flourished, the great game of illicit romance was played out in Rome, by then already notorious as the city that represented *la dolce vita*, 'the good life'. The moment that first photograph of them kissing was published, Taylor and Burton became the most famous and in-demand couple in the world.

With Joan Collins dumped and a new cast and director in place, after a desultory spell shooting in rainswept England, filming on *Cleopatra* finally began on 28 September 1960, nearly two years after the film was first slated. From the beginning, Twentieth Century Fox were convinced they could exceed the 'sword and sandal' success of MGM's 1959 *Ben-Hur*. Sure, they had a chariot race, but *Cleopatra* had a big barge, and onboard was the voluptuous Taylor, surely a bigger enticement than even the muscular Charlton Heston?

The ancient Egyptian capital of Alexandria had been reconstructed on a 20-acre site at Pinewood Studios, but from early on, *Cleopatra* was doomed. Even the weather was against the production, and eventually the Pinewood sets were torn down as the rain continued to pour. The costly decision was made and filming switched to Italy. After the sets had been expensively rebuilt in Rome, the beleaguered production recommenced in 1961, with a new director, Joseph L. Mankiewicz, now at the helm. The original male leads (Stephen Boyd and Peter Finch) were also replaced by Richard Burton and Rex Harrison.

Once in Rome, the newly christened paparazzi clustered like bees around the honeypot of the besotted Burton and Taylor. Respective wives and husbands seethed from the side-lines, while thousands of miles away, as the Telexes buzzed, each with tales of greater extravagance, Hollywood executives were tearing their hair out at the spiralling budget.

The making of *Cleopatra* was a titanic struggle from the very beginning: original director Rouben Mamoulian was replaced after four months of filming and a finished script proved as elusive as a sunny day in Buckinghamshire. All the while, Taylor's recurring illnesses saw production grind to a halt again and again – at one point the star was officially pronounced dead.

In desperation, in February 1961, Lloyd's of London were contacted and the venerable London insurance firm agreed to carry on insuring the troubled production. Incredible as it seems, the one name that would guarantee the production of *Cleopatra* to proceed was Marilyn Monroe. So successful was the blanket of secrecy over Marilyn that, had Lloyd's known of her paranoia, insecurities and reliance on prescribed medication, they would never have suggested her. It surely would have added innumerable zeroes to the ballooning *Cleopatra* budget had Marilyn acceded.

Following the turbulence of 1960's *The Misfits*, even the lightweight comedy, the unfinished *Something's Got to Give*, caused Fox executives further headaches. Marilyn was eventually sacked by the studio. It beggars belief to even imagine the troubled Monroe at the centre of the turmoil that swathed *Cleopatra*.

If not Marilyn, Lloyd's intriguingly revealed they would accept three other actresses for the title role: Kim Novak, Shirley MacLaine and

Rossanna Podesta. Novak was an established star in the Monroe mould; MacLaine was on the way up, following an Oscar-nominated performance in *The Apartment*, while Podesta was an unknown quantity to audiences outside Italy. In the end, it was a given. The film's producer Walter Wanger emphasised in telegramese, 'No Liz, no *Cleo*'.

While filming was underway at Pinewood, there was even a trade union battle over the star's choice of hairdresser. The British unions wanted their members to fashion the star's hair; she insisted on her own personal hairdresser. By the time the production ground to a soggy halt in England, only a meagre eight minutes of film would ever make it to the finished film. Those precious 480 seconds came at a cost of $6.45 million. Even by Hollywood standards, such extravagance was unheralded and unacceptable.

This was crunch time: would Twentieth Century Fox persevere with the already troubled production in the UK and pray that Taylor's health would hold? Or would the studio bite the bullet and pull the plug, thereby saving what would no doubt prove to be further prohibitive costs?

Who would put their head above the parapet and take responsibility for the catastrophe? Somewhere along the line the decision was taken. Nobody could sanction the loss of nearly $7 million with nothing to show for it. So, in its wisdom, the studio crossed its collective fingers and decided to proceed with the production.

Rather eerily, while writing this, I read of a similar predicament. In August 2022, David Zaslav, CEO of Warner Bros decided, following 'disastrous test screenings', to pull the plug on *Batgirl*. It was felt that the $90 million already spent would have been doubled if the film were released globally, so the decision was taken to write it off completely and bin the finished film.

For Twentieth Century Fox, over half a century before, writing off a seven-figure sum was chastening, but eventually approved. A move from rainy Buckinghamshire would help the beleaguered production, so the location switched to Rome. With Taylor returned to good health and relocated to the sunnier climes of Italy, what else could possibly go wrong?

It was when Burton arrived on set that further fuel was added to the fire. The actor had first set foot in Rome in September 1961 – and then, typically, had to wait for four solid months before he delivered a single line.

However, on 22 January 1962, when the first scene between Marc Antony and Cleopatra was filmed, the electricity was unmistakable. Ironically, Elizabeth Taylor's last day of filming was 23 June 1962 – and her final scene? The day Cleopatra first met Marc Antony!

For all the health issues, vanity and ego, as she approached 30, Elizabeth Taylor had never looked more glamorous. As Cleopatra, she was at her most seductive, ideally placed to play history's most desirable woman. As Marc Antony, Burton exuded rugged charisma. That first day when he arrived on set, an onlooker found him 'handsome, arrogant and vigorous'. Almost immediately, it became apparent that the love scenes between Burton and Taylor were more than simply well acted.

Within days of their first scene together, the director was informing the producer that 'Liz and Burton are not just *playing* Antony and Cleopatra'. Before long, the whole world knew of '*le scandale*'. From backstreet gossip in Warrington to presidential mansions in Washington, the world was intrigued. For example, on arrival at the White House as the story broke, PR executive Warren Cowan was buttonholed by the wife of the president, Jacqueline Kennedy, the second best-known woman in the Western world, who breathlessly inquired, 'Warren, do you think Elizabeth Taylor will marry Richard Burton?'

By April 1962, the *Los Angeles Times* confirmed, 'Probably no news event in modern times has affected so many people personally. Nuclear testing, disarmament, Berlin, Vietnam and the struggle between Russia and China are nothing comparable to the Elizabeth Taylor story.'

Burton and Taylor were front-page news everywhere – the world was spellbound, their affair trumping the Eichmann trial, America's first man in space, the Cuban missile crisis, and the Telstar satellite linking the US and UK. Such was the scandal that the couple were publicly denounced by the Vatican. Neither cared, they plunged headlong into the affair. Burton was spellbound by the intoxicating Taylor and left his wife, Sybil. Taylor was captivated and lost little time in ditching her husband.

It was not the sexual shenanigans for which the film is remembered today, however. Even by Hollywood's lavish standards, the scale of extravagance on *Cleopatra* was mind-boggling. It was not just Taylor's record-breaking million-dollar salary. She travelled to Italy accompanied by personal secretaries, doctors, cooks, hairdressers and her very own maître d', and later, when she moved her base in Rome, she took 156 suitcases with her. Food was flown in from her favourite deli – in New York.

The supporting cast were equally coddled in their Roman exile. Richard O'Sullivan, playing the boy king Ptolemy, was scheduled for a six-week shoot; he waited twelve weeks on full salary (flying back to London every weekend to watch Chelsea FC play) until he appeared in his first scene.

George Cole's role as the deaf-mute slave Flavius was originally scheduled for fourteen weeks but he ended up staying in Rome for eighteen months. Years later, Cole remained awestruck by the scale and spectacle of the production, but felt confined, 'We were already barred from leaving the [set] and now we called it "house arrest". I had no lines to learn, which was hardly surprising as I was a deaf mute, and no matter how beautiful Rome undoubtedly is, you can get bored very quickly there.'

Actor Carroll O'Connor estimated that his original fifteen-week contract stretched to ten months – during which time he actually worked on just seventeen days. Veteran Hume Cronyn recalled in a *Vanity Fair* feature that he arrived on set the same day as Burton, 19 September 1961, yet neither one of us worked until after Christmas'.

The truly epic scale of *Cleopatra*'s profligacy can be seen if you compare the production with that of *Ben-Hur*, the Charlton Heston Oscar winner which, four years earlier, had been filmed in Rome at the same studio as *Cleopatra*. *Ben-Hur* went on to become the most lauded film in Academy Award history, garnering a record eleven Oscars in 1959. But, despite the film's unforgettable chariot race, costly naval battles and spectacular sets, director William Wyler still managed to bring *Ben-Hur* in at a manageable $15 million – barely a third of the final cost of *Cleopatra*.

Poor Joseph L. Mankiewicz, who replaced the original director, found himself directing during the day then attempting to fashion a screenplay by night. He was buoyed by drugs to fuel him during daylight hours, then more drugs to make him sleep. No wonder he had been heard bemoaning on the Italian set, 'I'm not biting my fingernails, I'm biting my knuckles. I finished the fingernails months ago.' Immediately prior to the film's opening, journalists watched as the director donned white cotton gloves to stop him 'clawing at his cuticles'.

When *Cleopatra* finally did open in the summer of 1963, everything was resting on the film's success. Not just Twentieth Century Fox, the studio which financed the film, but the whole of Hollywood held its breath to see if the off-screen magic could be transferred into box office receipts.

*Cleopatra* received nine Oscar nominations, but the on-screen talent and screenplay were ignored. Due to a technical error, Roddy McDowall was denied a Best Supporting Actor nomination, for which the studio had to publicly apologise. The film triumphed only in the less glamorous technical categories: Art Direction, Costume Design, Special Effects, and Cinematography. *Cleopatra*'s director of photography, Leon Shamroy, was also nominated for his work on Otto Preminger's lengthy *The Cardinal* – which led presenter James Stewart to comment, 'Gee, that's five years out of a man's life right there.' Even Shamroy appeared baffled when accepting his *Cleopatra* award, whispering to the star, 'Which one did I win for?'

*Cleopatra* all but finished Joseph L. Mankiewicz's career as a director. He remembered it in *My Life With Cleopatra* as 'the toughest *three* pictures I ever made ... it was conceived in a state of emergency, shot in confusion and wound up in a blind panic.' He had always envisaged his epic as two separate films, one telling the story of Caesar and Cleopatra, the other that of Cleopatra and Marc Antony. He never lived to see his imagined two-part epic released but wound up a victim of a turbo-powered romance, studio chicanery and, unwittingly, the changing times.

Film making is always a battle. Revered set designer Richard Sylbert told Julie Salamon, in her spellbinding account of the making of another box-office flop, *The Devil's Candy: The Bonfire of the Vanities Goes* to *Hollywood* (1992), 'A movie is a war … The war is between the people with the ideas, and the people with the money. The crazies versus the bean counters.'*

The studio, Twentieth Century Fox, could only stand by in far-away Hollywood and watch in horror as, in Italy, *Cleopatra*'s budget spiralled and money was haemorrhaged. By the time *Cleopatra* finally premiered on 12 June 1963 – five years after it was first mooted – the film had cost a staggering $44 million.

Despite going on to become the highest-grossing film of 1963, the film's cinema receipts came nowhere near to matching its vast production costs. *Cleopatra* was in danger of withering and dying at the box office. And it very nearly took the studio with it.

In the end, Twentieth Century Fox was only saved two years later – by a modest little musical which unexpectedly broke all records. *The Sound of Music* was a Rodgers & Hammerstein musical which had already proved itself a hit on the stage, but no one was prepared for the sheer scale of its cinematic success. With the sixties already in full swing, the wholesome Julie Andrews vehicle (which came in at a modest $8 million) amazed everyone by becoming the most successful film release since *Gone with the Wind*, a quarter of a century before!

Financially, the success of *The Sound of Music* saved Twentieth Century Fox. But the terrible folly of *Cleopatra* could not be erased. It remained an embarrassment, a beached whale of a film that continued to haunt the studio, resulting in hirings and firings and vicious boardroom battles. It filleted the studio, with Fox having to sell off its backlot to try and recoup costs.

Ensuing years have seen other films fail on a grand scale – *Mutiny on the Bounty, Heaven's Gate, Waterworld, Ishtar,* the 2004 remake of *The Alamo, Cats* – the list goes on and on. All the executives felt, like Marty Bauer, director Brian De Palma's agent, who commented on seeing the previews for the mega-flop *Bonfire of the Vanities*, 'Maybe they're

---

* It's funny how the best books about film are always about the worst movies. See also Stephen Bach's chronicle of the catastrophic *Heaven's Gate – Final Cut: Art, Money and Ego in the Making of Heaven's Gate* (1999).

not going to execute us. Maybe there's a light at the end of the tunnel. We've been sitting in that chair and somebody's called the governor. The phone is ringing. Maybe we'll get a reprieve.'

He never got that call; the film was vilified. Somehow, the public can smell a stinker. Based on a much-loved global musical success and a cast which included Idris Elba and Taylor Swift, 2019's *Cats* lowered the bar. Even now, though, more than half a century on, it is *Cleopatra* that remains synonymous with eye-watering budgets, reckless extravagance and unparalleled cinematic excess.

And after all that, it really isn't a terribly good film; even its pivotal star appreciated that. After viewing the finished film for the first time, Elizabeth Taylor exited the cinema, repaired to her hotel suite and vomited.

The full story of the making of *Cleopatra* has all the ingredients for a truly compelling film itself. It is an epic tale of love and lust, gossip, money and sex; of hubris and movie-star madness, studio politics and paparazzi journalism. Within the saga of *Cleopatra* lies the end of an era and the making of a legend. That one film effectively ended half a century of Hollywood's studio system. In it lie the seeds of the Swinging Sixties, and the stuff of timeless movie legend.

☥

Elizabeth Taylor was synonymous with Cleopatra. She had been famous before and she would continue to be famous after its release. But *Cleopatra* was what enshrined her in the public eye as a voluptuous, immoral idol. For her co-star, *Cleopatra* elevated Richard Burton from a respected stage actor into a film celebrity. But more than the sum of its parts, *Cleopatra* is still one of the most expensive films ever made.

By the time *Cleopatra* finally opened to the paying public in June 1963, it had cost $44 million to bring it to the screen.* Today's

---

\* With a running time approaching four hours, it was almost certainly one of the longest commercial films ever released. One estimate had each cinema print weighing in at a hefty 600lb – the press pack alone weighed 10lb. The original release also entered the record books as the longest commercially made American film released in America.

money has that estimated at a staggering $400 million. Even today, Cleopatra makes *Avatar* look like a home movie. Allowing for inflation, it is difficult to adjust production costs. In real terms, the cost easily eclipses that of every other film (including *Titanic* and *The Lord of the Rings*). By 2023, at $533 million, *Stars Wars: The Force Awakens* had eclipsed *Cleopatra*.

I never liked the film. Few people did. Following a successful first year, when '*le scandale*' had died down and the Burtons married, the audience for *Cleopatra* drifted away. Epic predecessors, such as *Lawrence of Arabia*, *The Longest Day*, *How the West was Won* and *El Cid*, had performed spectacularly well at the box office. Epics conveying the grandeur of the Roman Empire had also scored – *Ben-Hur*, *Spartacus* and *King of Kings* had all been substantial box-office successes immediately prior to the opening of *Cleopatra*. This was proof that people were prepared to pay for big screen, stereophonic, 65mm, bright, colourful cinema entertainment. Britain, after all, didn't get colour television until 1968, five years after *Cleopatra* opened.

However, once the word got out that the *real* story of *Cleopatra* was being written off screen, the damning reviews did not help, and audiences were not as committed as Fox had hoped. The initial box-office returns from Italy, France, Germany and even the Soviet Union were encouraging, but Fox still had some way to go before the film recovered its enormous production costs.

When the film was shown on television in 1966, the ABC network paid $5 million for the privilege – that helped. Film historian Sheldon Hall wrote in a magazine article, 'By 1966 worldwide rentals had reached $38,042,000, including $23,500,000 from the US. This was far short of original expectations (producer Walter Wanger had predicted a world gross of $100,000,000). The film ultimately went into profit not from its theatrical release but from a sale to television.'

'The accounting procedure for films is labyrinthine,' John French wrote in his compelling biography of the actor Robert Shaw:

From the money that comes into the cinema box office, the cinemas (exhibitors) take their cut, usually 30% and then hand the remaining

70% over to the distributors. This is then set against the enormous cost of prints … and advertising which is calculated to be 2.4 times the cost of actually making the film. Only when this huge sum of money has been recouped by the distributors do they pass anything on to the producers to set against the negative cost of the film (i.e., the cost of producing the negative). Only *after this* [my italics] cost is fully recouped does the film go into profit.

By that reckoning, *Cleopatra* had to take an eye-watering $105.6 million before it even broke even. Over the years, and with subsequent video, DVD and Blu-ray sales, *Cleopatra* did finally inch into profit, and at least managed to cover its enormous costs. Fox executive David Brown later wryly commented, 'It did go into profit, but the studio went missing.'

What *Cleopatra* could bring to UK cinema audiences at the time was something that they definitely couldn't get in costume dramas on either of their two black and white television channels: sex! What *Cleopatra* had going for it was its reputation. The Burton and Taylor affair remained front-page news; their infidelity was widely known. Endless snatched newspaper photos showed the couple canoodling. There had been shots from the set taken by Taylor's friend Roddy McDowall, which had appeared in *Playboy* – shots of the actress discreetly draped and one nipple voluptuously appearing behind a gossamer thin gown.

Without their actually venturing such an opinion, it was this sexually charged element which, the studio hoped, was what would differentiate *Cleopatra* from such respectful and reverential costume epics as *Ben-Hur* or *King of Kings*. Sexual liberation in the cinema lay in the future – 1969's *Midnight Cowboy* was the first X-rated film to win an Oscar. While embarrassed at the unintended publicity the film had received during production, in the end, *Cleopatra* would need all the help it could get.

However undistinguished the finished film was, what ultimately makes *Cleopatra* so compelling is its legend. It was, after all, the film that all but bankrupted Hollywood. In film terms, *Cleopatra* was singlehandedly responsible for substantially undermining the studio system which had serviced the world well for over half a century.

In the near sixty years since its premiere, *Cleopatra* has come to represent the worst excesses of the film industry: this was a production running rampant, whose production stretched over half a decade, whose filming extended to over two entire years. It was a pre-fax, pre-email era; transatlantic telephone calls had to be booked in advance. Telegrams and telexes could only tell half the story. From its Los Angeles sanctuary, Fox watched as the film ran riot in faraway Italy, the budget spiralling daily out of control.

It was not only the capricious behaviour of its stars that prolonged production. The fact that the film was allowed to proceed without a finished script in a faraway country of which US executives knew little hiked up the costs. And while she was never keen to take the role, it had been a whim that dictated Elizabeth Taylor's million-dollar request. The fact that the studio had acceded raised the bar. Who was more foolish? Taylor for demanding her mega-bucks, or the studio for agreeing to pay her?

That fee cemented Elizabeth Taylor's stature as a star, with all the vivacious, luminous, incandescent presence that implies. There had been stars before. There had been films prior to *Cleopatra*. But in all the cynical, greedy, magical, histrionic history of the movies, there had never been a combination like that of Elizabeth Taylor and *Cleopatra*.

I suppose, in hindsight, over the years I have become fascinated by the impact the mere rumour of Elizabeth Taylor's presence had on my dear, late mother. The very prospect of such a screen goddess descending from her starry heaven to south-east London was so tantalising. Even then, aged 12, I knew she was more than a mere film star. I knew that Elizabeth Taylor was a legend. Today, that legend may have diminished. However, that night in 1964 was another story. And it was all due to the botched glory of that one film. But in a sense, for me, it was as much a personal quest to find out why it mattered so much to my mother, the night that *Cleopatra* came to town.

# 1

# 'Place called Hollywood ...'

From the shtetls and ghettoes of Eastern Europe they came. Hounded by Czarist pogroms, chased by the knout and harried by the lash, they fled. In their millions they came, from east to west. From beyond the pale to the land of the brave and the home of the free, they quit the old, splintered Europe for the new welcoming world, offering up the United States.

The immigrants were shepherded through Ellis Island. Like the wide-eyed exiles captured in *The Godfather, Part II*, the wary newcomers came in their untold millions. Fleeing in fear, all looking for a new beginning. Once ashore, a further shedding of their troubled past came in the almost random renaming. While the old world had long since ebbed over the horizon, the new world was wary of this influx. To compensate, they were given new identities. On arrival, they anglicised their birth names, names which were redolent of old Poland, medieval Hungary or Romanov Russia. All were now lost in a fresh branding.

Crammed into New York tenements, those 'poor huddled masses' clung together, fashioning fresh ghettoes – the close-knit Little Italy, the predominantly Jewish Lower East Side, the Russian Little Odessa. For entertainment, they had the music, the folk tales and shared memories of their birthplace. But as they gradually assimilated into their new world, a new form of entertainment was making its mark on the early twentieth century.

Moving pictures moved in noiseless splendour, the rapid black-and-white images reaching silently out in their simplicity to the immigrant audiences. No language was needed to watch the pictures move. No English was necessary to understand the on-screen emotion. The stories they told were simple and affecting.

These early moving pictures were not attempting anything aesthetic. There was no thought of 'art' in the flickering frames projected as a vaudeville interlude or circus novelty. Kinetoscopes, zoetropes, cinematographs, Nickelodeons – all had blazed bright, but brief, at the tail end of the nineteenth century and the dawn of the new millennium. Blink and you miss them – sixty-second shorts demonstrating the craft of the blacksmith, the arrival of a train, a horse-drawn cab in a Lyon square. This was the film fodder for those early audiences, happily spellbound by pictures that moved.

It was not until 1903 that what could be called the narrative film arrived with a bang. *The Great Train Robbery* told a story, albeit over only ten minutes, but it was a beginning. Still ensconced in penny arcades, moving pictures were a fairground diversion. But within a few years, film was growing out of its sideshow origins: the men who would become the moguls who came to dominate the studio system for the next half a century all cut their teeth in the cinema auditoria which sprang up in the years before the Great War.

By 1908, there were 8,000 Nickelodeons across the United States. The cinema experience of 1910 would be recognisable to audiences today: the buildings had the shape of a cinema, seats arranged in serried rows facing a screen onto which the spellbinding films were projected. A programme of short films, a main feature, advertisements and musical accompaniment was on offer.

A decade after *The Great Train Robbery*, a young director called Cecil B. DeMille was instructed to shoot another Western, *The Squaw Man*, on location in Flagstaff, Arizona. But persistent rain led DeMille to presciently cable, 'Flagstaff no good for our purpose. Have proceeded to California. Want authority to rent barn in place called Hollywood.'

Julie Salamon reflected:

Hollywood had always been seen as the land of opportunity. Its founding fathers were Jewish entrepreneurs, mostly immigrants, who saw in the movies a way to build fortunes in the new world where they could create the rules of respectability. Back east these rag peddlers from Eastern Europe would never be accepted either by the WASP establishment or by the German Jewish elite. Hollywood was, however, virgin turf for a new class system ... Having been excluded from the traditional corridors of power, the moguls built their own world and made themselves its rulers.

In the decade between 1910 and 1920, Hollywood's population rose from 5,000 to 36,000. Even then, such was the magnetism of the movies that the Hollywood Chamber of Commerce was warning newcomers to stay away. Full-page adverts ran, 'Don't Try To Break Into Movies In Hollywood [...] Out of 100,000 persons who started at the Bottom of the Screen's Ladder of Fame *only five reached the top*'. But even that statistic didn't halt the flood – maybe *they* could be one of the lucky five!

Flickering film trickled on, but it took the confidence of cinema's first genius, the auteur David Wark Griffith, to nudge the fledgling form towards art and further away from novelty. As the Great War ravaged Europe, and as America dithered about its involvement, Griffith's films, *The Birth of a Nation* (1915) and *Intolerance* (1916), projected spectacle quite unlike anything anyone had ever witnessed on a cinema screen before.

Hailed as the first film masterpiece, *The Birth of a Nation* makes for uncomfortable viewing to twenty-first-century audiences. In mitigation, the film was screened to veterans of the Civil War, which it depicted; those attitudes that had inspired the conflict were, therefore, within living memory. To audiences watching *The Birth of a Nation* when it opened, the Civil War was a lot nearer to them than the Second World War is to us today. However, it is embarrassing watching the pantomime African American slaves, who are patently white actors blacked up, as they threaten winsome Confederate belles. The Southern beauties come to be rescued by the unpalatable heroics of the Ku Klax Klan, whose actions Griffith glowingly celebrates. Worryingly, by celebrating that 'heroism', *The Birth of a Nation* unwittingly helped fuel a revival of interest in the racist Klan.

As cinema, to crowds in 1915, *The Birth of a Nation* was nothing short of a miracle. And even today, in it Griffith virtually invented the language of cinema – pioneering the technique of the cut, close-up, zoom, wipe, dissolve and the tracking shot. And all played out on an epic scale. Its awesome battle scenes, its thousands of extras, its panoramic sweep remain breath-taking to watch.

Today, in the wake of the 2020 issues that HBO found with its showings of *Gone with the Wind*, *The Birth of a Nation* is rarely seen, and it does make for uneasy viewing. However, with audiences properly alerted, even now, projected at the right speed, on a large screen with orchestral accompaniment, the audacity and scale of *The Birth of a Nation* is still capable of dazzling, as it did when first seen by President Woodrow Wilson, who described the epic, 'like history written by lightning'.

With the development of film, the locations for its appreciation became equally grand. By 1926, movie theatres were offering thousands of seats to accommodate the growing audiences. Early mogul Adolph Zukor traced the development: 'The Nickelodeon had to go, theatres replaced shooting galleries, temples replaced theatres and cathedrals replaced temples.'

The arrival of *The Birth of a Nation* came less than twenty years after the first moving picture had been screened in the United States to a paying audience. And with it came the confirmation of cinema as the popular art form of the early twentieth century. With the cinema established, in the decade of silence before talking pictures ushered in another new era came its stars. Paying audiences around the world came to recognise and adore such names as Mary Pickford, Douglas Fairbanks, Lillian Gish, Theda Bara, Fatty Arbuckle, John Barrymore, Rudolph Valentino, Clara Bow and Buster Keaton. All stars. All famous. All adored. Then there was Chaplin.

A teenage music hall knockabout in London, the son of an alcoholic father and mentally unstable mother and reared in Dickensian poverty bordered by the public house and the workhouse, Charlie Chaplin first appeared in his trademark tramp costume in 1914. By the end of the 'war to end wars', he was the most famous man in the world. For all his grace and talent, what makes Chaplin so enduring and fascinating is that he was a 'superstar' half a century before the word was coined. Chaplin's success and fame was on a level that had been unparalleled in human history.

There had, of course, been famous people before Chaplin – eminent scientists and respected politicians, explorers, monarchs, sportsmen, architects and authors – but Charlie's fame was on a scale that was unimaginable. Charles Dickens and Oscar Wilde had undertaken American lecture tours and readings before capacity houses, and eminent thespians such as David Garrick and Edmund Kean were acclaimed. In 1886, Sarah Bernhardt undertook a world tour. But relatively few people had actually *seen* them. It took a new type of technology to bring a new type of star to the world. Thanks to the ubiquity of the movies, everyone knew Charlie. From the moment he donned the tramp costume, Chaplin rocketed into a whole new galaxy.

Chaplin lived until the age of 88, verging on the immortal, but while he was in the ascendant, the star system suffered its first fatality. In 1926, barely out of his twenties, the brooding Rudolph Valentino died. The national outpouring of grief was only occasionally repeated, such as when James Dean, President Kennedy and Elvis Presley died. Film stardom ensured you immortality; Valentino's premature death reminded fans of their idols' mortality.

The stars, the names above the titles, were what drew the audiences. But even when their voices could not be heard, narratives and stories were necessary to keep the wheels of the Dream Factory turning. From early on, Hollywood ransacked the best writers, luring them from Broadway or away from the novels they should have been writing. Aldous Huxley, H.G. Wells and Somerset Maugham were only some of those who ventured west.

The money was the lure. The films they worked on impressed them less. As Spencer Tracy hurled himself into the sinister transformation from Dr Jekyll into the malevolent Mr Hyde, watching from off screen, a less-than-impressed Somerset Maugham inquired, 'Which one is he supposed to be now?'

Typical was the telegram from Herman J. Mankiewicz, the brother of the future director of *Cleopatra* and the co-author of *Citizen Kane*. 'Mank' wired fellow playwright Ben Hecht in New York from Hollywood in 1926, 'There are millions to be grabbed out here and your only competition is idiots. Stop. Don't let this get around.'

At the same time, mogul Samuel Goldwyn was sucking up all of the talent, from everywhere. He famously cabled the great(est) Russian director, Sergei Eisenstein, 'I have seen your film *Battleship Potemkin* and admired it very much indeed. What we should like you to do now would be something of the same kind, but rather cheaper, for Ronald Colman.'

Their chutzpah knew no bounds. Did David O. Selznick really try contacting the deposed Czar Nicholas II with an offer?:

When I was a boy in Russia your police treated my people very badly. However no hard feelings. Hear you are now out of work. If you come to New York can give you fine position acting in pictures. Salary no object. Reply my expense. Regards to you and family.

It was late in 1927 when the tectonic plates of the cinema industry shifted. Silence had been golden and the studios saw no reason why their stranglehold should be loosened. They had the stars and the stories; they had the studios and the climate. If people wanted to hear actors talk, they should go to a theatre.

The place of *The Jazz Singer* is cemented in cinema history as the first 'talking picture'. Initially dismissed as a novelty, the studios were overwhelmed by the public's demand for talkies. No more need for silent, smouldering action or captions to convey emotion. Soon audiences were expecting – *demanding* – talking pictures. As the star of *The Jazz Singer*, Al Jolson promised its awestruck audience from the screen at that premiere, 'You ain't heard nothin' yet'.

The Golden Age of Hollywood was undeniably the 1930s, when the stars were near-divinities, shielded from the public eye and only ever seen on screen, thus ensuring their mystique. Their every move was slavishly recorded in the burgeoning fan magazine market. With no television and only radio to keep you at home, the cinema was the focal point of social activity for a global audience of millions every week.

As the Wall Street Crash of 1929 led to the Great Depression of the 1930s, for many, the movies became their only escape. The Dream Factory poured out a succession of diverting vehicles, all populated by a new breed of screen star. Even today, the lustrous names linger on: Bette Davis, Clark Gable, Joan Crawford, Cary Grant, Jean Harlow, Gary Cooper, Katherine Hepburn, James Stewart, Mae West, Marlene Dietrich, Barbara Stanwyck, Errol Flynn, Greta Garbo.

Throughout the 1930s, Hollywood kept the world entranced, whether it was the scintillating terpsichorean symmetry of Fred Astaire and Ginger Rogers, or the 'eighth wonder of the world', *King Kong*. Perhaps it was the amiable anarchy of the Marx Brothers, or the animated fantasy of Disney's *Snow White* which drew you to the warm cinema. You could marvel at the chilling vision of a future posited in *Things to Come* or wallow in the good-natured optimism when *Mr Deeds Comes to Town*. There was the luminous Technicolor green of Sherwood Forest in the swashbuckling *Adventures of Robin Hood* or the claustrophobic tumble of John Ford's *Stagecoach*. You could stalk the Yorkshire Moors of *Wuthering Heights* or settle down for tea and crumpets in *Goodbye Mr Chips*. You could follow the Yellow Brick Road in *The Wizard of Oz*.

Then there was *Gone with the Wind*. By 1939, the Hollywood studios were making up to 400 movies a year, eagerly devoured by the 80 million Americans who attended the cinema every week. And every single one of them was looking forward to the most eagerly awaited motion picture of all time.

Margaret Mitchell had begun her only novel in the basement of her Atlanta apartment, which she called 'the dump'. It took ten years and an estimated fifty drafts to arrive at the finished 1,024 pages when it was first published in 1936. At one point, the finished manuscript of *Tote that Weary Load* (with its heroine 'Pansy O'Hara') was taller than its diminutive author.

On its release in 1939, *Gone with the Wind* was a sensation. As Hitler launched his Polish blitzkrieg in far-away Europe, American cinema audiences could lose themselves in a world of 'cavaliers and cotton fields'.

The film ran in London for four years during the Second World War. It remained the most successful film release of all time for over a quarter of a century. Even now, though, while its box office take may have been exceeded, it is estimated that *Gone with the Wind* has been seen by more people than any other film on the planet.

The premiere of *Gone with the Wind* was held in Atlanta, Georgia, the location of the fictional 'Tara', though every frame of this tribute to Confederate resistance was actually shot in Hollywood. The after-show party was segregated, but the studio thought that the all-white guests should be greeted by a choir of black children, so they contacted the local choirmaster to supply them. Which explains why a 10-year-old Martin Luther King Jr was one of those who serenaded the white guests on arrival.

For the next six years, a second war spread across the world. As the Nazi regime was vanquished and Japan succumbed to the atom bomb, the world wanted peace and escapism. And where else to find that sanctuary than your local cinema?

The high watermark of cinema-going in the UK was in 1946, when it was estimated that 73 per cent of the population paid entry, with half of them attending more than once a week. That first post-war year saw a record 1.65 billion cinema admissions.

In America, however, a new threat was emerging, almost unnoticed. In 1949, there were barely a million TV sets across the country, but cinema admissions were soon down – even if you could drive, why go out when staying in saw the stars come to you? There was a 40 per cent drop in ticket sales. And soon, television was in danger of all but destroying cinema attendances. However, Hollywood fought back with Technicolor, VistaVision, Cinerama, Todd-AO, drive-ins – and the stars.

Once the pre-eminent art form of the first half of the twentieth century, film faded. It had, in dazzling procession, the glory years –

the majestic silent parade of the 1920s; the star-studded grandeur of the 1930s; the reflective noir of the 1940s; the blazing Technicolor of the 1950s.

From those early, stilted, silent images, exhibited as a sideshow novelty, by the end of the Second World War cinema-going had become an international force of habit. And what drew the crowds, in their millions and millions every week, week after week, were rarely the stories. It was not the novelty of film noir nor the use of *mise-en-scène*. It was not directorial emphasis nor auteur flourish. It was not the elaborate sets nor the stylish cinematography.

No, what lured the crowds in were the stars. Those larger-than-life icons; those household names. Those names *above* the title. And few blazed brighter nor were lit more luminous than that of the future star of *Cleopatra*.

# 2

# National Velvet

Although she was born in Hampstead and was later a Dame of the British Empire, Elizabeth Taylor's parents were American. Her father, Francis, had been born in Illinois at the tail end of the nineteenth century. Her mother, Sara, was from Kansas. They married in 1926, and soon began their art-collecting business, which took them all over Europe in the heady years before the rise of fascism. Lifelong Anglophiles, Francis and Sara Taylor soon settled in London, where their only daughter was born, on 27 February 1932.

From high on Hampstead Heath, Francis Taylor would descend to his art gallery on Old Bond Street in Mayfair. Contemporaries recall the parents of the future star as an odd couple. Sara was keen to court the British aristocracy, while Francis was happier mingling with Bohemian artists. Through evident friction, the Taylors created a loving home for Elizabeth and her brother Howard, the elder by three years.

Rarely given to retrospection, Elizabeth Taylor occasionally reflected on what her life would have been had she stayed in England, and imagined a life as a debutante, with an early marriage into the aristocracy, where she would have rooted, surrounded by a growing family. But events in Europe were to overtake any homegrown ambitions.

Although she only lived at Heathwood for seven years, Elizabeth Taylor retained fond memories of its six bedrooms, tennis court and semi-rural location. Just behind the Taylors' Hampstead home was a wood, where the young Elizabeth would play happily for hours.

Among the Taylors' acquaintances was connoisseur Victor Cazalet, a Conservative Member of Parliament, who shared Sara Taylor's Christian Scientist beliefs. This drew him closer to the family – he was Elizabeth's godfather. Cazalet was an aristocratic MP, and, typical of his class in the mid-1930s, an admirer of Mussolini's Fascist Party. This was at a time when fascism was widely viewed as an acceptable ideology rather than a genocidal obscenity.

Cazalet – like many of the British upper classes – also approved of the draconian measures Hitler was taking in hauling Germany out of its morass. As the decade progressed, however, and the full extent of the Nazi evilness became evident, Cazalet found himself in a minority, associating himself with the maverick Winston Churchill. Both men saw the danger in appeasing Hitler as he slowly devoured the Rhineland, Austria and Czechoslovakia.

Like most of their friends, customers and contemporaries, the Taylors of Hampstead were capable of ignoring events on the Continent with equanimity. Through Cazalet, though, they were better informed about the true nature of Hitler's ambitions. By 1938, when the Allies sold Czechoslovakia down the river at Munich, it became apparent that Hitler could never be appeased. Twenty five years after 'the war to end wars' began, the armies of Europe were once again preparing for Armageddon.

Victor Cazalet alerted Francis Taylor of the impending danger during the Easter of 1939, and within a fortnight, accompanied by her mother, Elizabeth Taylor was crossing the Atlantic to the country that would provide her with a home and a career for the rest of her life.

Sara Taylor had been an actress until she was 30, but her stage gestures had not translated onto the coming medium of cinema, and on her marriage, Sara left the stage behind – but not her dreams of glory. If she could not savour the spotlight, then with her help off screen, her precociously beautiful daughter might.

While hindsight might have Sara pushing Elizabeth Taylor into the limelight, more prosaically, the family's reason for moving to Pasadena, on the outskirts of Hollywood, was more to do with its location, as the home of Sara's father, who offered his daughter and grandchildren free accommodation. And by Christmas 1939, three months after the outbreak of the Second World War, Francis Taylor rejoined his family in California, and within a few months, his Hollywood art gallery was established.

Hollywood, in 1940, was in its heyday. War in far-away Europe made little impact on the lotus-eating aristocrats of the film capital. The crushing of Poland was less noteworthy than the news that 'Garbo Laughs!' in *Ninotchka*. A momentary pang at the fall of Paris was soon superseded by the romance of Hitchcock's *Rebecca*. And all was overshadowed by the all-consuming triumph of David O. Selznick's *Gone with the Wind*, which, during 1940, enjoyed nationwide release in America while, across the Atlantic, the democracies tumbled. (Legend has it that the young Elizabeth was considered for the role of Rhett and Scarlett's daughter, Bonnie Blue, but her mother put her foot down.)

By that fateful summer of 1940, only England stood unconquered, and the Taylors' old English friend Victor Cazalet was at Churchill's side as the prime minister snarled defiance at the Nazi hordes, poised barely 20 miles across the thin strip of English Channel. While Joe Kennedy and Charles Lindbergh preached non-involvement in a European war, the Taylor family were among the few in sunny, far-off California who were able to appreciate the immediacy and proximity of Hitler's threat to Great Britain.

Their daughter's childhood had been uneventful, but when a customer at the Taylor Gallery became enchanted by the young Elizabeth's beauty, all that changed. The customer informed her fiancé, who conveniently ran Universal Studios. This was where the 9-year-old Elizabeth began her film career. She languished for less than a year at Universal, allowed only one cough-and-spit role in 1942's *There's One Born Every Minute*.

Her contract was not renewed and it looked as though the 10-year-old might well join the pile of has-been child stars, chewed up and spat out by the Hollywood machine. But Elizabeth Taylor was not to be discarded so carelessly, and in a story straight out of a Hollywood melodrama, the girl was given a further golden opportunity.

The young star of *Lassie Come Home* was proving unsuitable to Metro-Goldwyn-Mayer (MGM), and the urgent hunt was on for a youngster with an English accent. Hollywood had been impressed by Britain's triumphant stand against the Nazi threat during the summer of 1940, and the moguls reflected the interest in all things English in their films. *Waterloo Bridge*, *Lady Hamilton*, *Random Harvest*, *Forever and a Day* and, particularly, *Mrs Miniver* ('worth a squadron of battleships', according to Churchill) were only some of the depictions of plucky olde England which flowed from Hollywood in the days leading up to and after Pearl Harbor.

*Lassie Come Home* may not have had a wartime setting but its heart was in the apple orchards, stately homes, gas-lamp-lit cobbled streets and winding country lanes that was the England the studios of California were so fond of conjuring up. As well as Elizabeth, and her young co-star – Herne Hill-born Roddy McDowall – *Lassie Come Home* displayed the expatriate Brits *in excelsis*: Nigel Bruce, Dame May Whitty, Donald Crisp, Elsa Lanchester and Edmund Gwenn were in evidence; only the grand old man, C. Aubrey Smith, was absent.

*Lassie Come Home* went on to become a hit and it gave Elizabeth Taylor a foothold in Hollywood, though it should be noted that her weekly salary of $100 was easily eclipsed by that of her canine co-star – Lassie was clearing $250 a week. In the 1944 sequel, *Son of Lassie,* the adult Elizabeth's role was taken by June Lockhart, who did not enjoy the same relationship with the dog 'Pal', playing Lassie, 'the only star who could play a bitch better than Bette Davis'.

While her salary may have trailed that of a dog, *Lassie Come Home* provided a valuable boost. There was something immediately arresting in the young English girl. Although she was uncredited in both *Jane Eyre* and *The White Cliffs of Dover*, it was apparent that the camera loved the pre-teen beauty. And it soon led to her breakthrough role, in MGM's *National Velvet*.

Later, Elizabeth admitted that, along with its polar opposite, *Who's Afraid of Virginia Woolf*, the 1944 film *National Velvet* was her own favourite of all her starring roles. It's hard to believe now that the story of a *girl* winning the Grand National could inspire a best-selling novel and box-office triumph. Perhaps even at her young age sensing this was a make or break opportunity, Elizabeth Taylor invested a great deal of her 12-year-old self into the role of Velvet Brown.

Always at her side was her mother. MGM executives clearly remember Sara Taylor standing just out of shot, but clearly in Elizabeth's sight-line on set. With memories of her own nascent acting career having been cut short twenty years before, Sara Taylor invested a great deal in developing her daughter's. She would chivvy, goad and, occasionally, encourage Elizabeth from the sidelines. Sara was an overbearing stage mother, who invested all her hopes and dreams in her only daughter.

Such single-minded commitment frequently led to conflict. Elizabeth's short tenure at Universal was in part attributed to the fact that, according to one observer, 'her mother is an overbearing bitch'.

Under her mother's tutelage, and with nurturing from MGM, Elizabeth Taylor bloomed. Like many before and after, her childhood was sacrificed for film stardom. Over two decades, MGM was Elizabeth Taylor's home. She was educated at the studio school, and was made up, fed and clothed by MGM. As one of the more distinguished 4,000 MGM employees, she filmed on one of the twenty-five MGM sound stages. She ate in the studio's cafeteria, was treated in the studio's own hospital, and was protected by the MGM fire department in the event of fire. For safety, like all of the studio's stars, she was protected by the studio's own police force.

And, like all the other major Hollywood studios, MGM was swathed by its collective security, which protected its stars from the morality of others. All were told on arrival, 'If you get into trouble, don't call the police; don't call the hospital; don't call your lawyer. Call Howard [Strickling, MGM's Head of Publicity]'. So, when criminal charges loomed, when drink and drugs, infidelity and sexual scandals – even murder – arose, the studio took care of it.

Thus were the stars isolated and insulated. It was done to elevate the mortals into the pantheon of screen immortality, into a world where the most beautiful women had even more beauty painstakingly applied and where their every on-screen movement was sheathed in swishing, exotic gowns. That big-screen beauty was accentuated by lighting, voices nuanced and remodelled by MGM craftsmen. Here was a place on earth where there were 'More stars than there are in Heaven', as MGM famously boasted. It was here that Louis B. Mayer's dream of a perfect world was lavishly fashioned.

Like many of the Hollywood moguls, Mayer was an immigrant who had fled Czarist Russia. When he became the highest-paid executive in the nation, the image of America that Mayer projected was bound by family values, strict morality, patriotism and respect for figures of authority. Here, set designers, master craftsmen, cinematographers, couturiers, hairdressers, composers and stars – above all, stars – laboured to create an earthbound Paradise.

This was the world that Elizabeth Taylor entered when she was 12 years old, and in a sense, it was a world she never left.

# 3

# Elizabeth's Place in the Sun

From early on as a teenager, Elizabeth Taylor was a stunning screen star, beloved by the camera. It was the heady combination of childhood innocence and the desire to please, with the perceived womanly allure of a siren that made her a star and subjected her to the wrong kind of attention at an indecently early age in her career. Looking back, she famously reflected, 'I've been able to wear a plunging neckline since I was 14 years old and ever since then people have expected me to act as old as I look. My troubles all started because I have a woman's body and a child's emotions.'

In Hollywood, the transition from child star to actress had proven a rocky path. Even before her tenth birthday, Shirley Temple was the biggest film star in the world, but adult roles had proved harder to sustain. Barely into her twenties her star had diminished. And loyalty had not featured in the studio vocabulary when the star had waned. Years later, Goldie Hawn's character in *The First Wives Club* ruefully remarked, 'There are only three stages for women in Hollywood – babe, District Attorney and *Driving Miss Daisy*.'

Cinema is at its best capturing forever a fleeting moment, a look, an expression, a brief insight into character. It finds difficulty in sustaining, and handling the transition from the child to the adult. Audiences are like parents, who fall in love with the child but, like all parents, are reluctant to let their children grow and thus leave their innocence behind.

From early on Elizabeth Taylor possessed a determination, a driven quality on screen, even in her breakthrough role in *National Velvet*, aged only 12. By her mid-teens, the eternal beauty of Elizabeth Taylor was blossoming. It ran in tandem with a pushy mother and a sense within the teenager's heart that she might be able to translate mere beauty into a talent.

It is said that before the birth of screen rebels like James Dean, or rock 'n' roll idols like Elvis Presley, there were no such things as 'teenagers'; there were young adults, who endeavoured to emulate their parents in both look and outlook. There is certainly a fascination in looking at the films of Elizabeth Taylor from the late 1940s and early 1950s, just as she was transforming from a determined child star into a teenage ingenue. She does not look like the sort of teenager we would imagine of the period; she looks like a young girl striving to look like her mother, and indeed, when photographed together at the time, the similarities between Elizabeth and Sara Taylor were striking.

Even from those early photo sessions and film roles, Elizabeth Taylor's beauty is striking, with her large blue eyes framed by a corral of jet-black hair. It was an arresting face, and when she turned it full on, there was no denying its power.

☥

*National Velvet* had hinted at the genuine talent Elizabeth Taylor was capable of displaying, but she soon slipped into contract limbo at MGM – who, today, remembers the teenager's roles in *Cynthia*, *A Date with Judy* or *The Big Hangover*? As with all contract players, the regularity of a studio contract did throw up the odd diamond in the rough. Aged only 17, Elizabeth was charming in *Little Women* and, at 18, held her own with Spencer Tracy in *Father of the Bride*.

But as with all film stars making obeisance to their studio under contract, Elizabeth had little say in the choice of roles offered. For example, Humphrey Bogart followed up the timeless *Casablanca* with *Action in the North Atlantic* and following Rhett Butler, Clark Gable was in *Strange Cargo*. But in truth, Elizabeth had little real interest in developing a career; for her, acting was something to occupy her prior to marriage.

However, that all changed when Elizabeth Taylor fought to be cast in *A Place in the Sun*. It was a role she knew would demand that she be taken seriously as an actress. She found herself loaned out to a new studio, Paramount, under the watchful eye of director George Stevens and working alongside Montgomery Clift.

Although he had only made four films before *A Place in the Sun*, Montgomery Clift was already established as the next big thing in the Hollywood of the late 1940s. He had established himself on Broadway, then exploded opposite John Wayne in 1948's *Red River*. As Matthew Garth, Clift displayed sensitivity and vulnerability, offering up a pensive and reflective hero for a post-nuclear age.

For all his undeniable talent, Montgomery Clift was thwarted by indecision about the direction his career should take. He was relying on drink and drugs to fend off the torment caused by his homosexuality, which could terminate his career. Nervous and highly strung, Clift had just turned 30 when he came to *A Place in the Sun*.

Montgomery Clift had a pretty low opinion of Elizabeth Taylor prior to filming. He was dimly aware of her being fed through MGM properties like they were a sausage factory. Clift came from a strict theatrical discipline. He was an actor who immersed himself in his roles, who was 'methodic' in his approach to his craft. Not like this teenager, who he sense treated her roles like bangles and baubles.

The studio thought it would be a good idea, as Taylor and Clift were playing lovers in *A Place in the Sun*, for them to be seen out together, and so it engaged them to attend the premiere of Clift's new film, *The Heiress*, where they would be photographed together prior to filming. Clift was not keen on the idea, especially as he was in the midst of gearing himself up to play George Eastman. Clift's character is executed at the conclusion of *A Place in the Sun*. As an example of Clift's commitment, and to fully empathise with Eastman's torment, the actor had just spent a night on San Quentin's death row – the last thing he needed was to be seen at a glitzy premiere on the arm of some chattering actress.

Within moments of their prearranged meeting, though, both were smitten. At the party after the premiere, the great and the good of the movie industry were in attendance in abundance, but the focus of attention was the couple, who were to remain close for the next seventeen years. Diana Lynn, a guest at that party in 1949, remembered their entrance to Clift's biographer, Patricia Bosworth:

> The combination of their beauty was staggering. Elizabeth was hyp-
> notically beautiful – almost embarrassingly so. She was a perfect
> voluptuous little doll. And those great violet eyes fringed by double
> lashes. But there was an enigmatic power and magnetism behind her
> looks which gave her beauty – and his – a sultry depth. One could see
> her as goddess, mother, seductress, wife. One could see him as prince,
> saint and madman.

Elizabeth Taylor commented that when filming began on *A Place in the Sun* in October 1949, it marked the beginning of her development as an actress. And that blooming was as much to do with Monty Clift as with director George Stevens. Although she was not yet 18, Stevens cast Elizabeth Taylor as Angela Vickers because of that 'hypnotic beauty', which was so immediate and enrapturing. For Angela, George Eastman is willing to go to any lengths, including the murder of his own wife. The audiences who flocked to *A Place in the Sun* when it finally opened in 1951 had to believe that the object of his desire was worth going to those lengths for.

For Montgomery Clift, Elizabeth Taylor was always 'Bessie Mae', a pet name for the only woman the gay actor ever seriously cared about. Indeed, right up until the eve of her first marriage, to millionaire hotelier Nicky Hilton, in May 1950, friends (and gossip columnists) insisted that Elizabeth was still hoping to snare Monty.

Between films and marriage, Elizabeth Taylor and Montgomery Clift remained close. Elizabeth's star was in the ascendant, with the box office success of undemanding costume dramas like *Ivanhoe* and *Beau Brummell* and prestige productions like *Giant*. Clift achieved critical plaudits for *From Here to Eternity* and Hitchcock's *I Confess*. Finally, Elizabeth Taylor and Montgomery Clift were reunited for MGM's *Raintree County*, a Civil War drama that the studio hoped would rekindle the magic of *Gone with the Wind*, a generation before.

But a near-fatal car crash nearly ended it all. When The Clash came to write a song about Montgomery Clift, they called it 'The Right Profile', because that was the actor's best side after he was hideously mutilated in a car crash following a party at Elizabeth Taylor's home on the night of 12 May 1956.

Clift eventually left the Taylors' Coldwater Canyon house to drive himself home. On the winding canyon roads, Clift lost control of the car and it crashed. Somehow, the actor miraculously survived, but at a cost – his nose was broken, his jaw shattered and his head swollen to six times its normal size.

Elizabeth Taylor was the first on the scene and clambered into the wreck to cradle Clift's head in her arms. It was her quick thinking which saved his life, by reaching down his throat and yanking out the two front teeth which would otherwise have choked him to death. 'Montgomery Clift survived that night and lived for ten more years,' wrote Patricia Bosworth, in her biography *Montgomery Clift* (1978), 'but his real death occurred as he lay bleeding and half-conscious in Elizabeth Taylor's arms.'

As one of the movies' most mesmerising beauties, just who Elizabeth Taylor was going to marry was forever front-page speculation in the fan magazines. Her first marriage, at the age of 18, to Nicky Hilton was immaculately choreographed by MGM, which sadly had no say in their star's choice of husbands. Hilton was a heavy drinker, a compulsive gambler and a brutal husband. The fairy-tale marriage would be over almost before it even began, and even all the powers of MGM couldn't patch that one back together. After eight miserable months, their marriage was dissolved.

The following year, Elizabeth announced her second husband. Michael Wilding was 20 years older than his bride, an amiable, sophisticated man about town and a capable actor, who never took his profession or celebrity that seriously. Wilding was soon swept along by Elizabeth Taylor's headlong rush into marriage. He had muddled along as an actor and listed his ambitions as 'to be rich and not have to work too hard'. He had never met anyone quite like Elizabeth Taylor. She saw something of the father figure in him and wanted security, following the brutality of her first marriage. Wilding became the star's second husband in February 1952 in London, where Elizabeth had just finished filming *Ivanhoe*.

The hysteria was something London was unused to. Thousands of fans clamoured around the sedate Caxton Hall to catch a glimpse of a genuine Hollywood movie star. For Elizabeth, this was part and parcel of her life. The easy-going Wilding was baffled by the mob. One contemporary account read, 'The bride wore a dove gray suit, the groom wore an air of surprise!'

Wilding was a shy and retiring character, quite unused to the hullaballoo that accompanied his new bride. He was happy to play second fiddle and Elizabeth found him to be a steady, comforting presence; friends used the term 'father figure'. 'I thought Michael Wilding, twenty years older than I, was a sort of an island, an oasis ... He represented tranquillity, security, maturity – all the things I needed in myself.' The couple were together for five years and had two sons.

By the time Elizabeth went on location to Texas for *Giant* during 1955, her marriage to Wilding was in trouble. Elizabeth was enchanted by the moody and truculent James Dean. With two starring roles under his belt, Dean immersed himself in the chippy Jett Rink, at odds with the film's other lead, Rock Hudson. Dean forged a bond with Elizabeth. She was devastated when Dean died in a car crash, days after he had finished shooting the Texan epic in September 1955.

In 1956, still nominally man and wife, Elizabeth Taylor and Michael Wilding were invited for a weekend cruise off the coast of Santa Barbara. Their host was a flamboyant film producer called Mike Todd.

Born Avrom Goldenbogen in Minneapolis in 1907, Todd was a truly larger-than-life figure, even in an industry populated by giants. By the time they first met, Todd had run bootleg whisky out of Canada during Prohibition and been married twice and bankrupted twice. He produced over twenty shows, including musicals, peep shows, burlesque and variety.

He immediately captivated Elizabeth Taylor and, for a while, even convinced Sara Taylor, although her reserve crumbled when Todd was revealed not to be an Italian charmster but a Jewish huckster. Elizabeth's mother's veneer cracked completely as her daughter's third husband regularly introduced his wife as 'my fat little Jewish broad'. But Elizabeth was determined to marry the mogul, who swept her off her feet. He was the one man Elizabeth Taylor claimed really stole her heart.

Mike Todd hustled his way through his professional life; everything he did was eleven on a scale of ten. Tired of being perceived as a small-scale promoter of peep shows, Todd went for the biggest of the big-screen processes. Throughout the 1950s, with cinema audiences in decline, the moguls didn't have to look far for the cause – television. They fought back with a bigger-is-better strategy; using larger-than-life stars in epic productions that filled massive screens with stereo and Technicolor.

Todd had been one of the pioneers of Cinerama, a three-camera technique that had been premiered at the 1939 World's Fair but was first seen in cinemas with the 1952 release *This is Cinerama*. Todd sold his shares to concentrate on his new 65mm project, named with typical modesty, Todd-AO. The process was displayed to full effect on the 1955 film *Oklahoma!*, where the corn really did seem as high as an elephant's eye when it was witnessed in Todd-AO!

Mike Todd was big on promises, and for his own first film, promised the world that they 'ain't seen nothin' yet'! *Around the World in 80 Days* was a new type of motion picture. There had been big films before, but Todd dazzled with his production. It was shot in thirteen countries with 60,000 extras and a host of stars. For his adaptation of the Jules Verne classic, Todd introduced the concept of the cameo appearance.

Cameos were not new to movies. Stars would often pop up in one of their studio's projects, or there would be one-off gag sightings (Bing Crosby spotted in a Bob Hope picture; Humphrey Bogart in the Ealing comedy, *The Love Lottery*). But it took Mike Todd to elevate the novelty into a high concept in *Around the World in 80 Days*. By chutzpah, persistence and sheer force of will, Todd inveigled the likes of Frank Sinatra, Noel Coward, Marlene Dietrich, Ronald Colman, Charles Boyer, John Gielgud and Buster Keaton into his picture.

Against all odds, *Around the World in 80 Days* became a box-office smash. Its weekly costs of $329,000 were a regular drain on Todd, which he came up with by blagging, charming and coercing friends into investing into his film. At one point, he was offered $10 million for the rights to the film and the Todd-A0 process. Todd declined and somehow managed to keep the production wheels turning.

Todd applied the same grandiose techniques in pursuing Elizabeth Taylor – 200 red roses arrived on the Kentucky location of *Raintree County*; the 100-degree heat was kept at bay by the crushed ice in which Todd wrapped the flowers. Filming was interrupted when Mike Todd flew in to whisk Elizabeth off for lunch in Chicago on a chartered plane. On a whim, he took Elizabeth gambling in Reno, where he gambled $1,000 chips 'like they were quarters'.

It was courtship on a scale that impressed even Elizabeth Taylor with its persistence, scale and extravagance. When he finally got round to proposing, Mike Todd handed his fiancée a 29.5-carat diamond ring, valued at $92,000. 'Mike says 30 carats would be vulgar and in bad taste,' Todd's publicist dutifully reported.

Following their marriage in Mexico in February 1957, Mrs Mike Todd found that her honeymoon was a jaunt that conveniently coincided with European premieres of *Around the World in 80 Days*. The Todds' steamer trunks soon all but disappeared underneath a colourful kaleidoscope of labels – Athens, Cannes, Madrid, Paris, Rome. For the party following the London premiere, Todd hired Battersea Fun Fair, where he entertained 2,000 guests with champagne and fish and chips.

Elizabeth Taylor Todd returned to the city of her birth in triumph. Only 26, thrice married and mother of two (soon to be three; Mike and Elizabeth's only child Liza was born a month after the *Around the World in 80 Days* extravaganza in London), Elizabeth was a bona-fide screen goddess. Her English fans were disappointed that her marriage to Michael Wilding had melted away and they wished there was something Mr Todd would do to conceal his vulgarity. But the divine Elizabeth seemed happy enough.

*Around the World in 80 Days* went on to win the Oscar for Best Film of 1956. Its success fired Mike Todd to further great expectations. A cigar clamped between his lips, barking orders to secretaries and assistants and simultaneously juggling five telephones, Mike Todd was central casting's ideal of a movie mogul. The triumph of *Around the World in 80 Days* proved that Todd knew what the public wanted, and he was determined to give them that – and more!

Among the projects Todd was juggling was a remake of *Anna Karenina*, with his wife in the role made memorable by Garbo and Vivien Leigh. While Russian tanks had only recently rolled into Hungary to crush the uprising, Mike Todd took his wife to Moscow to try to persuade Premier Khrushchev to let him utilise Soviet troops for a screen version of *War and Peace*, with Elizabeth as Natasha. By the time that fell through, Mike Todd was off 'renting Spain' for a production of *Don Quixote*. Typically, Todd spoke to Picasso about designing the film's poster. A role would be found for Elizabeth, who never missed the opportunity to say that marriage to Mike Todd was 'for keeps'.

All that could be found from the wreckage of Mike Todd's chartered Lockheed Lodestar, ironically named *The Liz*, was his gold wedding ring. On his way to New York for an awards ceremony, on the night of 22 March 1958, Todd's plane crashed in the mountains of New Mexico. The weather was stormy and the plane's wings iced up.

The crash took the lives of Todd's biographer, Art Cohn (who'd been looking for a 'good ending' to his biography), the pilot, co-pilot and Mike Todd, aged only 49. Their bodies were destroyed by fire on impact. Fate played a hand for the future director of *Cleopatra*, however – Joseph L. Mankiewicz was scheduled to be on that fatal flight, but a premonition found him switching planes and surviving.

Elizabeth Taylor was desolated. The death of her third husband sent her into hysterics, a state exacerbated by the hysteria that surrounded Todd's funeral in Chicago. Thousands of fans had camped by the cemetery to catch a glimpse of the stars and the beautiful, grieving widow. Picnickers craned their necks and voyeurs chewed gum and drank Coca-Cola as the celebrities filed by. An estimated crowd of 20,000 made a holiday out of the funeral.

Shell-shocked by the tragedy, Elizabeth finished filming *Cat on a Hot Tin Roof* two months after the funeral. She was still evidently in mourning for the man she claimed was the one true love of her life. As the scale of her loss and the gap left by the larger-than-life Mike Todd became apparent, Elizabeth was inconsolable.

As the beautiful, mourning widow, Elizabeth Taylor cut an irresistible figure to fans and the world press. Her every public appearance attracted a tidal wave of ghoulish appreciation. So, she stopped going out.

One of the few visitors she welcomed was the singer Eddie Fisher, the best friend of her late husband. Fisher emulated Todd's style: the big cigars and the sharp clothes. Fisher was a bobby sox idol in the Sinatra mould and had been mesmerised by Mike Todd. Unlike Sinatra, Fisher had never made the transition to film acting ('I was to acting what Laurence Olivier was to pop music,' he later claimed). But as a singer, particularly in America, Fisher was a star. His stature was cemented when he married Debbie Reynolds in September 1955. Gossip queen Louella Parsons soon dubbed the couple 'America's Sweethearts'.

Eddie and Debbie were more than a couple; they somehow seemed to embody the clean-cut, white-bread security of the Eisenhower presidency. 'People believed in Debbie and me,' Fisher later wrote in his autobiography. 'I think they saw us as representative of the young couples who were beginning to shape America's future.'

Elizabeth Taylor found plenty to chat about to Debbie Reynolds, reminiscing about their childhoods sacrificed to MGM. But the differences were more marked. Elizabeth was a sultry, dark-haired beauty, whose violet eyes were flashing invitations to the bedroom. Debbie was domestic and blonde, a cosy ingenue suggesting that her idea of a hot night out was ten-pin bowling. Debbie's determination had seen her prise herself up from rural deprivation in Texas to become a much-loved singing and dancing star, the kind of girl every mother wanted their son to marry.

Even in her shattered widowhood, Elizabeth Taylor gave the impression that she spent her every waking moment in low-cut dresses in equally low dives, with a cigarette and cocktail never far from her flame-red lips. Debbie Reynolds looked like she preferred milk to Martini and was never happier than when changing a nappy on the family ironing board while waffles singed in the toaster.

The Todd–Taylor, Fisher–Reynolds couples made an agreeable pairing. They were photographed together at Royal Ascot, and while he was alive, Eddie and Debbie trailed, awestruck, in the wake of the comet that was Mike Todd.

Like Elizabeth, Eddie Fisher was devastated by his mentor's death and named his son Todd in his memory. He was a regular visitor to comfort Elizabeth, and one summer evening in August 1958, five months after Mike's death, he was summoned by her. She wanted to give Fisher one of her late husband's money clips as a souvenir. She had had it engraved with one of Todd's regular gags, 'I've been broke lots of times, but I've never been poor'.

Fisher was one of the few who truly shared the scale of Taylor's loss. Bound by mutual mourning, Elizabeth and Eddie grew close during late 1958. Only gradually did it become apparent to both of them that the time they were spending together was having less and less to do with remembering Mike Todd and more and more with their apparent attraction to each other.

When Elizabeth attended Eddie's opening night in Las Vegas, six months after her husband's death, the press were alerted. And soon everyone was aware of the romance that would preoccupy the world in a way no other love had done since a king gave up his throne for the woman he loved. It was a foretaste of things to come. Off screen, Elizabeth Taylor's life was one of sin and scandal.

With freedom from her MGM contract on the horizon, Elizabeth would be able to pick and choose her own roles. Tiring of the slavery of the studio system, Elizabeth relished the prospect of independence. While she was still in her 20s, liberation beckoned.

However, the carrot of a million-dollar contract was not to be sniffed at. The studio that dangled that carrot anticipated that some of that off-screen lustrous charm could be captured in an epic about one of history's greatest seductresses.

♀

For all that had gone before and the tsunami that came afterwards, Elizabeth Taylor would always be identified with the Queen of the Nile. Director Andrew Sinclair recalled shooting her cameo in his 1971 film *Under Milk Wood*, with Richard Burton as First Voice. Cast as 'a Welsh port whore of the 1930s', she kept the crew waiting for three hours, according to a feature in the *Daily Telegraph Magazine*. Sinclair remonstrated with his star about this and her elaborate make-up. 'I always look like Cleopatra,' she responded, 'and that is how I'm coming out.'

At the height of her fame, there were dozens of Elizabeth Taylor biographies. Typical of the *Cleopatra* period was Cy Rice's 1962 *Cleopatra in Mink*, which was sold as 'the life, husbands and loves of legendary Liz – magnificent image of history's greatest minx!' (For all her fame and for reasons best known to herself, however, Taylor always refused to let a replica be exhibited at Madame Tussaud's.)

While she was admired the world over, the bulk of the actresses' friends were in the same profession. She remained close to Roddy McDowall, Montgomery Clift, James Dean, Rock Hudson and Laurence Harvey throughout their lives. The reason for Elizabeth Taylor's fondness for, and proximity to, the gay community became clear when it was revealed that her father, Francis, was bisexual. Although he remained married to Elizabeth's mother, Sara, until his death in 1968, Francis Taylor also enjoyed a number of relationships with men, which some biographers have speculated played a part in his daughter's friendships.

For audiences of the later twentieth century, she was better known for her activism on behalf of AIDS victims. She was one of the few Hollywood stars who acknowledged, let alone fought for, AIDS sufferers.

Freed from her studio contract, together with Richard Burton in *The V.I.P.s*, she took two years off following the rigours of *Cleopatra*. Her career roller-coastered: a well-deserved Oscar for *Who's Afraid of Virginia Woolf* and the Shakespearean romp *The Taming of the Shrew* were highlights. *Reflections in a Golden* Eye was audacious, although the pairing with Marlon Brando failed to produce the much-needed on-screen chemistry. Throughout the late 1960s and into the 1970s, she made some bold choices, but films such as *The Only Game in Town*, *Hammersmith is Out* and *Zee and Co.* did her few favours.

The public, however, remained fascinated by the Burtons. The brand was still a potent draw. 'They say we generate more business activity than one of the smaller African nations,' Burton reflected in amazement. Of the dozen or so films they made together, only 1968's *Boom* was a complete box-office disaster.

During the 1970s, Elizabeth Taylor was more familiar as newspaper fodder than screen goddess. I always think of her cinema farewell as the doomed Marina Rudd in 1980's guilty pleasure, *The Mirror Crack'd*. The dame appeared to relish her glamorously bitchy exchanges with Kim Novak in this Agatha Christie romp.

Asked by *The Guardian* in 2019 which woman he most identified with, Elton John replied, 'I would love to have been Elizabeth Taylor, because (a) she was f*****g talented and brilliant, (b) she was beautiful, (c) she had a lot of sex, and (d) she had the most fantastic jewellery. And she became one of the world's greatest philanthropists.'

Her friendship with Michael Jackson was heartfelt. She wrote a glowing testimonial to his 1995 hits collection *HIStory* ('his sensitivity and concern [...] and especially all the children of the world over [...] one of the least devious people I have ever met in my life [...] I think he is one of the finest people on the planet'). Indeed, the last photo in the lavish fifty-two page booklet is a Photoshop image of the singer posing behind Elizabeth Taylor – as Cleopatra.

After *Cleopatra*, Elizabeth found it hard to adapt to the changing mores of late 1960s and 1970s cinema. As someone who has studied her career assiduously, writer Andrew Batt observed:

Elizabeth's dilemma was that, given her beauty and celebrity in the mid-sixties, her options were deceptively limited. Her almost lifelong stardom and extraordinary features meant she could never participate in the more down-to-earth, naturalistic films now being made in Hollywood. She was simply too big a star to allow her to inhabit stories about the lives of ordinary women – casting her as a waitress, a teacher or even a housewife seems absurd – nobody ever lived next door to Elizabeth Taylor.

So if Hollywood was rejected, and a move to the counter culture impossible, one of the few avenues left to her was to become Queen of the art house, where she could have made intelligent and interesting if not always massively commercial films. It seems she did in fact try to do this, but like Burton she lacked the discipline and drive to really maintain a firm handle on the direction of her career. For one that had begun so young it is perhaps unsurprising that she lacked the desire to maintain a meaningful career at this stage.

Instead, she became, and remained, 'Elizabeth Taylor' – an iconic, revered, superstar survivor, one of the few whose career spanned Hollywood's Golden Age. She retired from the cinema screen following a dispiriting cameo in 1994's *The Flintstones*.

Created a dame in 2000, her death in 2011 was front-page news. Much of the coverage reflected on *'le scandale'*, the relationship with Richard Burton, forty years before. With her passing came the end of an era. I think it was Mike Nichols, who directed her in *Virginia Woolf*, who said, 'One thing about Elizabeth was that she never had a cruel word to say about anybody. And she was *never* on time.' Typically, the notoriously tardy star had it written into her will that her burial be delayed for fifteen minutes, so that she *could* be late for her own funeral.

# 4

# Queens of the Nile

When Elizabeth Taylor agreed to appear as Cleopatra, there seemed a perfect symbiosis: the world's most fabled film star playing one of history's most notorious seductresses. According to legend, so beautiful was the Egyptian queen that, like the Gorgon of myth, the very sight of her cast a lethal spell.

It was the Roman historian Plutarch who popularised the story; he remains virtually the sole source, although he was writing 150 years after Cleopatra died. It was Plutarch whose story was later taken up by, among others, Chaucer and Shakespeare, that Cleopatra so bewitched Marc Antony that he gave up the world for her.

Her luminous power was legendary. However, Plutarch emphasised that it was her personality which truly captivated. And, speculating on how history can be altered by the tiniest of incidents, such as Napoleon's piles at Waterloo, Franz Joseph's chauffeur taking a wrong turn, and Hitler's failure as an artist in Vienna, the seventeenth-century philosopher Pascal famously wrote, 'Cleopatra's nose, had it been shorter, the whole face of the world would have been changed'.

Like Taylor herself, Cleopatra came to maturity early – she was believed to be only 17 when she ascended the throne. Her beauty was almost certainly idealised. The name was Macedonian, and to keep his kingdom secure, her father, Pharaoh Ptolemy Auletes relied on the support of the mighty Roman Empire. The family was a psychiatrist's delight – Cleopatra spent her life looking over her shoulder as her mother, uncles and her own children all kept their eyes on the prize of the pharaoh's throne. As historian Duncan Sprott told me, 'The degree of domestic nastiness (sororicide, infanticide, fratricide, etc.) can seem rather hyped up and overblown. On the other hand … it could all be true.'

Married to her younger brother, Ptolemy XIII, when her time came to succeed, Cleopatra knew she had to rely on the power of Rome to maintain her throne. Thus, she seduced the most powerful Roman of them all, Julius Caesar, and is believed to have borne him a son. She was famously smuggled into Caesar's presence rolled up in a carpet, and the Roman was immediately smitten. Duly enthroned and with any claimants done away with, Cleopatra remained in Rome until the fateful Ides of March.

Returning to Egypt, Cleopatra set out to seduce an equally powerful Roman, Marc Antony, in a vessel determined to impress, 'The barge she sat in, like a burnished throne, burned on the water [...] purple the sails, and so perfumed that the winds were love sick with them.' The Bard based this on historical fact. By all accounts, Cleopatra soaked the sails of her barge with scents, including frankincense, myrrh, jasmine and juniper, so that the Roman could sense her arrival in the air before he even saw her.

The romance flourished but, defeated at the Battle of Actium, Marc Antony was beaten by Octavian, his troops deserted and he committed suicide. As, famously, did Cleopatra, the famous asp applied to her fateful bosom. Historians later asserted her death was almost certainly caused by a poison she drank. Her body was never found.

But the legend of Cleopatra has persisted down millennia. History now has her seen as an astute ruler in recognising that, for her reign to continue, she needed the support of Rome. Historians now believe that by elevating her beauty, the Romans could argue that neither of their most powerful and celebrated leaders and warriors were weak men, who were seduced by a scheming woman. Revisionist history of the twenty-first century liberated her from her role as the 'great seductress' and elevated her as the ruler who was a devious brand manager, wise ruler and deft strategist. In the 1963 film, Rex Harrison's Caesar remarks, 'Were she not a woman, she could be considered to be an intellectual.'

Islam cast Cleopatra as a sage and philosopher, and in the 1920s she became an icon for Arab nationalists. By the 1990s, feminists and historians argued that, with her ancestry, she could have been Black, which sparked new interest in her life and person.

Near the end of 2020, *Wonder Woman* star Gal Gadot announced a new film version of Cleopatra's story. However, although benefitting from herself as producer along with a female director and scriptwriter, the project ran into controversy as soon as it was announced.

In *The Guardian*, Hanna Flint complained of the casting as:

> ... an example of cultural ventriloquism that sees the continued bias towards light-skinned minorities who adhere to a western aesthetic [...] So given what we now understand about the Queen of Egypt's heritage, and while the battle for better representation for ethnic minorities continues, it seems like a missed opportunity that Cleopatra's next appearance will be more representative of Hollywood's past than North Africa's present.

In 2018, an 'immersive new pop musical' about Cleopatra opened in New York, with RuPaul Drag Race contestant Dusty Ray Bottoms as 'the legendary Queen of the Nile'. Then, in 2021, plans were announced for another Cleopatra musical.

This, then, was the woman who has spellbound dramatists and performers down the centuries. Among those who have tackled the role over the years, on stage and on screen, are Claudette Colbert, Sophia Loren, Vivien Leigh, Vanessa Redgrave, Glenda Jackson, Judi Dench, Hildegarde Neill, Maggie Smith, Helen Mirren (three times), Frances de la Tour, Sophie Okonedo, Amanda Barrie – and Mark Rylance.

It is 28 September 1960. The first day on which filming of *Cleopatra* commences.

It is a very different world. Filming begins in the year that marks one of history's most turbulent decades, the one that went on to become known as the Swinging Sixties.

In America, President Dwight D. Eisenhower is coming to the end of his second term. The youthful Democratic contender John F. Kennedy has just undertaken the first televised presidential debate with Republican candidate Richard M. Nixon. Kennedy has sought advice for this crucial television appearance from his brother-in-law, the actor Peter Lawford, who gave Elizabeth Taylor her first real screen kiss in *Julia Misbehaves*.

In London, residents grumble at the 1*d* increase on a pint of beer. Teenagers list to one side, their pockets weighed down with the heavy pre-decimal coinage they need to press Button A in the public phone boxes. Penguin Books say they will fight for their right to publish D.H. Lawrence's *Lady Chatterley's Lover*, while 344 unlucky motorists peel the capital's first parking tickets from their windscreens.

In Hamburg, a quintet of British teenagers calling themselves The Beatles have just begun their first residency at the seedy Indra Club off Hamburg's Reeperbahn. In Hollywood, Elvis Presley, recently demobbed from the US Army, finishes filming *Flaming Star*. In Minneapolis, 19-year-old Robert Zimmerman has begun performing under the name 'Bob Dylan'.

In Edinburgh, a late-night satirical review called *Beyond the Fringe* opens. In Germany, the Communist East closes its border with West Berlin. American pilot Gary Powers is put on trial on spying charges in Moscow. In Rome, a young light-heavyweight boxer called Cassius Clay wins an Olympic gold medal. Little interest is shown outside Iraq, Iran, Kuwait and Saudi Arabia when the Organisation of Petroleum Exporting Countries is formed.

In the UK, The Shadows' 'Apache' was concluding its five-week run at No. 1. In the US pop charts, the No. 1 has Chubby Checker introducing a dance sensation that's sweeping the nation, 'The Twist'. Television audiences in Britain stay in for *Take Your Pick*, *Wagon Train*, *Bonanza*, *Danger Man* and *Maigret*.

In the theatre, Albert Finney stars in *Billy Liar*, and Lionel Bart's *Oliver!* and Robert Bolt's *A Man for all Seasons* premier. In literature, a new realism is reflected by the first publication of Lynne Reid Banks's *The L-Shaped Room*, Stan Barstow's *A Kind of Loving* and David Storey's *This Sporting Life*.

Cinema audiences are spellbound by Billy Wilder's *The Apartment*, shocked by Michael Powell's *Peeping Tom* and stunned by Alfred Hitchcock's *Psycho*. At the Cannes Film Festival, Federico Fellini's *La Dolce Vita* wins the Palm D'or. The film introduces the word 'paparazzi' into common language.

$$\frac{\varphi}{\,}$$

Elizabeth Taylor as Cleopatra was undeniably sensational casting, but not altogether unexpected. There had been something about the Queen of the Nile and her kingdom which had fascinated Hollywood for all its existence. Indeed, many of the vast picture houses of the period featured ancient Egyptian decorations, with hieroglyphics and pyramids. Even before the first twentieth-century film, Georges Melies had made a two-minute short in 1899, *Robbing Cleopatra's Tomb* (with the press release boasting effects 'as sensational as they are mind-boggling').

Helen Gardener ('the brightest luminary in the motion picture firmament') starred as Cleopatra in a 100-minute 1912 version, but it was in 1917 that the vamp Theda Bara captivated as Cleo, 'the siren of the Nile that wrecked Empires'.

Much was made of this lavish production ('Never before in the history of photo-dramatic production ...' trumpeted the publicity on release) and Bara's fifty spectacular costumes. The publicity went into meltdown over this woman of mystery: her name was an anagram of 'Arab Death'; she suckled on snake venom; she was born within spitting distance of the Pyramids.

In fact, the sultry Theda was born Theodosia Goodman in Cincinnati. The Theda Bara *Cleopatra* was lost in a studio fire and remains the most eagerly sought missing silent film. Fragments have emerged from production stills but they only hint at the scale of the production.

*The Sheik* (1921) gave cinema one of its first superstars, as Rudolph Valentino romped across North African deserts. The appeal of Ancient Egypt and the Land of the Pharaohs was given further lustre following the discovery of Tutankhamen's tomb in 1922. The golden treasure of 'wonderful things' revealed the grandiose scale of the Egyptian dynasties.

Cecil C. DeMille raised the ante in 1934. His winning mix of ancient wisdom and sex rarely failed. Claudette Colbert played the queen as a sassy, screwball, modern woman. She was scheming and coquettish, though critics today might not succumb to her line 'I am no longer a queen, I am a woman'. Henry Wilcoxon's Marc Antony was as wooden as one of the figureheads on Cleopatra's barge. The film, however, was a storming success, with a raft of merchandising tie-ins – shoes, cigarettes, gowns, sandals and Cleopatra bangs for only $10.

Not to be outdone, and with the author's approval, Gabriel Pascal helmed 1945's *Caesar & Cleopatra*, based on the play by George Bernard Shaw.* In the immediate aftermath of the Second World War it was, at the time, the most expensive film made by a British studio. Questions were even asked in the House of Commons about the escalating costs. But the kittenish Vivien Leigh and the suave Claude Rains couldn't light cinematic fire under the title roles. It was a costly failure, and on release, *Caesar & Cleopatra* suffered unfavourable comparisons with Leigh's husband, Laurence Olivier's successful adaptation of *Henry V.*

So, the Queen of the Nile did have a track record, and for the 1958 Twentieth Century Fox production the plan was that producer Walter Wanger would begin *Cleopatra* after he completed filming Albert Camus's aptly titled *The Fall*. That existential movie never happened, and there must have been times when even the veteran producer must have wished his next project had been stillborn.

Walter Wanger's history was that of a Hollywood veteran. Beginning as Garbo's producer in 1933, Wanger went on to shepherd other cinema legends – John Wayne, Hedy Lamarr, Laurel and Hardy. He had worked

---

* One of the spear carriers in *Caesar & Cleopatra* was Michael Wilding, Elizabeth Taylor's second husband.

alongside legendary directors John Ford and Alfred Hitchcock. In 1951, Wanger himself became news when he shot ('in the balls') Jennings Lang, who he was convinced was having an affair with his wife, the actress Joan Bennett. After a thirty-year career at the helm, Wanger was ready for anything Hollywood had to offer.

The film capital had come to appreciate that to combat the stay-at-home power of television, the movies needed to retaliate on a grandiose scale. They needed to push the moral boundaries, to tantalise, titillate and entice.

The Production Code Association (PCA) was a self-censoring organisation which had been introduced to Hollywood *by* Hollywood in 1934. Even by 1963, the PCA was concerned that 'no picture shall be produced which will lower the standards of those who see it'. Its initial response to the original script of *Cleopatra*, which Wanger submitted, under the heading of 'Miscellaneous Sociological Factors', noted 'pagan religious rites'. Ironically, given the Burton and Taylor furore to come, the PCA lighted on 'illicit sex', listed disparagingly as 'an important story point'.

The Catholic organisation the Legion of Decency, also formed in 1934, found in their first sighting of the *Cleopatra* script 'immodest costuming, boldly suggestive posturing, dancing and situations'. The trade industry the Motion Picture Association was concerned at its initial read-through of the first draft of *Cleopatra*, stating on 8 May 1959:

> While the basic story seems acceptable under the provisions of the production code, the present version would seem to contain certain elements which would have to be corrected before a picture based on it could be approved.
>
> Specifically it seems to us that there should be a little more definite voice for morality regarding Cleopatra's conduct with both Caesar and Antony.

The MPA then went on to single out particular points, such as 'There should be no open-mouth kisses. Lucius should not conduct himself in a way that would characterize him as a fairy.' They also found fault with the 'lustfulness lyrics of the legionnaires' song [which] are offensively blunt'. By the time these revisions had been made in August 1960, the MPA's Geoffrey M. Sherlock was writing to Frank McCarthy, stating emphatically that 'There should be no scenes showing Cleopatra nude while she is bathing'.

On 16 June 1959, Fox submitted their first Cross Plot. In a pre-computer age, this 3ft square document was a scene-by-scene breakdown for their production of *Cleopatra*. The original budget came in at below $3 million, although, by December 1959, Wanger was told he had 'an early Christmas present' – Twentieth Century Fox had bought an Italian film of *Cleopatra* outright 'to keep it off the market'. So, that was another $500,000 added to the budget, right off the bat.

A realistic sixty-four shooting days were originally envisaged. Production would take place in California, so a watchful eye could be kept on any escalating costs. It's hard to believe, knowing what we know now, that in the studio's second Cross Plot of August 1959 the number of shooting days were actually cut to fifty-four!

It had been way back in September 1958 when *Variety* announced that Walter Wanger had purchased the rights to C.M. Franzero's *The Life and Times of Cleopatra* for a 'top-budgeted epic'. By the time they had got round to reading the script for the 1917 *Cleopatra* (which had only needed 'a little rewriting'), the studio dimly realised it was a silent film, so all the script contained were captions and camera positions. It had been a lifelong ambition of Wanger's to make a movie about Cleopatra. He paid $15,000 for the film rights to the Franzero title. 'A modest beginning,' he later admitted, 'for the most expensive picture of all time.'

# 5

# Rain Stops Play

Once she had signed on, for her own tax purposes Elizabeth Taylor was insistent that the filming of *Cleopatra* should take place outside America. Executives made an expensive trip to Turkey for locations but returned with doubts about the country's suitability. Italy was considered, but a studio memo diplomatically pointed out, 'There is a gulf between our way and the Italian way of making films'. So, reluctantly, the decision to film in the UK was made. It was to prove a costly error.

The reason the UK was selected was due, in no small part, to the country's Eady Levy, where American film productions received tax breaks if a certain percentage of the cast and crew employed were British. A large number of the actors shortlisted for the film were British, which would make the UK Exchequer happy, and British craftsmen were renowned for their skill, so there shouldn't be a behind-the-camera problem either.

Leaving aside any climatic conditions, the Hollywood moguls had not calculated, when it came to crunching the numbers, that there just weren't enough behind-the-scenes experts on hand. Downsizing a switch to Pinewood would undeniably entail financial advantages. However, to replicate the ancient grandeur of Alexandria, sky-scraping and jaw-dropping sets were required.

To erect the huge sets at Pinewood, once the scaffolding was in place, plasterers were needed – a *lot* of plasterers – 300–400 might be able to do it. At Pinewood, the most they could muster would be fewer than 20. From far-away New York or California, the Americans appeared baffled by the Brits. Executives found that the Pinewood craftsmen were more interested in tending their gardens, Association Football, a cup of tea or the public house than the financial inducements on offer.

However, the difference between the UK and US styles of film-making need not necessarily be a deal breaker. The warm climate of Italy had been inviting, but the might of Twentieth Century Fox could not compete with the Olympic Games. Even in its original modest form, if the production of *Cleopatra* had switched to Rome in 1960, there wouldn't be a spare hotel room to be had in the Olympic-mad Italian capital.

Finally committed to the UK location, Twentieth Century Fox had already invested $600,000 in sets alone. The splendour of ancient Alexandria covered 20 acres at Pinewood Studios. Towering over the set were sphinxes, which loomed over 50ft high into the grey English skies. In order to replicate the Mediterranean locale, palm trees had been imported from America to Buckinghamshire.

The film's star was in her suite at the Dorchester Hotel. For her, this was her London base. As a youngster, she had watched the coronation of George VI from the balcony of the hotel. A quarter of a century later, she was in residence as one of the most famous women in the world – only George VI's daughter and the wife of the President of the United States could equal her celebrity.

Miss Taylor's hotel bills were covered and she was drawing ample expenses on top of her agreed salary, which has already accounted for £1 million of the *Cleopatra* budget. For the waiting world, Elizabeth Taylor *is* Cleopatra. But Taylor informed the production office that, alas, due to a sore throat, she would not be making the 20-mile journey from Park Lane to Pinewood.

Even before the official start of filming, there was concern over *Cleopatra*. It took two years to get to Pinewood and Taylor's fee was causing disquiet in the studio boardrooms. There were also worries that the veteran director, the 63-year-old Rouben Mamoulian, might not be up to the arduous task, and the script remained 'a work in progress'.

There was a convulsive sigh of relief that, at least – *at last* – the filming had begun. But not for long ...

By the first day's end, there had been not one but two stoppages – by the film's hairdressers. The powerful British trade union objected to the on-set presence of Elizabeth Taylor's personal hairdresser! An understanding was eventually reached whereby Miss Taylor's hair was prepared at the Dorchester and then adjusted on set at Pinewood.

By the end of the first day of filming, not one usable foot of exposed film had been shot. It was a symbolic start and marked only the beginning of the problems surrounding the production of *Cleopatra*.

On the second day of shooting, Mamoulian was informed that Miss Taylor's sore throat had developed into a cold and she would not be able to appear on the *Cleopatra* set – again. The director was sanguine; with the sets in place, he could at least shoot around his absent heroine.

However, the glowering skies would never lighten for long enough. The drizzle and rain just would not stop. Even when the showers ceased, the grey sky over Buckinghamshire remained sombre and unforgiving. What Mamoulian needed were magnificent white clouds, sailing like galleons over a Mediterranean blue sky. Instead, he was getting a truculent grey shroud, defeating his every effort at suggesting tranquil Middle Eastern promise. The autumn weather continued, and at one point the replica of the harbour at Alexandria, which already contained 1 million gallons of water, was in danger of overflowing due to the incessant rain.

Around 5,000 extras, elaborately clad in authentic period costumes, all daubed with brown body paint for 'authenticity', huddled under the looming sets, sheltering from the rain and shivering in the cold. They were occasionally called out from their shelter to populate the sets between showers, but the calls grew more and more infrequent.

One of those shivering in the unremitting rain for his £15 a day was future Led Zeppelin manager and former Robert Morley stand-in, Peter Grant. 'I always remember her turning up on set,' Grant recalled of the film's star, 'in a white Phantom 5 car, wearing a fur coat. She'd get out of the car, decide it was too chilly, and go straight back to the hotel.'

Just to get the extras to Pinewood was a logistical nightmare. Twenty-eight extra tube trains were laid on from London to Uxbridge, then thirty buses transported them from the station to 'Alexandria'.

Like the massive sets, the huge Todd-AO cameras stood idle, at the mercy of the inclement English climate. The skies remained grey and overcast, and all too often the clouds wept voluminous showers. Hollywood always preferred studio shooting – that way you could control the environment.

Location filming was always going to be a precarious business, posing such problems as dealing with truculent natives and background distractions. Not to mention the weather; shooting out of doors posed a further variety of problems. But now, trying to recreate the Middle Eastern grandeur, the splendour of the ancient world of Egypt in 48BC in the damp English countryside suddenly seemed not such a wise decision.

A fortnight into filming, the Pinewood location was offering barely two minutes of sunshine every day. By October, the producer noted a typical day's event: 'We had called 500 extras and could hardly find them on the set in the fog.'

Cold was another factor. The provincial English autumn can be notoriously chilly. 'It was sheer lunacy,' Mamoulian remembered in *The Cleopatra Papers*. 'Rain, mud, slush. On a good day, whenever a word was spoken, you could see the vapour coming out of the actors' mouths.'

The chief financial reason for filming in England was eroding. However enticing the financial inducements had been, they did not take into account the unyielding British weather. The early October of 1960 meant that no filming could actually take place on the *Cleopatra* sets, which stood magnificent and unpopulated under the drizzle and biting winds. The palm trees were lashed by the blustering wind and rain of an unseasonably early and harsh English autumn. To ensure their Middle Eastern lustre was maintained, fresh fronds were flown in daily to Pinewood from Egypt. Such expense was never envisaged in the film's original budget.

The massive sets were already in place, towering over the fields. But there was no likelihood that the slate skies could be mistaken for the turquoise blue of the Mediterranean. Grey as the skies were, the two-storey sets representing the imperial harbour of ancient Alexandria were awesome in their detail and scale. A photo at the time with the sets under construction has an ironic hoarding saying, 'Rome Was Not Built In A Day'.

It was here at Alexandria, in Pinewood, that Julius Caesar would land; the first step ashore in a journey that would have the ruler of the world's biggest empire wooing the queen of a distant, sunlit and mysterious land. It was here that the saga of *Cleopatra* would begin.

As with all other films, the epic was shot out of sequence, relying on the stars' availability, but above all, the weather. However, such was the elaborate and complex construction of a film of this scale that the availability of Peter Finch, the actor cast as Caesar was jeopardised.

At Pinewood, the rain and drizzle just wouldn't cease long enough for any filming to be seriously undertaken. Shots would be snatched between showers, but the cumbersome process of film-making meant that the unwieldy, bulky cameras, camera tracks and cranes, huge lights and colossal sound equipment were rarely synchronised with the temperamental weather. By the time director Rouben Mamoulian shouted, 'Action!', more often than not the rain came lashing down, washing out another day's shooting.

As grey September slipped into chill October, on the rare occasion when the crew could snatch a shot, too often the steam of cold breath could be seen issuing from the mouths and noses of actors and horses. Even a casual glance at the day's rushes revealed that Ancient Egypt this was not.

Already, madness was in the air. Film-making has its fair share of folly, whether in casting (Ronald Reagan in *Casablanca*?), location (Stanley Kubrick's decision to recreate Vietnam in Beckton, east London) or cost (of his *Raise The Titanic*, Lew Grade admitted, 'It would have been cheaper to lower the Atlantic!'). But nothing came close to the epic folly of *Cleopatra* during its troubled five-year production.

# 6

# 'No Liz, No Cleo!'

What early 1960s madness had a multimillion-dollar production convinced it could recreate the magnificent grandeur of a sunlit, ancient kingdom in a rain-sodden location west of London during the first chill of autumn?

By the third day of shooting, Elizabeth Taylor was still ill. Typically, with the health of this troubled star, the cold turned into a fever and for the ensuing five weeks, the star did not leave her suite. Already the future of the film was in the balance; without Miss Taylor, there simply was no *Cleopatra*.

Taylor had been dogged by illness for most of her adult life. By 1970, she was on her twenty-eighth operation. Among the health issues affecting her was a glandular condition, hypertrichosis, an ulcerated eye, ruptured spinal disc, phlebitis, pneumonia, Asian flu, laryngitis, meningitis and bronchitis.

On the night of 4 March 1961, the star came perilously close to death. Gasping for breath in her Dorchester suite, she started to turn blue. Fortuitously, a doctor and specialist in respiration techniques was rushed to the room and brought her back to consciousness. Taken to the London Clinic (which was soon besieged by the media), she underwent a tracheotomy so she could breathe, which left a 2in scar in her throat. The wound was like a medal, a symbol of her unerring ability to survive.

Within a week she had recovered and was swigging champagne with Truman Capote. 'It was like riding on a rough ocean,' she told the waspish author of her near-death experience. 'Then slipping over the edge of the horizon. With the roar of the ocean in my head, which I suppose was really the noise of my trying to breathe.'

Elizabeth Taylor was bedridden for weeks. The world held its breath for her recovery. No longer was she Elizabeth Taylor, the immoral husband stealer, but rather Liz, the survivor.

Opinion was still divided over the 1960 Best Actress Oscar she received for *Butterfield 8* (a film she loathed). She was good, but undeniably better in *Cat on a Hot Tin Roof*, *Suddenly Last Summer* and even *Raintree County* – she received nominations for all three performances. Cynics, however, suggested that the Oscar she was allowed to take home for *Butterfield 8* was due to the star's indomitability; it was her survival that won her that coveted statue. It was also a sign that Hollywood had forgiven her transgressions.

The sympathy vote was an undeniable factor. Los Angeles newspapers, with banner headlines screaming 'Liz Dying', were on the newsstands the same day that Academy members received their ballot papers.

Days stretched into weeks as the news from London had the star hovering between life and death. Her competitors (Melina Mercouri, Greer Garson, Deborah Kerr, Shirley MacLaine) were resigned. 'I lost to a tracheotomy,' MacLaine later acknowledged.

The indefatigable Taylor had recovered enough to collect her Oscar in person. On the night, Hollywood welcomed her back into the fold. 'Hell,' the cuckolded Debbie Reynolds admitted, 'even *I* voted for her.'

At Pinewood, Rouben Mamoulian made the best of it he could, shooting around the star on whom the fate of the entire film rested. He filmed the pick-up shots or – when the weather permitted – had Caesar in long-shot arriving in Alexandria. Peter Finch, already reluctant to play second fiddle to his leading lady, was noticeably unhappy. The situation was not helped by the prolonged absence of Taylor and the lack of a coherent script.

The novelist Nigel Balchin had been given first crack. His books included the tense novel *Small Back Room* (atmospherically filmed by

Powell and Pressburger) and the brooding *Mine Own Executioner*. His screenplays included the spellbinding wartime thriller *The Man Who Never Was* and the *Cleopatra* competitor, 1962's *Barabbas*. He never received a credit for *Cleopatra*. Neither did Nunally Johnson, Ben Hecht nor Lawrence Durrell.

Elizabeth Taylor's choice verged on the surreal: Paddy Chayevsky, who had won the Oscar for *Marty*, an intimate two-hander set in the Bronx. The film's eventual director, Joe Mankiewicz, dismissed the earlier scripts as 'a frustrating mixture of an American soap opera virgin and a hysterical Slavic vamp'.

Peter Finch had arrived in Pinewood immediately following his triumph playing Oscar Wilde. A versatile actor, Finch had been cast to play Caesar opposite Stephen Boyd (fresh from *Ben-Hur*) as Marc Antony. So immersed had Finch become in the role of Caesar that when his agent came to visit him, he failed to recognise her, and only responded in character as the Roman Emperor.

The *longueurs* of the Pinewood shoot also took their toll. Finch was on the verge of a nervous breakdown, and after a fortnight in a sanatorium in England, early in 1961 he was shipped over to Jamaica on holiday to recover. By the time he was better, studio executives no longer felt he had the box office appeal required and he was replaced.

When interviewed at the time, Finch was rueful, as he reflected in his biography:

> They have postponed the picture at least six months, maybe longer [...] If they ever use that set again it will have to be done over entirely. The paint is practically gone and the plaster is falling of everything [...] After *Cleopatra* closed down a fellow came to me and asked if I'd like to play Pontius Pilate. I told him, 'I never want to see another toga as long as I live'.

Stephen Boyd, as Marc Antony, was equally disenchanted. He went to *Cleopatra* hot on the heels of his success as Messala, opposite Charlton Heston in *Ben-Hur*. Boyd grew tired of kicking his heels beneath his toga. Even in a business where hanging around was an occupational hazard, *Cleopatra* had already taken the inactivity to Olympian heights.

In 1966, Boyd was asked by *Film Review* if he had any regrets about withdrawing from *Cleopatra*:

> My only regret is never having been seen on the screen with Elizabeth Taylor, whom I consider to be one of our great actresses. But I've never been sorry I handed in my Marc Antony uniform when they scrapped the first ill-fated attempts we made at Pinewood.

☥

The casting for *Cleopatra* is a tale in itself. There was fascinating documentation to be found. Twentieth Century Fox in Hollywood wrote to its London office on 6 May 1959, announcing that its *Cleopatra* project would go into production in June and asking for London's advice on casting.

The correspondence sheds intriguing light on Hollywood's attitude to its foreign empire. Lest we forget, this was when *Cleopatra* was envisaged as a modest Twentieth Century Fox project. According to the studio, the names bandied around for the eponymous lead included Joanne Woodward, on the back of her Oscar-winning role in *Three Faces of Eve*, but also, of equal importance, under contract to Twentieth Century Fox. Susan Hayward was another player on the Fox payroll, again in the frame, thanks to an Oscar-winning performance in *I Want to Live*. In fact, it was Hayward who was the preferred choice of the Fox board, but as she was already in her early forties, the studio thought it unlikely that audiences would accept her as the ingénue queen. And anyway, producer Walter Wanger only ever envisaged Elizabeth Taylor for his Queen of the Nile.

'Marie Versing and Jeanne Moreau' were names that the London office suggested, 'but we do not know much about them. Apparently they are either Italian or French and if they have accents, then we cannot consider them.'

The Australian actress Jackie Lane was keenly considered as 'she looked very attractive'. She had starred in a number of low-grade UK films of the 1950s, when critics dubbed her 'the British Bardot'. But she missed out on *Cleopatra* and her career never took off subsequently. Rebranded as 'Jocelyn Lane', she starred alongside Elvis Presley in one of his formulaic films of the period, *Tickle Me*. Writer David Bret, who valiantly sat through all the Presley movies for his book *Elvis: The Hollywood Years*, felt that Lane, the once possible Queen of the Nile, 'probably ranks as Elvis's least talented and certainly least charismatic leading lady'.

London responded to the Hollywood request with its usual thoroughness on 26 May 1959. In hindsight, it makes for fascinating reading. For the title role, Fox suggested a long list of lovely likelies, including Janette Scott, Lee Remick, Mandy Miller, Jean Simmons, Claire Bloom, Dana Wynter, Cyd Charisse, Kim Novak and Joan Collins. The future dame was a strong contender; she was another one under contract to Fox and let it be known that she was 'dying to play it'. The studio were equally keen and screen tested the actress. Producer Walter Wanger wrote witheringly in 1959, 'Hermes Pan is working with Joan, trying to improve her posture and walk so she will have the grace and dignity of Cleopatra.' As a flavour of the times, the biographer of Fox head Spyros Skouras wrote that Collins had 'eyes bigger than boobs'.

Although she missed out on the Queen of the Nile, Collins had high hopes for the sandy spectacle *Land of the Pharaohs* (1955). She scored as the scheming Princess Nellifer ('Her Treachery Stained Every Stone Of The Pyramid') but the Warner Bros epic flopped. Audrey Hepburn was keen, but her studio, Paramount, would not lend her to its rival, Fox. And there, nestling at No. 17 on the original list, was Elizabeth Taylor.

Taylor said she only took the role on as a whim. Newly independent and free from studio contracts for the first time in over fifteen years, the star admitted, 'I was in my bath when my lawyer called and asked me what I wanted to do about the "*Cleopatra* thing". I thought I would dispose of it by asking something impossible. "Tell him I'll do it for a million against 10 per cent of the gross".'

In his autobiography, Eddie Fisher claims the credit. 'Elizabeth was in the bathroom brushing her teeth and I shouted in to her, "Elizabeth, you should do this for a million bucks".' It was an impossible demand –

Marilyn Monroe only received $500,000 for 1959's *Some Like it Hot* and Marlon Brando and William Holden had edged up to the magical million, but when they reached the mark, it included percentages of the gross. Elizabeth Taylor was the first screen star to receive a million up front.

Serious or not, when Taylor signed that seven-figure contract on 15 October 1959, it made headlines around the world. For the actress it was a liberation; it would be the first film she made after being a contract player at MGM for her entire acting career to date. Her final film for the studio that had groomed her since *National Velvet* was one that she detested – *Butterfield 8*, the story of a vengeful call girl. One reason for undertaking the role – which would go on to land her an Oscar – was that it provided husband Eddie Fisher with a part.

For the role of Julius Caesar, it really was the usual suspects: Larry Olivier, Ralph Richardson and Johnny Gielgud, as well as the cream of Equity – Michael Redgrave, James Mason, Jack Hawkins, David Farrar, Richard Todd, Leo Genn and James Donald. There were also those stars of the Hollywood Raj: David Niven, Basil Rathbone, Vincent Price, Ray Milland and George Sanders.

Distinguished American stars such as Yul Brynner, Joseph Cotten, Walter Pidgeon and Orson Welles were also put forward. Two maverick suggestions were Noel Coward and the Canadian who would soon find fame as the boss of the Ponderosa, Lorne Greene, star of TVs *Bonanza*. Rex Harrison made it at No. 12.*

Rufio, Antony's comrade, was eventually played by Martin Landau, after Stanley Baker passed. Agrippa (Andrew Keir) was offered to Harry Andrews. For Apollodorus (Cesare Danova), London had two tantalising suggestions: long before *Airplane* and *The Naked Gun*, young Leslie Nielsen was suggested; and hot from *Darby O'Gill and the Little People*, Sean Connery. While Richard O'Sullivan eventually secured the role of Ptolemy, Twentieth Century Fox originally had Fabian in mind.

Someone who was cast and actually made it onto the Pinewood set was Keith Baxter, as Octavius. In the 2000 documentary about the film, he recalled a nominal eight-week contract at the notable sum of

---

\* Harrison's road to the role of Julius Caesar is detailed in Chapter 16.

£2,000 per week. He is seen in costume in a 1960 Pathé News short –
Prince Philip was attending a charity dinner at Pinewood and is seen
being conducted over the *Cleopatra* set by Baxter. But with the shoot
dragging on to no avail, Baxter soon fell by the wayside.

With Taylor's prolonged absence, the English winter drew in
around Pinewood. October turned to November, and exterior shooting on the sprawling sets became wholly impractical. The director was
also unhappy with the script he was sporadically shooting from. But
hanging like a pall over the already troubled production was Elizabeth
Taylor – or rather the lack of the star. So much of *Cleopatra* hung on
Taylor that to think of filming without her was … unthinkable.

Ultimately, it was the weather that decided it. The English autumn
shrouded John DeCuir's magnificent sets, which stood largely unused
and unusable in the intemperate climate. Taylor was cloistered at the
Dorchester Hotel. The two principal male stars (Finch and Boyd) were
plainly unhappy with any visible progress. The sets and extras stood
idle. The rain wouldn't stop.

The studio in sunny, far-away Los Angeles was equally frantic at the
absence of progress. Before fax and email, the only speedy way of com-
munication was by cable and transatlantic phone. But it was a lengthy,
time-consuming and slow process to communicate between London
and Los Angeles all those years ago.

Executives could not believe the figures that were screamed daily
down the crackling phone line. *Cleopatra* was haemorrhaging cash, with
nothing to show for it. By May 1960, Wanger was told that 'the abso-
lute limit' on the Cleopatra budget was $4 million, but he responded,
'We've spent half of that already and haven't got a foot of film.'

There had been slow starters in the studio's history before, but at
least they had something to show for it. There had been cumbersome
productions prior to *Cleopatra*, but they were at least manageable when
shot in Hollywood. If you wanted a desert or an ocean, you simply
went to the western reaches of California.

*Cleopatra* was drowning in the corner of a foreign field at a cost of
$120,000 a day – every day; $15,000 an hour – every hour, whether
Elizabeth Taylor left the Dorchester or not. At today's prices, *Cleopatra*

was in danger of costing £1 million a day. Try as the studio might to search for a scapegoat, the decision to cut costs by filming in England was the cause of the escalating budget. And while the press might point the finger at Taylor's absence, she was not crying off with just a bad cold. Her health issues soon became undeniably life-threatening.

It soon became apparent that the much-anticipated *Cleopatra* was grinding to an inexorable halt. Eventually, the decision was made to pause filming and shut the production down, have a complete script overhaul and recommence filming during the early part of 1961. There were plans to recast the male leads, but keep hold of Elizabeth Taylor at all costs, and switch the location to sunnier climes.

Studio head Spyros Skouras flew in to London in June 1960. The Greek executive had plenty to fiddle with on his worry beads. Despite being shown weather forecasts and predictions, he shrugged and affirmed, 'The weather is going to be fine.' He did, however, concede that the desert scenes would be more convincing if filmed on location – in Egypt.

This location opened up another can of worms. President Nasser's Egyptian government was beguiled by Skouras, who promised a further five films to be made by Fox in Egypt. Its eyes watering at the prospect of Gina Lollobrigida in their country for a future production, the government offered up 10,000 members of its army for the *Cleopatra* battle scenes. However, they would not welcome Taylor, following her marriage to Mike Todd, who was a convert to Judaism. Things were not helped by a throwaway comment of Taylor's in a magazine interview, 'It will be fun to be the first Jewish Queen of Egypt'.[*]

Israel, on the other hand, might have welcomed the production and its star, but not as the film in question was set in Egypt. Even though the film depicted events of 2,000 years before, the Middle East has long memories.

The lack of progress on *Cleopatra* was sending shockwaves not just through Twentieth Century Fox, but all the major Hollywood studios.

---

[*] In the end, second-unit filming did take place in Egypt but, typically, the army extras promised did not materialise. When extras recruited from Alexandria arrived on location in the desert, fierce fights broke out with the locals. The equipment was held up in Italy and ended up arriving via Beirut.

In the first year of the new decade, profligacy – something which Hollywood had accepted as part and parcel of movie making – was sprawling out of control, far from the canyons of Beverly Hills.

After nearly two months of production, when Twentieth Century Fox finally pulled the plug on the English leg of *Cleopatra* on 18 November 1960, director Rouben Mamoulian did not have a single frame of film featuring the film's much-touted star. It was a knock-out combination of the star's serious health condition and the unyielding English weather that finally scuppered the production.

At the end of the Pinewood stretch of *Cleopatra*, and through no fault of his own, Rouben Mamoulian had painstakingly accumulated eight minutes of finished film at a cost approaching $8 million. To put this into some sort of financial perspective, the total cost of mounting the Coronation of Her Majesty Queen Elizabeth II in 1953, a mere seven years before the English segment of *Cleopatra* was finally wound down, was estimated at £2 million.

By the beginning of 1961, the Pinewood sets were standing idle and peeling and Rouben Mamoulian had resigned. He granted an interview to a young reporter on the *Daily Mail*, Barry Norman. The film 'cannot be made the way I wanted it […] When I began fifteen months ago I had a dream, an artistic conception of the way the film should be'.

And what was it that saw that dream unrealised, Norman asked?

'Elements,' replied the director enigmatically.

Producer Walter Wanger called the Pinewood experience 'a fiasco […] We didn't make the film, we didn't even get the hairdressers' strike settled.'

By January 1961, with Mamoulian gone, this was crunch time for the already turbulent production. Did the studio bite the bullet, swallow a multimillion-dollar loss, take it on the chin and cancel the film? Or did they persevere and continue plunging money into a production which could, which just *might*, save Twentieth Century Fox from extinction? Many years later, Fox executive David Brown was quoted in the 2017 book chronicling the studio's history: 'We never gave up, we were fuelled by an obsession and the idea that every obsession makes money.'

It would have taken a brave executive to pull the plug on a production which had already eaten up over $8 million of the studio's finances.

Given the gift of foresight, that would obviously have been the right decision, rather than see *Cleopatra* bogged down in the maw of escalating costs and a fantastically extended production. But then, as the rain lashed the Pinewood sets, could anyone – *anyone* – have anticipated it would be more than two long years before the film finally opened?

By March 1961, the Pinewood sets, so painfully and painstakingly erected, were laboriously torn down (but not before one crafty English production nipped in and carried them off to use later). The original cast were paid off; an estimated 99 per cent of the Pinewood footage was scrapped; Taylor's health remained precarious. A finished script was a chimera.

Three years into production new locations in Greece, Spain, Egypt and Italy were scouted and a new director and leading stars had been signed up. The production then finally decided to switch to post-Olympic Rome. And despite all the problems that had gone before, *that* was when the real problems facing *Cleopatra* began.

# 7

# The Three Lives of
# Richard Burton

It is an eerie experience reading through the contemporary accounts of the filming of *Cleopatra*. It is dislocating to appreciate that John F. Kennedy was president, alert and occupying the Oval Office and inhabiting the West Wing – not a legend, not a martyr, not a tarnished idol, but an active, living president. And Dallas, Texas, was a faraway place about which we knew little.

Crew-cut kids gleam from the pages of the American newspapers – no long hair on boys back then. Pop music was at its blandest. Everything was so ... *normal*. All eyes were on America for automobiles, refrigerators, hamburgers, music and films. Marlon Brando's attendance at a CORE (Commission of Racial Equality) rally was worthy of front-page news. Pop Art was bafflingly introduced as 'the latest thing'. The old guard still held sway over the new releases.

London was still scarred by the ravages of the Blitz only a few years before. Before *Billy Liar*, Bond and The Beatles, American studio representatives were little more than staging posts for Hollywood releases. But the film capital's reach was long, and far away, before filming began, Twentieth Century Fox advised its London office that for the role of Marc Antony the actor should be 'around 40, very active and good physique'. Final director Joe Mankiewicz was keen to cast Marlon Brando, who had played the role so well under his watch on the 1953 production of *Julius Caesar*, but Brando proved unavailable.

Among the names conjured up were Stephen Boyd, who was – briefly – cast. Other names cited were Richard Johnson, Peter O'Toole, Peter Finch, Laurence Harvey, John Justin, Rock Hudson, Tony Curtis, Christopher Plummer, Tab Hunter, Dirk Bogarde and Richard Todd.

At No. 10 was an actor whose career was going through one of his customary bumps. Following the forgettable *Sea Wife*, *Bramble Bush* and *Ice Palace*, the glory days of Richard Burton appeared to be over. Turning his back on theatre, he had been criticised for his role as the original Angry Young Man in the film of John Osborne's *Look Back in Anger*. It was not just that he was too old for the role; it was more that Burton did not seem capable of scaling down his performances for film.

Burton, however, was keen to establish himself as a film star. Before too long, he would achieve his ambition on a scale that even the ambitious Richard Burton could not have imagined.

When Richard Burton died in the Swiss village of Celigny in 1984, he was so far removed – by career, geography and name – from his origins that it was as if you were talking of at least three quite distinct and separate lives. The first is that of a young miner's child, Richie Jenkins, growing up in poverty in the close-knit coal-mining community of the Welsh Valleys. Pontrhydyfen was a place and time barely on nodding terms with the twentieth century. As the boy Rich grew, 'The bridge over the ford across two rivers' was just beginning to emerge from the Great Depression. A career below earth looked like all he was set for.

The second life concerns that of the teenage Richard Burton, who took the name of an avuncular teacher and lifted the boy from the Valleys to the London stage. This was the Richard Burton who mesmerised theatre-goers in the immediate years following the end of the Second World War. Hailed as the successor to Olivier, Gielgud, Redgrave and Richardson, Burton invested Shakespeare with a sensuous immediacy. His performances made the Bard sexy.

The third life is that of Richard Burton, film star and celebrity, his every jet-setting move and record-breaking jewellery purchase dutifully recorded. That Burton is synonymous with extravagance and ostentation, with the diminishment of an undeniable talent. That rise, and subsequent fall, are inextricably linked with Elizabeth Taylor and the film which first bound them together, *Cleopatra*.

Richard Burton's life was seismically split by *Cleopatra*. Prior to that film, Burton was a middle-ranking film star, who had eschewed the promise of early stage triumphs for a career amid the froth and frivolity of Hollywood. Burton was arrogant and impetuous, and his film career pre-*Cleopatra* was a roller-coaster. After *Cleopatra*, he became the cynosure for the world's press, a personality elevated to an unimaginable strata of celebrity. So familiar was Burton on the arm of his second wife that his abilities as an actor were all too often overlooked. Yet, by his own admission, he was willing to sacrifice that early talent on the altar of fame and wealth.

Such ambition was not remarkable: as a dirt-poor miner's son growing up during the grim Depression of the 1930s, when the wealth came his way, Burton relished it. On stage, he was a titanic figure, and critical plaudits were all very well. The same critics set stage acting high above mere film performances, but Burton was happy to savour the salaries the latter brought. And, in fairness, even while he was regarded as 'Mr Elizabeth Taylor', Burton did deliver some outstanding performances and could elevate humdrum movies with his electric screen presence.

Interestingly, one of those roles was as Doctor Faustus. In a 1967 film version of Christopher Marlowe's sixteenth-century play, Burton played the character who sells his soul to the Devil for everything he wants while alive on earth. To further tempt him, Faustus is seduced by Helen of Troy, the world's most beautiful siren ('was this the face that launched a thousand ships? [...] Her lips suck forth my soul [...]'). The cameo was played by Burton's wife, Elizabeth Taylor, then at the height of her sexual allure. The irony of the plot would not have escaped Richard Burton, nor his mischievous wife.

Filmed at the height of the couple's power as 'The Burtons', there was little that was starry in their commitment to the production. For all her regal bearing and elevated status, there was a kind, soft side to Elizabeth Taylor. David Wood wrote an affectionate portrait when she came to Oxford to appear in the college production of *Dr Faustus*. It is full of small acts of kindness, gifts and a genuine down-to-earth personality that was unrecognisable from the steely hearted seductress of tabloid legend. Burton too seemed content in college cloisters; indeed, a long-felt want of the actor's was to return to Oxford in a tutoring capacity.

When he burst like a comet onto the London stage in the early 1950s, Burton was immediately elected as heir apparent to Laurence Olivier – both brought a fiery sensuality to Shakespeare and both were dusted by greatness. But there was something in Olivier, the clergyman's son from the sedate south coast of England, which allowed him to balance the very best of the English stage and the better-paying allure of Hollywood. At that stage of his career, Olivier was capable of being spellbinding on stage but was equally adept at reigning in and delivering measured performances on screen.

It was a compromise that somehow Richard Burton never managed. As soon as Hollywood beckoned, Burton was there like a shot. While his Hamlet was felt to have been the finest post-war interpretation of the prince, almost simultaneously Burton was churning out Hollywood gruel like *The Rains of Ranchipur*. When they were working on a film together, he was asked by the actor Gabriel Byrne why he made so many films instead of going back to the theatre. Burton responded, 'Because I couldn't bear not to have somewhere to go in the mornings.'

At his worst, when his drinking was at its most addictive, the discipline of a live performance was unthinkable. On film, the benefit of retakes was irresistible.

What made it all the worse was that Burton knew how low he had sunk. And while, in the words of Oscar Wilde, he could lie in the gutter and still look at the stars, he was patently more comfortable in the artistic gutter. Within Burton's reach was the mantle of Olivier, but it required a stretch, and within easier grasp was the lucrative temptation of film stardom.

The former was denied to him; the latter came too easily. Burton made his own choices, and, indeed, Elizabeth Taylor was in thrall to

Burton's mastery of his craft and spellbound by his talent. Throughout their lives together, she was always encouraging him to return to the live stage.

The reason for that loss, and for that never-to-be-recaptured promise, lay in the sprawling production of *Cleopatra* and the voluptuous appeal of its star. In *Cleopatra* lay the seeds of the destruction of Richard Burton. It was no one's fault but his own. From early on, the actor appreciated the demands made by theatre and the benefits the film set offered. Critics may well have felt that Richard Burton sold his soul; at least, throughout his cinema career, the Welshman ensured that he got a good price for it.

♀

Richard Walter Jenkins was born on 10 November 1925 in Pontrhydyfen, a small mining village in South Wales. The twelfth child of a miner, Richard's father, *Dic Bach* ('Little Dick') (1876–1957) stood barely more than 5ft high and had spent the bulk of his life toiling underground at the coal face. Richard's mother, Edith, had been born in Swansea but moved to the Valleys where, as a teenager, Edith worked as a barmaid at the Miners' Arms. One of its most frequent visitors was *Dic Bach* Jenkins.

The couple were married on Christmas Eve 1900, when the groom was 24 and the bride was only 17. The Jenkins family began immediately: Thomas (1901), Cecilia (1905), Ifor (1906), William (1911), David (1914), Verdun (1916), Hilda (1918), Catherine (1921), Edith (1922), Richard (1925) and Graham (1927). Edith had also given birth to two daughters who died in infancy.

Edith Burton, the mother Richard never knew, died when she was only 44 years old, in 1927. Her husband's drinking and the grind of rearing eleven children had taken its toll. In later years, and from his film star eyrie, Burton never forgave his father. On his father's death, Burton did not even attend the funeral. Such was the gap in ages in the Jenkins family, and following his mother's tragic death, baby Richard was sent off to live with his eldest sister Cecilia (Cis) and her husband, Elfed James, also a miner, in Port Talbot.

The fledgling years of the young Rich are ably chronicled by his brother, Graham Jenkins, in his 1988 biography, *Richard Burton: My Brother*. Burton made much of his impoverished Welsh childhood, and it was plainly not exaggerated. As a miner's child, there were few doubts about young Rich's destination: the mines were what fuelled the Welsh economy and, for most of the country's youth, that was where the men eked out their working lives, either deep in the bowels of the earth or, for the luckier ones, working above ground at the pit-head.

It was a hard life. Burton's early life was bordered by the pit, the pub and the chapel. But at school, the young Richie Jenkins displayed a flair. He was precocious and cocky and possessed a phenomenal memory; he was soon memorising swathes of poetry, prose and drama. It was a good way of showing off and attracting girls. But more substantially, and fortuitously for the boy, that flair was picked up by Philip Burton. This was the man who would become the young Rich's mentor and whose name the teenaged Welsh boy would take as the first step on a road to unparalleled riches and unimagined fame.

Back at Pontrhydyfen, Rich was skiving school, scrounging cigarettes and losing himself in the dream world of Hollywood films. With Graham, Richard went along to the Taibach Picture Dome as a teenager, and one of the first films the boys remember seeing was a revival of Cecil B. De Mille's *Cleopatra*.

Working as a 15-year-old at the Co-op got Richard Jenkins out of the pit. Mentors from school helped the boy achieve a further education. At Easter 1943 Philip Burton offered Richard accommodation in his lodgings, which he shared with a widow and her two daughters in Port Talbot. The extraordinary menage was soon legalised – Philip Burton was too young to adopt the boy, but instead became his legal guardian.

'The change in Rich in the first months of his life with Philip Burton was apparent to everyone,' Graham Jenkins later wrote:

Intellectually and socially, he acquired a confidence which quite over-awed the younger members of the family. He dressed well, at Phil's expense, adopted manners which some miners might have thought a trifle fussy and talked fluently on topics outside the normal run of conversation.

While he remained a bachelor, there is no evidence that Philip Burton's interest in Richard Jenkins was anything more than an older man encouraging and nourishing the intellectual and aesthetic interests of a younger man. By his mentor, Richard Jenkins had the rough edges sanded off. Under Burton's tuition, the boy's voice developed, his appreciation of culture was honed. But for all his polishing, while Philip Burton could take the boy away from the Valleys, he could never wholly take the Valleys out of the boy. Philip Burton gave Richard Jenkins a future and a name. He was born in 1905, and Penny Junor, Richard Burton's biographer, noted in *Burton: The Man Behind the Myth* (1985):

> [Philip] Burton never married, nor had girlfriends worth noting. His lonely childhood had turned him into a very private person. He kept himself to himself. What is certain, however, is that having no children of his own through whom he could try and live his thwarted ambitions, he sought out potential candidates from the boys he taught.

One of those was the fiery 17-year-old Richard Jenkins. On the teenager's enlisting for the RAF, Philip Burton found that recruits could apply for short university courses at Oxford or Cambridge. He reasoned that Richard showed enormous potential, but would benefit further by appearing to be the son of a schoolmaster, which is why, on 17 December 1943, 18 year-old Richard Jenkins was legally transformed into Richard Burton.

In April 1944, Burton went up to Exeter College, Oxford. It was a curious hybrid of fresh-faced students and undergraduates interrupting their military service. Oxford was Burton's idyll, the Eden to which he periodically returned and from which he was even more frequently exiled. In later life, Burton envisaged an academic career – he possessed a phenomenal memory, was a voluminous reader, an enthusiastic diarist and, if he applied himself, a potentially good writer.

These were qualities he hoped would overshadow his celebrity. In a dream alternative life, in an Oxford he was familiar with, a begowned Richard Burton would stride the dusty halls of academe, respected as a nurturing tutor. In college, Professor Burton would dazzle with his photographic memory and equally beguile his students in lengthy perorations in the university pubs. It was not to be. It was never to be.

Even while he was the most famous film actor in the world, at his peak post-*Cleopatra* in the mid-1960s, Burton cherished a dream to return to the cloistered bliss of Oxford, where he would teach his beloved Shakespeare, passing on his hard-won knowledge to successive generations. It was a pipe dream. Richard Burton was too famous for Oxford, too rich for Stratford, too well known and too rich to be anyone but tax exile Richard Burton. In his heart of hearts, there was a sense that Richard Burton would gladly have returned to life as Richard Jenkins. It was an unrealistic dream.

It was while he was at Oxford during the war that Richard Burton received his next big break. Emlyn Williams was looking for 'a Welsh boy actor' for the West End run of his play, *The Druid's Rest*. Casting director Daphne Rye was alerted to that indefinable, alluring 'something' in the teenage Burton.

Following his six-month stint at Oxford and a spell on the West End stage, the RAF recalled Burton into its ranks. Training took place on the south coast before Burton was posted to Canada in early 1945 to train as a navigator. Fortunately, the war with Germany ended (in May 1945) before the services of LAFC Burton were required. But Burton had known boys who did not return from the war and, throughout his life, he maintained an antipathy to all things German – at the height of his fame, he was even wont to spit at a passing Mercedes.

Following Burton's discharge, Emlyn Williams came to his rescue once again, casting him in the 1948 film *The Last Days of Dolwyn*, on the set of which Burton met his wife-to-be, an 18-year-old actress, Sybil Williams. They were married on 5 February 1949 at Kensington Registry Office. Together, as struggling actors and newlyweds, they were happy. The couple had two children, Kate (1957) and Jessie (1959).

The esteemed Gainsborough leading lady Phylis Calvert had been impressed by the young Burton in *The Lady's not for Burning*, which led to him starring alongside her in the 1951 film *The Woman with no Name*. She told Brian McFarlane of the newlyweds' plans:

> He told me he had saved some money and had just taken out a mortgage on a house. It had three floors, he had the middle flat, and he intended to let the upper and lowers flats. He said, 'I will never have to work again'. That's sweet, isn't it?

Following his marriage, Burton was immediately off on tour in plays by Terence Rattigan and Christopher Fry. And it was in a Fry play, *The Boy with the Cart* at the Lyric Hammersmith, that Burton was noticed by Anthony Quayle, who was putting together a cycle of Shakespeare's history plays, including *Richard II*, *Henry I, II & IV* and *Henry V*, for the Royal Shakespeare Company. The Stratford season of 1951 was historic and Richard Burton was selected to be one the season's leading lights. Burton's Prince Hal was eulogised by hard-to-please Kenneth Tynan in his review for *The Observer*:

> He is never a roaming boy; he sits, hunched or sprawled with dark, unwinking eyes; he hopes to be amused by his bully companions, but the eyes constantly move beyond them into a time when he must steady himself for the crown … Fluent and sparing of nature, compact and spruce of build, Burton smiles where other Hals have guffawed; relaxes where they have strained.

Even more significant audience members were struck by the youngster's blazing talent. On visiting Stratford, Humphrey Bogart and his wife Lauren Bacall were spellbound. 'He was just marvellous,' the sultry Bacall enthused.

Another cinematic co-star was less enthusiastic. Honor Blackman starred alongside Burton in 1951's *Green Grow the Rushes*, the last film he made before the leap to Hollywood. Talking to Brian McFarlane, she admitted:

As to Richard Burton, I have to say I didn't take to him very much because he was pretty arrogant and often drunk. I remember that they asked us to go and give out prizes at a church hall or something silly, to publicize the film, and he made such a fuss about it. He was a serious actor, he didn't want to do trivial stuff like publicity. It was ironic when you think he lived the rest of his life on publicity! He was a fine actor but he practically chucked it in Hollywood.

Another co-star who was similarly unimpressed was Olivia de Havilland. She told Roger Lewis in one of her last magazine interviews:

She couldn't stand the man. She hated the way he cheated on his nice wife Sybil. This was a decade or so before Elizabeth Taylor entered the scene. Olivia's view was that he was an unscrupulous chancer, coarse, and she enjoyed the way, in *My Cousin Rachel*, her character got to poison his character.

It had been in 1951 that Burton went under contract to Alexander Korda, who promptly assigned his charge to Hollywood. Like an Eastern potentate, Korda sold Burton to Twentieth Century Fox's Darryl F. Zanuck for £100,000 for a three-film deal, of which Korda kept 20 per cent.

'What parts are they offering?' Burton demanded.

'Don't worry,' was Korda's response. 'They'll think of something.'

It proved to be symptomatic of Burton's edgy relationship with the film capital. On his arrival from a UK still labouring under rationing, with its cities scarred by six years of sustained bombardment, Hollywood in 1952 seemed like a beautiful, untouched film set. Burton hurled himself into the lifestyles of the rich and famous; he partied hard with Greta Garbo, Jean Simmons, Cole Porter, Judy Garland, Stewart Granger, Humphrey Bogart and Lauren Bacall.

With early 1950s Hollywood selecting CinemaScope as the gimmick to lure audiences away from their television sets and back into the cinemas, in 1953, *The Robe* was selected as one of the early big-screen enticements. Twentieth Century Fox had acquired the rights to the process, which had been patented back in the 1920s, and studio head Spyros Skouras christened it CinemaScope. Fox decided to introduce the new process to audiences who were hungry for colour, scale and spectacle with a biblical production.

Tyrone Power and Laurence Olivier were offered, and declined, the role of Marcellus, the sensitive centurion who keeps Christ's robe after the crucifixion. When Burton's casting was announced, it prompted gossip queen Louella Parsons to hail him as 'the hottest thing in Hollywood'.

Hollywood's fondness for the Holy Land had begun even before pictures began to talk, and there were parallels between *The Robe* and *Cleopatra*, a decade later. *The Robe* was budgeted at an exorbitant $5 million, plus further millions to convert existing cinemas to show CinemaScope releases.

The gamble paid off. The film came on the back of a successful novel by Lloyd C. Douglas, and Fox pushed the boat out when it came to selling it on screen: 'The Miracle Story "reaching out" to encompass you in its awe-inspiring spectacle and breath-taking grandeur.'

*The Robe* may have done the right box office business but it was a mess that time has not been kind to – Burton looked uncomfortable in the short Roman centurion's skirt and declaimed loudly so that *everyone* in the cinema got their money's worth. The film was typical of the biblical costume dramas of the time: Christ is never seen, only glimpsed and spoken of reverentially. His disciples are all saintly, bearded types; the Romans are snarling chaps in cloaks. *The Robe* is remarkable for Jay Serling's Caligula, a carpet-chewing, furniture-bumping performance of such campness you wonder how it escaped without a parental warning.

*The Robe* went on to gross $18 million in North America alone. Most critics agree that the best performance in the film came from Victor Mature, the most disparaging of all the Hollywood stars: 'I'm no actor, and I've got sixty-four pictures to prove it.' But for all its many faults, it is the length and sense of awe which damn *The Robe*. There are a couple of remarkable moments that shine through: Richard Boone's querulous Pilate and Burton's spectral, shadowy encounter with the man who would be Judas.

☥

Burton's was a short-lived romance with the film capital. On completion of *The Robe*, the actor rankled at the fact that Twentieth Century Fox claimed to have him under a seven-year exclusive contract. Burton insisted that his agent signed that contract without his consent. Fox disagreed and sued the star for breach of contract. The case came to court in 1953, where Burton clashed with the powerful studio head, Darryl F. Zanuck, but he was extracted from the exclusivity. He did have to consent to make one film a year for the company for the next seven years. It was Fox that, of course, ultimately picked up the tab for *Cleopatra*.

The nadir of Burton's Hollywood career, certainly in the 1950s, came with *The Rains of Ranchipur*. A browned-up Burton knew it too, responding to a journalist, 'They do say it never rains but it Ranchipurs!'

For all the artistic compromise and critical sneering, Burton's spell in Hollywood had given him a taste for the high life. On his return to London, Burton constantly moaned about the quality of the roles he was offered, admiring Alec Guinness and James Mason. But it was pointed out that, while well-known to cinema audiences, these were essentially character actors who were happy to subsume themselves in a role. Richard Burton was undeniably, single-mindedly determined to become a film star.

# 8

# The Once and Future King

As Graham Jenkins observed of Richard at the time:

> For one thing he was beginning to enjoy the privileges of wealth ...
> It was quite something for a miner's son to return to the valley in a
> smart new Jaguar and with a roll of banknotes thick enough to buy
> out every beer cellar in the country. If he was looking for signs of
> approval from those who gave him his start, the show of wealth, solid
> proof of success, was more important than flattering reviews in the
> smart papers.

It was a dichotomy Burton faced throughout his professional career.
While he relished the money and fame that Hollywood hurled at him
for lousy film roles, Burton always believed he could redeem himself by
playing Shakespeare at Stratford or the Old Vic. But the dedication and
commitment required for the major Shakespearean roles was undermined by his reliance on alcohol. If he mucked up on a film set, a retake
was arranged; he didn't get a chance to retake on stage. And his acting
discipline was diminished by the shoddy and time-consuming film roles
he undertook.

Financially, Burton was getting a taste for the high life. On his return
to the London theatre after Hollywood in 1953, Burton agreed to go
straight into *Hamlet*, but the Old Vic fee was £45 a week and his weekly

living allowance, excluding salary, was £140. His salary for a six-week Hollywood film shoot was £82,000

The year 1953 could claim to be the high watermark of Richard Burton's professional career. It began on 25 January with the recording of Dylan Thomas' *Under Milk Wood* for BBC radio. For as long as there is electricity, there will always be an audience for Burton as 'First Voice' in what remains one of the timeless triumphs of radio. Even now, just to hear that sonorous voice – 'To begin at the beginning: It is Spring, moonless night in the small town, starless and bible-black' – still sends shivers.

An acclaimed *Hamlet* at the Old Vic followed. His film star fame drew in a younger audience, and Burton remained close to the tiny theatre on The Cut in Waterloo for the next few years. It was there he ran the Shakespearean gamut – as well as *Hamlet*, Burton appeared in *Twelfth Night*, *Coriolanus*, *The Tempest*, *Henry V* and *Othello*.

*Hamlet*, of course, was the one – the Everest for all actors. Burton swelled the coffers of the Old Vic, but not everyone was entranced – *Plays & Players* called his *Hamlet* one of the 'disappointments of the year'.[*] In its review of the year, the magazine reflected:

> Richard Burton lacks star personality ... Burton is a leading man who has arrived too early at the signpost. Where does he go from the Old Vic? Will he advance to tread the road that Olivier took before him, or is he for the Waste Land? Time will tell.

In a sense, it was as if Shakespeare proved too *easy* for Burton. He could recite chunks of the Bard backwards. He could accommodate the precise rhythms Shakespeare demanded. He commanded the stage, and of the great Shakespearean roles, only *King Lear* and *Macbeth* tantalisingly eluded him. Perhaps he felt there would be time in later years.

---

[*] On arriving backstage at the Old Vic to take the prince to dinner one night during the *Hamlet* run, that ever-reliable brick-dropper John Gielgud asked Burton, 'Shall I go ahead, or wait until you're better ... I mean, *ready?*'

However, once again, the lure of the lucre triumphed: Burton quit Waterloo for Hollywood. Kenneth Williams remembered Burton telling him, 'I shall go to Hollywood but it won't corrupt me. Sybil and I come from these valleys, and that's where our values are ... when I make money I will bring it back here and it will be jobs for the boys.'

It was not to be. He had made a strong impact in his first Hollywood film, *My Cousin Rachel*, and, save for a blonde *Alexander the Great*, the remainder of the 1950s passed in a series of unremarkable roles in long-forgotten films – *Sea Wife*, *The Bramble Bush*, *Ice Palace*. Burton appeared to put more effort into *Bitter Victory* (1957), an otherwise leaden Second World War drama, but he played his character, loosely based on T.E. Lawrence, with a rare reserve. Only in 1958's *Look Back in Anger* did Burton look like pushing himself. But on re-viewing, his performance as Jimmy Porter was not confined by the camera, bursting out of the screen and into the 1s 9d seats. Burton was also patently too old to be an adolescent hero.

With Hollywood on hold, but with his name as a box-office draw, Burton's return to the stage in 1960 was in an unlikely role. He found himself promoted from a prince (Hamlet) to a king (Arthur). *Camelot*, the Lerner and Loewe follow-up to *My Fair Lady*, was a musical based on the spellbinding novel *The Once and Future King* by T.H. White. While many considered the role to be beneath him, his performance as King Arthur made Burton the toast of Broadway and his king shone opposite co-star Julie Andrews as Queen Guinevere. While not a professional singer, Burton was Welsh and convincingly pulled it off.

It was during the run of *Camelot* that friends became seriously concerned about Burton's drinking. A doctor presciently analysed Burton's condition to Alan Jay Lerner, 'Welsh livers and kidneys seem to be made of some metallic alloy, quite unlike the rest of the human race. One day, like aeroplanes, they eventually show metal fatigue.'

'When any normal man would have been placed on the critical list,' Lerner told Penny Junor, 'Richard could stand firmly in the centre of the room, recite Dylan Thomas from "hello" to "goodbye" and rattle off any Shakespearean part he had ever performed.'

To be in the presence of such theatrical dynamism was overwhelming, but it could be a little ... trying. Author Stephen Birmingham recalled one occasion, a few years later, in a magazine article:

> Richard Burton, drunk as per usual, presented these wonderful oratories and poetry recitations – Shakespeare, Dylan Thomas, Burns, T.S. Eliot, the entire repertoire. Mind you, he would deliver these elocutions night after night until he became a livid bore. You couldn't converse with him, you could only listen.

It was during the *Camelot* run that Burton took lunch with producer Walter Wanger. Rather than his film work, Wanger had admired Burton in *Camelot* ('He exuded confidence, personality and sex appeal') and that was what led the actor to *Cleopatra*, Rome and his destiny. The wily Wanger felt he could discern a potential on-screen chemistry between Taylor and Burton, and pitched him the role in New York. Burton knew of the troubled production – the abandoned sets in England; Taylor's life-threatening illness; the problems Fox was having with casting. There was, however, something undeniably appealing in being asked to appear in such a prestigious production.

Burton was undeniably tempted. 'I've always wanted to play Antony,' he told his brother Graham, even if he added, 'This is maybe not quite what I had in mind, but it's a good second best.'

While it certainly wasn't Shakespeare, there were other enticements. Burton was offered a straight salary of $250,000, good money for what would probably be no more than a twelve-week shoot. The bonus was percentage points when the film went into profit. There were also to be generous expenses, including the use of a family villa outside Rome and two chauffeur-driven cars on permanent call.

'As an exciting diversion, *Cleopatra* was irresistible,' Graham diplomatically wrote. 'The film took Rich into a higher earning bracket, which was success of a sort, it offered another chance to conquer the big screen and it was a way out of family preoccupations.'

Those 'preoccupations' were priapic – he seemed wilfully determined to have a fling with every female co-star. His long-suffering wife and mother of his children, Sybil, turned a blind eye to her husband's transgressions. They had survived a tumultuous decade of marriage, and for all his errant ways, Burton always came back. Sybil and the family offered stability, a retreat from the silliness of cinema.

Wanger bought Burton out of his Broadway *Camelot* contract. Lyricist Alan Jay Lerner plucked the figure of $50,000 out of the air for the buy-out, which Wanger readily agreed. 'That was an easier way of making money than writing musicals,' Lerner joked. Symptomatic of the curse of *Cleopatra*, there had been no need to lavish money on getting Burton out of his Broadway contract – he could have finished the *Camelot* run, and then gone on to Rome, where filming had yet to commence.

At the lavish party that marked Burton's departure as the Once and Future King, *Camelot* director Moss Hart presciently toasted the star with the words:

> Great actors like you are born once in a lifetime. You are as big a personality off the stage as on the stage, and you are, in every sense, larger than life. I beg you not to waste your wonderful gifts. You must know you have it in you to be one of the greatest stage actors of this century.

It was as if Hart had been granted a glimpse into Burton's dark future. As if involved in a Greek tragedy, one cannot help but suspect that Burton was the author of his own subsequent misfortunes. However, as he quit New York for Rome, the future for Richard Burton burned bright.

# 9

# Pandora's Box Opens

After three months spent kicking his heels in luxury in Rome, Burton first appeared opposite Elizabeth Taylor on the *Cleopatra* set on 22 January 1962. The two had encountered each other before, in 1952 when Burton was in Hollywood filming *The Robe*. The 20-year-old Taylor had met him at a party to promote the film. (Burton: 'She was so extraordinarily beautiful that I nearly laughed out loud.' Taylor: 'My first impression was that he was rather full of himself.')

True to form, Burton's first day in Rome found him battling a raging hangover. You would have thought that the first day's filming of the most important film of his career might have led him to be prepared. You would be wrong. Hands trembling, he could barely raise a cup to his lips. His co-star took pity, immediately warmed to him, and responded, as one on-set observer recalled, 'like a needy child'.

When the two came together on the *Cleopatra* set, there was already an air of electric anticipation. Taylor's make-up man, Ron Berkeley, recalled the set already full of hangers-on, prurient sensation-seekers and the idly curious. There was an immediate frisson, which Berkeley reasoned was due to the fact that:

Elizabeth was not used to assertive men. Oh, they might put on an act for a while, but they nearly all ended up showing love by deference, paying tribute to her beauty. Only one other man had taken her by sheer force of personality. When she encountered Richard Burton it must have seemed to her that she had rediscovered Mike Todd.

In truth, Taylor was in awe of Burton's intellectual virility, and she admired his phenomenal memory and knowledge of the classics. Burton, though, felt Taylor was a movie actress. In fact, he learned much from her. Looking back, he reflected:

I did a scene with her one day, and I said, 'She doesn't *do* anything, what's she doing?' and a mutual friend said, 'Go and see her tomorrow, on the rushes' and I went to see her and she was doing everything! I think she's one of the world's greatest screen actresses.

Burton had overlooked the experience Taylor had acquired after twenty years spent in front of the camera. She rarely considered her own acting ability, but in her autobiography, did concede:

I think film acting can be an art, and certainly the camera can move in and grab hold of your mind – so the emotion has got to be there behind your eyes, behind your heart. You can never act superficially and get away with it. Stillness is a great asset on screen. You don't need to use your voice to the same degree as a stage actor. You don't need to use your body to such a degree. It all has to show in the eye. The slightest movement will speak volumes.

A week after their first scene together in Rome, there were already rumours of an affair, and within weeks, the first suggestive stories appeared in the world's press. 'There was a tremendous sense of being in the right place at the right time,' Jean Marsh told David Kamp. The actress, a decade away from *Upstairs Downstairs*, appeared in *Cleopatra*, bafflingly uncredited, as Octavia. Looking back on the time spent in Rome, she remembered, 'The film was so extravagant, so louche, it affected everyone's lives. It was a hotbed of romance – Richard and Elizabeth weren't the *only* people who had an affair.'

It was a different time. It might have been the 1960s, the decade that was later synonymous with freewheeling sex, but this was the very early 1960s. The moral shadow of the 1950s lay heavy: the liberating contraceptive pill would not be widely available for some years. Richard Burton was married to long-time (and long-suffering) wife Sybil. Loyalty was expected.

The fingers of one hand could just accommodate Taylor's marriages. When *Cleopatra* began, Taylor was married to crooner Eddie Fisher. The matrons of middle America despised the actress, because she had 'stolen' Fisher from his wife, and their sweetheart, Debbie Reynolds. Taylor got used to receiving hate mail, death threats and voodoo dolls with pins stuck in them. When Elizabeth arrived to witness Fisher begin his residency at Los Angeles' Tropicana, just prior to their wedding in April 1959, she was greeted by pickets waving 'Liz Go Home' and 'Liz Leave Town' signs.

This was the background against which the Burton–Taylor romance was played out. The scandal, like the slumbering volcano of Vesuvius further along the Neapolitan coast from the *Cleopatra* set, took time to erupt. 'In our little enclave in Wales,' Graham Jenkins wrote, 'the rumours were greeted with disbelief and anger. But as the rumours persisted, anger turned to fear that after all, something was seriously wrong.'

The Jenkins clan closed ranks: they liked Sybil, who had remained steadfastly loyal, despite her husband's manifest transgressions over the years. As the rumours persisted and escalated, the Jenkins family felt that Burton's beloved elder sister and surrogate mother Cis had to be protected from the gossip. In Rome, a smokescreen surrounded the golden couple, with the family simply not wanting to believe the truth of the persistent gossip.

'Many years afterwards,' Graham Jenkins wrote:

Rich told me that he and Elizabeth had been thrown together by events. I knew then what he meant, though if the comment had been made much earlier, I might have dismissed it as an easy excuse for adultery. From all that I discovered subsequently, I do believe that

Rich wanted to save his marriage, but could not bring himself to cut away cleanly from Elizabeth. Anyway, given that they had a picture to make, his problem could not be solved by a straight choice.

As the affair escalated, the comings and goings were luridly chronicled. The strait-laced mores of the 1950s had spilled over into the 1960s: marriage was for life; it was a commitment; it was a sanctity, not to be shaken by scandalous film stars. A husband may have 'played away', but always returned to the marital roost. However upsetting it might be, a wife loyally stood by her man. Marriage was not worn and discarded like last year's fashions.

Together, Burton and Taylor proved a potent cocktail for the fledgling paparazzi and insatiable media. Taylor was at her loveliest. She was being paid an unimaginable sum to portray cinema's sexiest siren and she was giving Twentieth Century Fox their money's worth. Burton was at his rugged best, before the booze took its toll and prior to squandering his talents. He had exploded onto the screen as a macho fireball. His sexual magnetism was evident on stage and on screen. The combination was just too good to miss.

When they weren't worried about the end of the world in Cuba or the escalating chill of the Cold War, the eyes of the world were focused on Rome. Sibyl Burton took the children to the family home in Switzerland, graciously commenting, 'It is best for Rich to be free to work out his own future'. Burton agreed to let Sibyl return from Switzerland in early February 1962 to try to save their marriage.

Elizabeth Taylor's husband flew to Rome to try to discover the truth behind the gossip; and later both Elizabeth and Eddie flew to Paris on the same salvage mission. But for all the diplomatic shuttles and high-level diplomacy, Burton and Taylor were still required on the *Cleopatra* set. It was there every day, under the harsh lights and the scrutiny of the world's press, that the world's most famous lovers were required to play – well, the world's most famous lovers.

'The problem for them both,' wrote Graham Jenkins, a close observer of his infamous elder brother at the time, 'was to do what they were paid to do – which was to fall in love on screen. With an actor of more celibate reputation and an actress of less obvious charms, this might have been possible. But they weren't and it wasn't.'

Elizabeth was immediately attracted to the fiery Welshman, drawn to his oratorical feats, his rugged athleticism. Too often, she underestimated her own on-screen abilities and belittled her lack of intellectual attributes. She was undeniably the star, but when Burton came into her orbit she could not help but be drawn to him.

In her autobiography, published in 1965, the year after their wedding, Elizabeth reflected on that seismic period:

> There was never any point at which Richard and I began. We just loved each other, and there was no discussion of it. I mean it was there – a fact of our lives. We didn't want it to happen because of Sybil and the children. She and I weren't close friends or anything but I admired Sybil tremendously and loved being around her. And Richard and I really fought and hurt each other tremendously to keep it from happening. My God, we told each other to leave a hundred times. It was really more off than on. According to the code of ethics today, I was, I suppose behaving wrongly because I broke conventions. But I didn't feel immoral then, though I knew what I was doing, loving Richard was wrong. I never felt dirty because it never was dirty. I felt terrible heartache because so many innocent people were involved. But I couldn't help loving Richard. I don't think that was without honour. I don't think that was dishonest. It was a fact I could not evade.

In a sense, Burton treated the whole thing as one enormous joke. Perhaps he did see his part in *le scandale* as simply that, 'a part'. At one point, as the whole thing was taking on an elaborate life of its own, Burton told Wanger, 'Walter, I never thought it would come to this.' In his cups, he envisaged a return to the Old Vic, as if the notoriety could be swept under the carpet. Sincerely, but rather implausibly, Taylor promised she'd quit acting and be out front in Waterloo, SE1 every night.

In fairness, following *Cleopatra* and *The V.I.P.s*, she did take a three-year sabbatical from cinema and was there for every performance of

Burton's *Hamlet* on Broadway. By then though, the whole affair had taken on a life of its own. After a decade of fame and prosperity, Burton was courting one of the world's most desired women and revelling in finding himself the centre of attention, with the prospect of unlimited wealth on the horizon.

As Taylor and Burton were locked together on set in each other's arms, Eddie Fisher flew to the family home in Gstaad in Switzerland, which he and Taylor had recently purchased, to escape the ignominy of being cuckolded by Richard Burton. In a sense, he was the one to suffer worst. Over the years, it seems that Sibyl came to accept that her husband, when appearing opposite the world's most beautiful women, 'played away'. Fisher was still scarred by the opposition to his divorce from Debbie and spellbound by his new wife. It can't have been easy that, on set in Rome, with little to occupy him, Fisher had the unenviable title of 'Mr Elizabeth Taylor' during the filming of *Cleopatra* while his wife's affair raged.

Sybil Burton flew to New York without telling her husband. As late as May 1963, while the affair played out in the full glare of worldwide publicity, Sybil was telling journalists, 'Richard is mine. He will always be mine. I will never give him up to Elizabeth Taylor or to any woman.'

Burton was committed to a two-day cameo in Darryl Zanuck's star-studded *The Longest Day*, which was being filmed in Paris. On his first day's filming of the D-Day epic, Burton was just another actor in a film full of cameos. When he came back a month later, with the news of *le scandale* reverberating, forty photographers and journalists greeted him at the airport and hounded him during his stay. Such was his notoriety that he found himself elevated into a whole new stratosphere of fame. Kenneth Haigh remembered Burton returning to the *Cleopatra* set and pointing out a huge pile of '300 scripts. The offers are piling up everywhere.'

On completing his role as Marc Antony, Burton intended to fly long-haul to New York to see Sibyl, to try to reconcile their union. But on 18 February 1962, the news broke of Elizabeth Taylor's suicide bid (it was actually food poisoning). So concerned was Burton that he immediately changed plans and flew straight to Rome.

In fact, the press had made a mountain out of a molehill. Taylor had taken sleeping pills, and, when her hairdresser on entering saw (a) the bottle and (b) Taylor asleep, it led to them rushing to the wrong conclusion. Within an hour of her being rushed to Rome's Salvator Mundi Hospital, doctors reported there was nothing wrong with Miss Taylor.

On arrival in Rome, Burton was swamped by the press. Huddled in a limousine, fleeing the airport with his publicist Chris Hoffa, he learned that Taylor was quite unharmed, but was dismayed to learn that no statement had been issued by the studio to that effect. It was as if the studio preferred to believe that silence lent a dignity to the escalating scandal. It only fuelled the rumours.

Burton was incensed, and in the back of the car with Hoffa, drafted a statement which began:

> For the past several days uncontrolled rumours have been growing about Elizabeth and myself. Statements attributed to me have been distorted out of proportion, and a series of coincidences has lent plausibility to a situation which has become damaging to Elizabeth.

The studio were furious and insisted Burton deny the statement, but the press had got hold of it, so Burton's press agent then admitted that his client had made the statement, which generated even more publicity.

The genie was out of the bottle. The Pandora's box of publicity had been hurled open and the bell could not be unrung. Publicists endeavoured to keep a diplomatic lid on things and bland reports from the set – 'With her co-stars Rex Harrison and Richard Burton, she is on the friendliest terms' – bore little relation to the Roman reality.

However much the principals tried to deny the rumours, the world was engrossed by the Burton–Taylor romance and on-set photos of the couple together were at a premium. One extra hid a camera in her bee-hive hairdo, while another even concealed a camera, attached to her bra and operated by manipulating her left breast, 'like a bell push'.

Still anticipating a 1962 opening, *Photoplay* looked ahead to the year and reported:

It is believed £4,000,000 will be the final cost of the production. *Cleopatra* has been jinxed like no other picture. The question is: will the jinx follow it to the box office? Despite all the troubles, Fox have battled bravely on. No film could deserve an audience more. And queues. Long queues.

In 1963, *Girl Television & Film Annual* began its coverage:

> When Cleopatra died from the bite of the snake that she held to her bosom, the enemies around her throne rubbed their hands with glee. However, when Elizabeth Taylor acted out the same scene in front of the film cameras in Rome, the emotion could best be described as one of relief!

The report ended, citing its '£13,000,000 expense, the most costly adventure in movie history'.

Hitherto, the highest status granted a VIP on a visit to Rome was a trip to the Vatican and to be granted a papal audience; in 1962, it was an invitation to the set of *Cleopatra*. A blue badge was issued to 'people directly connected with the picture'. A red badge was for on-set visitors. One journalist reported at the time, 'Precautions resembled those in force at Los Alamos atomic testing grounds.'

While Taylor celebrated her thirtieth birthday in Rome, Burton went to Switzerland for a family conference. Graham Jenkins remembered being told:

> Rich was actually frightened of what he had started. For the first time, the prospect of losing Sybil was real. And not just Sybil. With her would go his confidence and his stability. 'He won't take the risk' [Tom Jenkins told Graham] 'He's not that much of a fool'. But we reckoned without Elizabeth Taylor ...

Elizabeth was not a vengeful Harpy out to poach Burton from his wife. For all the alleged wantonness, she was quite an old-fashioned girl – no affairs for her, she *married* the men she loved. Her marriage to Eddie

Fisher was on the rocks by the time the Welshman appeared on the scene. She was quite simply blown away by Burton's virility, his swaggering bravado, and the fact that they were thrown together on set each day, every day.

The Jenkins clan took a long, hard look at what was developing and felt that Elizabeth's fatal commitment was that she had decided her marriage to Eddie Fisher was finished. And that opened up a dangerous door. Surrounded by the usual paparazzi on his return to Rome, Burton was surprised to find Taylor in a skittish mood and keen to take on their tormentors at their own game. 'They want pictures,' Elizabeth laughed. 'So let's give them pictures. Let's give them more pictures than they expect, more pictures than they could ever want. Let's give them so many pictures, they'll never want to point a camera at us again.'

The plan backfired. Graham Jenkins noted, 'Never once did it occur to him that Sybil or anyone else in the family would misinterpret the rush of scurrilous publicity. They would know it was just good old Rich having his game. Wouldn't they?'

The sanctity of marriage went beyond the Welsh Valleys. In those distant, pre-feminist times, it was Taylor's reputation that suffered: a man-eating adulteress; a serial marriage-breaker; a slut. Meanwhile, typical of the hypocrisy of the period, many people just raised an eyebrow, chuckled and nudge-nudged at rumours of the virile Burton's innumerable infidelities.

☥

While they were out on the town on 31 March 1962, the Burton–Taylor romance went stratospheric. The couple were photographed openly together, off set, hand in hand and evidently in love. Now they could no longer claim it was purely business. There was a scintilla of truth in the fact that, while on set as Marc Antony and Cleopatra, Richard Burton and Elizabeth Taylor were only acting. Evidently on the town, lapping up each other's company, now such strenuous denials were given the lie.

Sybil Burton was stoic, turning a blind eye to the rumours and gossip. But it was when accounts of the affair her husband was having with his co-star appeared in *The Sunday Times* that she began to fear the worst. Trusting and loyal, Mrs Burton could avoid the lurid scandal magazine coverage and ignore reports in far-off newspapers in America and Italy. But when the story broke in one of the most respected newspapers in the English-speaking world, it was time for action.

The next day, those paparazzi shots from Rome were on the front pages of every newspaper around the world. Inexorably and relentlessly, Burton had jumped on the slalom of unimagined fame, to his own delight. 'I had no idea she was so f\*\*\*\*\*g *famous!*' he chortled. He assumed the affair was a diversion, like so many before, or that the couple could control the tiger on whose back they now rode. It was a journey that would take Burton to the very heights of unparalleled success, but would leave a vacuum where the centre of his art and craft should have been.

The romance that blossomed between the two stars really was the love that dared not speak its name. When Elizabeth Taylor and Richard Burton played their first scene together, as the world's best-known lovers in the most fabled film in the history of sound cinema, the air was charged with the kind of static electricity that film publicists and newspaper editors only dream of. Until *Cleopatra*, film publicists were always keen to spark rumours of off-screen romances to generate interest in a film while in production.

Long after Burton filmed his first scene with Taylor, their pairing was fuelling the gossip mills. Producer Walter Wanger was concerned that the film's production executive, Peter Levathes, looking after on-set publicity, was a man incapable of controlling the escalating drama, 'the kind of man who would be right at home placing an ad for a shredded-wheat campaign, but he is over his head here'.

In their compelling account of the filming, *The Cleopatra Papers*, it is with incredulity that you read that Fox publicists Jack Brodsky and Nathan Weiss (who took over from Levathes) had been sent to Rome by the studio in 1961 because *Cleopatra* 'was not getting enough publicity'! 'Nobody wants this to get out,' Brodsky wrote to Weiss, with an eye on the box office effect, 'because they feel that the public will crucify her and picket the theaters if she breaks up another family.'

As the scandal took on a life of its own, Fox even tried to sue, invoking a morality clause. But Taylor knew she had the studio over a barrel. Her biographer, C. David Heymann, quoted scriptwriter Meade Roberts, who knew both Burton and Taylor, in *Liz* (1995), recalling her responding to the letter:

If I walk, I'll never work again. I'm not going to starve if I never work again. I'll be sued, but [Fox executive] Mr Levathes will lose his empire and 20th Century Fox will crumble. *Cleopatra* is three-quarters done, and it's too late for them to replace me, and if I walk out of here, Fox is as good as dead.

# 10

# *Le Scandale*

There had, of course, been precedents for the attention the world paid to illicit romances, like the one blossoming between Elizabeth Taylor and Richard Burton on the set of *Cleopatra*. For cinema, it had been the romance between Ingrid Bergman and Roberto Rossellini, a few years before. A Hollywood legend since before the war, Bergman had captivated in *Casablanca*, worked closely with Hitchcock, and later won an Oscar playing the engimatic title character in *Anastasia*. But it was her relationship (including an illegitimate child) with neo-Realist director Rossellini that all but killed her career. It provided, as Shawn Levy wrote, 'a nexus of newsreels, picture magazines and tabloid newspapers that actively sought to ferret out and broadcast intimate details about the lives of celebrities'.

Bergman's affair with Rossellini was conducted in the full glare of the paparazzi flashbulbs. She arrived in Rome in 1949 to film *Stromboli*. For the cinema-mad Italians, just her being in their country was enough. 'For us in Italy,' Fellini wrote in typically exuberant form in a newspaper greeting, 'it was as if the Virgin Mary had just descended upon us from Disneyland.'

For the generation between the wars, it had been the affair of King Edward VIII and American divorcee Wallis Simpson that had proved so spellbinding. It is hard to imagine now, in a world preoccupied with celebrity, with the media so intrusive, all-pervasive and immediate, how 'the affair which rocked the British monarchy' was handled.

With the newspapers censored by powerful press barons at the connivance of Stanley Baldwin's Conservative government, the British public were kept in blithe ignorance of the affair, while foreign newspapers indiscriminately reported every titillating detail of the burgeoning romance between a twice-divorced American commoner and the undisputed ruler of the largest Empire the world had ever known. If, however, foreign newspapers *did* sneak into Britain during the crisis, any reference was literally cut out by scissor-wielding customs officers. Only high society knew of the king's devotion to his lover.

As the Prince of Wales, the 42-year-old future Edward VIII cut as compelling a figure as Diana, Princess of Wales, half a century later. While his father, George V, had led his nation to victory through the turbulence of the First World War, but he was not an imaginative man – stamp collecting and shooting things occupied his off-duty hours. The monarch's eldest son, however, was keen to move Great Britain further on, and faster, towards the era of the Bright Young Things. But his father was concerned. 'After I am dead,' George V forecast with eerie prescience, a few months before his death, 'the boy will ruin himself in 12 months.'

The 'land fit for heroes' that Prime Minister Lloyd George had promised the returning survivors, scarred by the horrors of the 'war to end wars', proved to be an illusion. Britain was plunged into the Great Depression and the General Strike. Like a cancer, Fascism spread from the Continent. As a distraction, the Prince of Wales was the cynosure of all eyes. His dashing good looks, zeal for fashion and jaunty air made the man who would be king the centre of attention for a nation keen to have their minds taken off the daily grind.

However, the Prince of Wales was unmarried, and as his ascendancy edged nearer, questions were beginning to be asked of the bachelor prince. The rumours percolated among the smart set of the upper classes, trickling through drawing rooms and wafting across cocktail parties – no celibate was he. Then, when Mrs Simpson appeared on the scene, the gossip took a malicious turn.

This was a time when a divorced person could not enter the Royal Enclosure at Ascot or be presented at Court. So, the prospect of Edward VIII, Emperor of India, protector of the faith, sharing his throne with an American who had the temerity to be divorced, not once but *twice* (and with both husbands still alive), was quite literally unthinkable and inconceivable to the Establishment of the time.

While the affair of Edward and Mrs Simpson was common knowledge in the high-vaulted rooms of Mayfair and Belgravia, it was kept from his subjects who were labouring in the mines of Wigan, the factories of Manchester or office cubicles in the capital. Prime Minister Baldwin was vehemently opposed to the relationship, while Winston Churchill, an incurable romantic, was a loyal supporter of Edward VIII.

All manner of proposals were mooted. The king proposed a morganatic marriage. This would see Mrs Simpson become his wife but she would not accept any titles or partner him in royal duties. She could share his bed, but not his throne. However, this was deemed unworkable.

Even more unacceptable was the prospect of abdication, which shimmered like a phantom over all the negotiations and overshadowed the whole of 1936. It has been said in hindsight that the British government's attention to the detail of Edward and Mrs Simpson blinkered its awareness of the rise of Hitler. Casting aside the Versailles Treaty, by 1936 Hitler had systematically and legally begun the persecution of the Jews. He invaded the Rhineland and slavered for further conquest. And all the while, Edward dug his heels in, determined not to budge, not to concede an inch – he was to have his throne and share it with his love. When news of the affair finally did break, the nation was stunned.

Symbolically, the Crystal Palace burnt to the ground in 1936. It was a year that led to the unique 'Year of the Three Kings' (George V, Edward VIII, George VI), a year which notoriously marked the abdication of Edward VIII, Hitler's reoccupation of the Rhineland, the Jarrow March, the outbreak of the Spanish Civil War and Mussolini's poison gas attacks on hapless Abyssinia. The destruction of the Crystal Palace was seen, like that of Halley's Comet on the eve of the Great War, as a harbinger of the apocalypse to come.

The former king and the woman he loved went on to live their lives together. However, ostracised from his country, they pinballed the globe in a luxurious limbo. The notoriety and public fascination with Edward and Mrs Simpson presaged that of Burton and Taylor.

☥

In the interim, however, came another scandal, which exercised a strange fascination. In 1953, the eyes of the world were spellbound by the timeless pageantry of the coronation of 27-year-old Queen Elizabeth II, but it was the casual action of her sister that alerted the world to the next romance to mesmerise the globe.

For the first time, television audiences had been allowed to witness the sacred ceremony of a crowning in Westminster Abbey. Onlookers watched as, in an idle moment, the new queen's glamorous 23-year-old sister, Margaret, leaned across and was seen to pick a piece of fluff off the uniform of her father's aide-de-camp, Group Captain Peter Townsend.

It was the devoted act of a woman in love, an absent-minded deed that alerted the world to intimacy, and that was to rock the foundations of the British Establishment in a manner that had been unmatched since the abdication nearly twenty years before. It was not the fact that Townsend was demonstrably older than Princess Margaret, rather his status as a divorced man, which still sent spasms through the stuffy tweeds of the Establishment.

The Townsend affair did not have the same ramifications as that of Edward and Mrs Simpson. Margaret was never in line to ascend to the throne; she was merely the sister of a reigning monarch. Margaret was no defender of the faith, no monarch reigning over an empire upon which the sun was still reluctant to set. The fact that there was a romance, though, set pulses racing and tongues wagging.

Margaret ran with a fast set. Her beauty was more like that of a film star than a member of the British royal family. Margaret smoked, was no stranger to hard liquor, and she liked her rock and roll.

As the sister of the reigning queen, though, Margaret was subject to a different set of rules. Townsend was banished to Brussels and Princess Margaret undertook her royal duties, but, along with the rest of the world spellbound by the royal romance, she waited breathlessly for Townsend's return. When he did come back, the capital was convulsed. At one point, 300 photographers and journalists were camped outside Townsend's residence.

In the end, Margaret chose duty over love, and in October 1955 issued a statement which read, in part, that the princess was 'mindful of the Church's teaching that Christian marriage is indissoluble'. For critics of the Establishment, it was another triumph for the men in suits behind the railings of Buckingham Palace; their remit was shadowy, but their reach was long.

The media hysteria and public frenzy over another public romance, the marriage of actress Grace Kelly to Prince Rainier of Monaco in 1956, gave another foretaste of the romance of Burton and Taylor, six years later. A real-life prince marrying a bonafide film star made for irresistible reading.

Then followed the Taylor and Burton affair, but they were soon elbowed off the front pages in the UK by the Profumo affair, which exploded in 1963. With the Cold War very much in evidence, it was revealed that the Minister of Defence was having an affair with a call girl who was also sleeping with an official at the Russian Embassy. A jealous boyfriend, who she had met apparently searching for marijuana in a Notting Hill club, took pot-shots at the flat Christine Keeler shared with Mandy Rice-Davies. It really did have it all – sex in high and low places, drugs, espionage.

As the sordid details of the Profumo affair began to emerge, it really kicked open the door that was signposted 'The Swinging Sixties'. Newspapers began to describe orgies at stately homes, kinky sex in high places, and prostitutes sharing their favours with drug dealers, government ministers and Russian spies.

As well as the salacious aspects, it was the hypocrisy of the Profumo scandal that sent newspaper sales soaring during the summer of 1963.

Osteopath Stephen Ward, mentor to both Keeler and Rice-Davies, was the sacrificial lamb. Ward's suicide before a verdict was passed was seen as the Establishment getting away with it. People in high places just didn't *do* such things. No wonder that in faraway Hull, Philip Larkin wryly noted that, for him, like so many, sexual intercourse only began in 1963!

By the time *Cleopatra* premiered that same year, the public were sated with sensationalism. But such was the fervour of the Burton–Taylor affair that their magnetism still exercised a powerful hold. The question the director, the studio and Hollywood itself asked was would that be enough to recoup the film's $44 million budget?

The Burtons stop off for a pint. Richard once joked, 'I introduced her to beer; she introduced me to Bulgari!'

The only public screening of the film Elizabeth Taylor attended: a benefit for the Bolshoi Ballet in London, 19 August 1963.

One of the first publicity photos of an 11-year-old Elizabeth Taylor.

Taylor with her great friend Montgomery Clift, from *A Place in the Sun*, 1951.

On set with her *Giant* co-star James Dean.

A rare photo of Elizabeth's screen test for *Quo Vadis*, 1949. The role eventually went to Deborah Kerr.

Vivien Leigh as Cleopatra in 1945's *Caesar & Cleopatra*, at the time the most expensive British film ever made.

Claudette Colbert in Cecil B. DeMille's 1934 *Cleopatra*.

The *real* Cleopatra from a contemporary statue, now at the Altes Museum in Berlin.

Theda Bara in the 1917 silent film *Cleopatra*, all prints of which were later destroyed in a studio fire.

Elizabeth Taylor signs that historic million-dollar contract. On her right is 20th Century Fox head Buddy Adler, who died before the film opened, and on her left is producer Walter Wanger, whose career never recovered from the *Cleopatra* debacle.

A rare photo of Elizabeth Taylor with the teenage Francesca Annis, one of the few surviving stars of the film.

Richard Burton in the 1953 Old Vic production of *Hamlet*.

Burton and Taylor leave the fashionable Roman restaurant Ai Tre Scalini at the height of '*le scandale*'.

# The PLAYBILL ®

*For the Mark Hellinger Theatre*

## My Fair Lady

The original programme from the 1956 Broadway production of *My Fair Lady*, featuring Rex Harrison as Professor Higgins, his best-known role.

Director Joseph L. Mankiewicz on the set of *Cleopatra*, the film that virtually ended his career.

Cleopatra's entry into Rome. No CGI here – the Roman forum constructed for the film was twice the size of the original, and those are all costumed extras!

# 11

# The Burtons

The surfeit of publicity that greeted the couple's 'coming out' was manifestly manna for the *Cleopatra* publicists. But could there be a case that not all publicity was good publicity? Within days of the front-page romance, the Vatican issued a bulletin unmistakably addressed to Taylor. It commented on 'erotic vagrancy' (a charge Elizabeth would occasionally revel in). The missive went on to condemn 'the caprices of adult children', which, the Holy Father believed, offended 'the nobility of the heart which millions of married couples judge to be a beautiful and holy thing ... There remain three husbands buried, with no other motive than a greater love that killed the one before.'

Burton himself was not concerned by the pope's missive. 'He's never been on my party list,' he airily told his brother. But the reminder of moral rectitude found a welcome audience in America. The conservative congresswoman Iris Blitch was singularly upset, believing that Taylor 'lowered the prestige of American women abroad and damaged good will in foreign countries'. The *Washington Post* later reported that Ohio's Congressman Michael Feighan strongly felt that 'the State Department ought to show its regard for propriety by revoking the visa issued to Mr Richard Burton, the English actor'. Burton was unimpressed – but took issue with being described as an '*English* actor'.

While the off-screen romance kept the world captivated, the couple still had a film to make. The Vatican denunciation appeared the day before Taylor filmed her entry into Rome. It was the key scene of the film. This was 'the money shot': the one that director Joe Mankiewicz had elaborately choreographed so that jaws would drop. This would make the executives sit up and see where the money had gone. It would make audiences forget the gossip and marvel at the stupendous spectacle.

There was real concern that the thousands of Roman extras (Catholics to a man) would heckle and spoil the scene. The endless fascination with the affair undermined even Taylor's steely purpose. Those close to the star said they had never seen her so nervous before a scene. In the event, the scene was only undone on technical grounds – the thousands of extras greeting the star with real enthusiasm.

☥

And all the while, as the production costs soared, Mankiewicz grappled with his script and the Fox executives tore at what little hair they had, the film's stars were locked in their own world. For Graham, his brother was 'a prisoner of his own emotions. He loved Sibyl and was spellbound by Elizabeth. He lived from day to day hoping decisions would be made for him.' Elizabeth was equally besotted. Writing years later, she enthused, 'Richard was magnificent in every sense of the word [...] from those moments in Rome we were always madly and powerfully in love.'

Studio executives in Hollywood were in two minds about the scandal. It undeniably helped *Cleopatra* become the most talked-about film of the decade, but even they saw that with the pope and US congressmen and women lined up against it in a stern climate of moral rectitude, the orchestrated salaciousness could backfire.

In the end, when *Cleopatra* finally opened and the first scathing reviews appeared, Twentieth Century Fox were looking for scapegoats, whose heads they could place on the chopping block, someone to blame for the evident fiasco. 'The prime candidates,' Graham Jenkins reflected:

... were the Studio executives in Hollywood, who were in two minds about 'the scandal', and Elizabeth Taylor. However competent as performers, their personal shenanigans had distracted producer and director from their professional responsibilities. Another version of the charge sheet held that while the film was good, if not brilliant, family entertainment, the stars' behaviour destroyed its appeal at the box office.

In hindsight, making the stars bear the burden for the runaway catastrophe that was *Cleopatra* in production is unfair. Poor planning and budgeting, expensive location switches, beginning such an epic without a finished script and the Hollywood studio wavering in its commitment, plus the reckless behaviour of the principals, were what set the production on such a rocky route.

Even as the *Cleopatra* carnival left town, the furore surrounding the couple refused to abate. With an eye on the healthy publicity surrounding a film starring Burton and Taylor, MGM weren't slow off the mark to commission Terence Rattigan to come up with a script inspired by *Grand Hotel* called *The V.I.P.s*. The trailer left little doubt as to where the film's appeal was aimed at: 'The most talked about couple, the most famous couple in the entire world.' *The V.I.P.s* went on to become the studio's most successful film of 1963.

Graham Jenkins was his brother's stand-in during the shoot and observed first-hand over a period of weeks the immediate effect that the fishbowl of fame was having on Burton following *Cleopatra*. Always a heavy drinker, it is likely that the constant and unremitting life he was living under the media microscope and the public obsession with Elizabeth tipped him further down the unsteady road. Graham observed his brother's breakfast consisting solely of a series of large Bloody Marys. While filming *Becket*, in 1963, Burton began the day with vodka and wine, a whisky pick-me-up for lunch, then more whiskies, on and on, into the late evening.

It was while filming *The V.I.P.s* that Burton's marriage inevitably collapsed. Like the majority of the Jenkins clan, Graham had 'decided not to like Elizabeth Taylor. But the resolution went by the board almost as soon as I met her. I could see very clearly how she captivated Rich. If Sybil stood for security, Elizabeth was excitement.'

Taylor planned her campaign to woo the Jenkins clan as astutely as any general. She flew as many as would come to see Richard in *Hamlet* on Broadway. She paid particular attention to courting Cis, the woman Burton effectively saw as his mother, and Ifor, the brother her husband revered.

Five weeks into filming *The V.I.P.s*, Burton proposed to Taylor. Sibyl Burton received an estimated $1 million divorce settlement and set up home in New York. Eddie Fisher disappeared into the margins of showbiz notoriety, with his place in history as the man cuckolded by Richard Burton.

Burton's decision to divorce his wife and marry Elizabeth did not impact only his family. Sibyl was very popular with many of Burton's friends; his fellow Welshman and acting contemporary Stanley Baker and his wife, Ellen, sided with Sibyl. It caused a rift, which was later repaired when Burton agreed to deliver the narration for Baker's dream project *Zulu* free of charge.

And so the parade moved on. As 'The Burtons', they became the most photographed, talked about and envied couple in the world. Their every move was endlessly repeated and transported down the wires to an insatiable world's press.

For all the celebrity trappings and excess, while sober, Burton could still recognise a good script. *The Spy Who Came in From the Cold* (1965) reminded audiences that there was a depth to Burton beyond the jet-setting movie star. The *Daily Express*'s Leonard Mosley was not alone in writing:

> His performance makes you forgive him for every bad part he has ever played, every good part he has ever messed up, and every indiscretion he has ever committed off the screen or on. If he doesn't win an Oscar for it this year, there is not only no justice left in Hollywood, but no judgment either.

Burton was nominated, but that year's Oscar went to Lee Marvin in *Cat Ballou*.

Burton steamrollered through *Becket*, *Night of the Iguana* and *The V.I.P.s* in the immediate years of the post-*Cleopatra* madness. Arguably, 1965's *The Spy Who Came in From the Cold* was the best role of Burton's film career. He also played a nice cameo in *What's New Pussycat* and a tour-de-force pairing with Taylor in *Who's Afraid of Virginia Woolf* – a role which should have landed him that well-deserved, but never-received Oscar.

But as he played up to the public image of Mr Elizabeth Taylor, Burton found himself dogged by turkeys such as *The Sandpiper* ('The world's most headlined lovers dominate the screen again' screamed the film's poster). This 1965 romance failed to conjure up any sexual chemistry between its stars. The film portrayed a very Hollywood vision of artistic Bohemians, and Burton was lumbered with the role of an Episcopalian minister and lines like 'I cannot dispel you from my thoughts'.

One script that Burton did recognise in the immediate post-*Cleopatra* euphoria, and at the height of the Burton–Taylor frenzy, was *Hamlet*. The first prince he had seen was Gielgud's in Oxford while a student in 1943, and hearing that the knight was keen to stage the play in modern dress, Burton agreed to play the Prince of Denmark for the second time. Burton was terrified of the part: he hadn't played Shakespeare for a decade and hadn't appeared before a live audience since 1960. The press interest was solely focused on the infamy the couple hauled around with them, like the caravanserai of secretaries, bodyguards and childminders.

Burton's nerves translated into the rehearsal. Off her own bat, Taylor approached Burton's mentor and namesake, Philip Burton, and asked him to bring his considerable Shakespearian expertise to the thorny knot. The older Burton arrived in Toronto three days before the opening night, and together they knocked his protege's performance into shape.

Prior to its Broadway opening in August 1964, in Toronto, Burton estimated that Taylor's loyal presence in the audience added an extra eighteen minutes to the play's running time because of the crowds craning their necks to simply get a glimpse of the diva. But by the time the

*Hamlet* production hauled into New York, the Canadian frenzy had escalated into out-and-out hysteria.

The Beatles had arrived in America a few months before *Hamlet* opened at the Lunt-Fontanne Theater on 48th Street, so America was prepared for mass hysteria. But every night, 100 police kept the crowds at bay as Burton and Taylor fought through the mob to gain access to the stage door. The play's director, John Gielgud, recalled a machine-gun-toting guard patrolling outside the couple's hotel suite.

Audiences were thrilled as they heard Hamlet declaim lines such as 'Doubt that the stars are fire; Doubt that the sun doth move; Doubt truth to be a liar; But never doubt I love', knowing that the object of such veneration was likely in that same theatre. Gielgud reflected that if Burton had made his return to the stage in a less-showy role than *Hamlet* – *Macbeth*, say, or *Coriolanus* – the critical reception would have been kinder.

Age was a factor. Burton was edging 40 as he tackled the prince's adolescent angst. But there was no denying the production's success – Burton's *Hamlet* ran for eighteen weeks in New York, making it the most successful run of the play in the city's history. The reviews were generally favourable and Burton undeniably added another string to his bow following the *Cleopatra* debacle.

Even a year after the film's opening, though, the Burtons (they were married in Montreal on 15 March 1964) were up to their bejewelled necks in lawsuits. Burton must have reflected, like the Danish prince, 'When sorrows come, they come not as single spies, but in battalions.' In the immediate aftermath of *Cleopatra*, the Burtons had up to twenty lawyers working on their behalf through the legal minefields. By the summer of 1964, the lawsuits were flying as freely as the arrows at the Battle of Actium:

1   Walter Wanger sued Skouras, Zanuck, Fox and columnist Earl Wilson for defamation, demanding $2.6 million.
2   Skouras sued Wanger, Bantam Books and (co-author) Joe Hyams, alleging that 'he was held up to ridicule' in the book *My Life With Cleopatra*.

3  Elizabeth Taylor's company MCL films sued Twentieth Century Fox, alleging 'lack of sound business judgment in the distribution and exploitation of the film'.

4  Twentieth Century Fox claimed a total of a reported $50 million in damages, from Burton and Taylor, charging that 'the pair had depreciated the value of the film by their deportment during and subsequent to the making of the film'.

5  A chain of US cinema distributors sued Fox and the Burtons in their separate claim for $6 million. It was alleged that the couple's conduct 'during the *Cleopatra* production turned it into an inferior motion picture'.

One suit that occurred while filming was taking place came from the circus owner, Ennio Togni, who supplied the animals for Cleopatra's entry into Rome. He was originally asked to supply 100 elephants. That was reduced to ten and then only four elephants were required. As filming progressed, production assistants insisted that 'the elephants were unfit for film work', so Togni sued the film's producer because his elephants were 'slandered'.

The suits were eventually settled, and in the ensuing tsunami of what became the Swinging Sixties, *Cleopatra* was soon overshadowed. As the 1960s wound on, even 'The Burtons' found their fame eclipsed by younger contenders such as Paul McCartney and Jane Asher; Mick Jagger and Marianne Faithfull; Terence Stamp and Jean Shrimpton; Bob Dylan and Joan Baez; and David Bailey and Catherine Deneuve.

The *Cleopatra* stars were delighted when the spotlight shifted. For all the melodrama that she embraced, Elizabeth Taylor was a survivor. Burton lacked that resilience, and as the drink dissipated the desire, the talent too began to wane and Burton lost interest in the craft that had hauled him out of the valleys. 'I've done the most awful rubbish just for somewhere to go in the morning,' he once admitted.

The cheques and the desire to fill the daylight hours saw Burton's discernment wither – among the roles he declined were Napoleon in *Waterloo* and Bill Sikes in the film of *Oliver* (both opposite Peter O'Toole), which could have made fascinating films. Taylor herself wasn't too bothered; she declined to play Queen Elizabeth I in *The Queen and the Hives*. Mind you, audiences may have found it hard to imagine her as 'The Virgin Queen'.

Graham Jenkins observed the glitter come off the tarnished crown:

> It was not simply that bad movies predominated. What was worrying was the clearly perceptible slide in the popularity of the Taylor–Burton partnership. Younger audiences, on whom the industry increasingly depended, were no longer transfixed by the *Cleopatra* love story. It was so tame by the standards of the swinging sixties. What place was there for the Burtons in the age of The Beatles?

While filming the catastrophic *Candy* in 1968, where Burton played a bard based on Dylan Thomas, he and Elizabeth struck up a friendship with Ringo Starr. It was the dog days of the group and the drummer was looking for new avenues to explore. Here he was playing a Mexican gardener! Looking back, one of the highlights of the filming, the drummer recalled, was hearing Burton recite the lyrics of 'I am the Walrus' in that 'magnificent voice of his'. In truth, by then the public appeal of 'The Burtons', the plc brand of 'Dick & Liz', was in danger of waning.

☥

The writer Dick Clement was in a production office in Mayfair in 1970 when Burton 'stormed in' straight from Buckingham Palace, where he had been awarded his CBE. 'He was belligerent and angry and wanted a drink,' Clement later wrote:

> I can only assume he felt short-changed by his honour. A knighthood would have put him on a par with Gielgud, Guinness, Olivier and Richardson. Turning his back on the theatre and the lifestyle had cost him the accolade that he obviously coveted.

On and on, and down and down. For Burton, there were odd flurries – a stellar turn in *Equus* and a final flourish in *1984*. There was the family favourite, *Where Eagles Dare*. There were the unremarkable *The Assassination of Trotsky* and *Exorcist II: The Heretic*. But there were also the unforgivable – an ill-considered TV remake of *Brief Encounter*, and the films *The Klansman* and *The Wild Geese*.

There were the visible and lurid displays of impulse buying, ostentatious purchases of jewellery and displays of the couple's evident affluence on board yachts or for Elizabeth's fortieth birthday party in still-Communist Budapest. There was the visible divorce in 1974 then the farcical remarriage in a safari park soon after.

It is poignant to watch Burton's 1974 interview with Michael Parkinson. The actor, just out of rehab, is visibly nervous, puffing steadily on a succession of Benson & Hedges. He is engaging company, if subdued, but when he lets rip that magnificent voice, all manner of echoes emerge – *Hamlet*, Marc Antony, *Under Milk Wood*, *Where Eagles Dare* ('Broadsword calling Danny Boy ...'). There is a genuine, undermining sadness in seeing it, knowing the actor only has ten more years to live. Parkinson asks which of the many films he made does he look back on with fondness and he answers, 'Six or seven, which is a pretty bad batting average'. But Burton is wilful and determined, looking forward to the next *thirty* years.

At his funeral in Celigny in Switzerland, Burton's daughter Kate read the poem that linked her father with his homeland, and which could well act as his epitaph. Dylan Thomas's poem concludes, 'Do not go gentle into that good night/Rage, rage against the dying of the light.' And that was something Richard Burton excelled at: raging hard.

When the obituaries came, and they, too, came in battalions, most spoke of the wasted promise, of the talent dissipated by the drink, of the Faustian pact Burton made to wallow in the lavish lifestyle film fame gave him. And all the while, the regret at what might have been.

It was *Cleopatra* that was the making of Richard Burton, giving him a second chance at a career in film. He had dallied in film stardom in the 1950s, but it was *Cleopatra* that hurled him into the headlines, where he was to remain for the rest of his life. It was *Cleopatra* that proved to be Burton's excelsis and nemesis. It was wooing his Cleopatra that let him scale the heights of unimagined fame and fortune.

But it was being tied to that film's star which, perhaps needlessly, shackled his career. They were 'The Burtons', a commodity that guaranteed box-office gold. Not that Elizabeth Taylor ever held her husband back. She was in awe of Burton and his prodigious talent. She encouraged him to take roles that would stretch that talent. His ability at Shakespeare was enviable and, until the drink took its toll, inviolate.

It was a dilemma and dichotomy Burton battled with all his life. While filming *Who's Afraid of Virginia Woolf* in Northampton, Massachusetts, he was in reminiscing mode. An early stage appearance had elicited a glowing review from the *New Statesman*: 'In a wretched part, Richard Burton showed an exceptional ability.' Something triggered a memory in Burton:

> I would have become a preacher, a poet, a playwright, a scholar, a lawyer or something ... I would never have become this strange thing, an actor, sitting in a remote corner of the universe called Northampton, drinking a vodka and tonic, and waiting to learn the next line. He's got a bloody lot to answer for, that man.

In Richard Burton was a Shakespearian fatal flaw: he wanted the acclaim that dedication and commitment to his craft brought. And he wanted the money that well-paid film roles brought for relatively little effort. At the height of the *Cleopatra* scandal, Laurence Olivier telegrammed the boy who had been given house room at the Old Vic in Waterloo, just south of the Thames. It was a world away from the scandal surrounding the *Cleopatra* set in Rome. 'Make up your mind, dear heart. Do you want to be a great actor or a household word?'

Burton immediately cabled back, 'Both!'

Such vaunted ambition was to be both the making and breaking of him – as an actor, and as a man.

# 12

# 'Fasten Your Seat Belts'

It had been the box office triumph of 1951's *Quo Vadis* that had alerted Hollywood to the success of 'sword and sandal' productions. The studios had earlier opened the biblical floodgates with *David and Bathsheba* (1951), but it had been MGM's epic *Quo Vadis* that had demonstrated the viability of Italy as a production base. On chariot wheels, quickly after *The Robe* came *Salome* (both 1953), *Demetrius and the Gladiators* (1954) and *Solomon and Sheba* (1959). Most lavish of all, on home turf, came Cecil B. DeMille's *The Ten Commandments* (1956) – even Rome could not guarantee parting the Red Sea successfully.

All were cut from the same cloth: spectacular crowd scenes (with real crowds), reverential and homely when dealing with the Messiah, but with a tantalising suggestion of sex, thundering chariots and all-conquering legions. Power and corruption, faith and belief, decadence and spectacle, dissolution and depravity, sensuality and Christianity – all in lurid CinemaScope and booming in stereo. All were approved by the MPA and the Legion of Decency. But all were just titivating enough to cause stirrings in juvenile boys and to set teenage girls' pulses racing.

Peter Ustinov had a theory about the genre's success, as he told Brian McFarlane:

> I think the Americans are the only people who can do ancient Roman films for the simple reason they are *like* the ancient Romans. If you go

into the Chase National Bank to get a loan you are taken into a room with columns of Gorgonzola and, in the middle of this, a furled flag and an eagle behind him … the bank manager is saying, 'Why don't we go home and continue this conversation by the atrium?'

*Cleopatra*, in fact, was not Elizabeth Taylor's only appearance in a toga saga. In fact, the actress was the original choice for the role of Lygia in *Quo Vadis*, with Elizabeth going as far as having costume tests. But scheduling saw the role taken by Deborah Kerr.

While on honeymoon in Rome with her first husband Nicky Hilton, a plainly unhappy Taylor made her way to the *Quo Vadis* location one night. There, she bumped into old friends from MGM and, without too much difficulty, was persuaded into costume, appearing as an unpaid extra in one of the film's huge crowd scenes. Also among the 30,000 extras was the young Sofia Scicolone, who would later change her name to Sophia Loren.

In 1950, to encourage native film production, the Italian government severely restricted the release of US films. In the five years since the liberation, a studio like MGM would have accumulated literally billions of lire but could only access it by spending money on production *in* Italy. In 1950, the shooting of MGM's *Quo Vadis* helped eat up 4 billion lire ($6.4 million).

Starring Robert Taylor and Deborah Kerr, *Quo Vadis* had a script as purple as Nero's robes ('Hair with the sheen of a young raven', 'Guard her well, my grey-haired Colossus'). Here was bread and circuses writ large. However stern and plodding *Quo Vadis* appears to today's audiences, it nonetheless remains a full-scale example of the sort of pious spectacle laced with sexiness that Hollywood used to fight back against TV during the desperate 1950s – formulaic acres of CinemaScopic spectacle, screeds of Christianity and a bit of sexual allure, with the usual conflict between faith and belief. The opening narration sets the scene: 'On a Roman cross in Judea, a Man died to make men free, to spread the Gospel of love and redemption. Soon that humble cross is destined to replace the proud eagles atop the victorious Roman standards.'

As Nero, Peter Ustinov heads over the top at the drop of a slave's toga. The unlikely figure of Scots pensioner Finlay Currie was a regular player in these epics, while Leo Genn adds dignity, as you would expect from a Nuremberg prosecutor and early visitor to the hell of Belsen.

Even before Hollywood began dipping its toes into the Tiber, there was something about the ancient world that had fascinated contemporary societies – Shakespeare's *Julius Caesar* and *Antony and Cleopatra*, for example, and the seventeenth-century unearthing of Pompeii, then the paintings of Joseph Wright and Alma-Tadema, who always dealt with their subject on a substantial scale. When Edward Gibbon handed a copy of his monumental *Decline and Fall of the Roman Empire* (1776/1789) to the Duke of Gloucester, he was disconcerted to be told, 'Another damned, thick, square book! Always scribble, scribble, scribble, eh, Mr Gibbon?'

But even scholars, historians, earlier efforts and rival studios were unprepared for the scale of Twentieth Century Fox's tortuous production of *Cleopatra*. The decision to persevere post-Pinewood was to prove prohibitively expensive. With Italy decided and the Cinecitta studios block-booked for the production, the 'new' *Cleopatra*, with Joseph L. Mankiewicz at the helm, was scheduled to begin filming in September 1961.

On 13 August, the long-suffering producer, Walter Wanger, despaired. 'England all over again: we do not have a script, the sets aren't ready, costumes aren't ready. The props are not ready either and we need more than a million dollars' worth.'

In Italy, the vertiginous costs continued: a crew of over 1,000 laboured every day on set. Once filming began, a crew of 235 grafted behind the cameras and 1,800 kilowatts of electricity were generated daily.

More cement was used over the 20-acre set of the Roman Forum than was used for the 1960 Olympic stadium. True to form with the troubled production, typically, the film Forum was twice the size of the original. Thirty buildings, using 6,000 tons of cement, were constructed on the huge site; 160 statues over 12ft tall were erected.

Over 26,000 gallons of paint were splashed out during the production of *Cleopatra*. A team of armourers produced 10,000 spears and 150,000 arrows for firing. For detail, 460 pieces of pottery were specially made.

The money flowed as freely as the wine was consumed. Budgetary considerations were never a factor. *Nobody* seemed in control. Paper cups alone accounted for $100,000 of the budget. Five thousand wigs were made, only to remain unseen beneath centurions' helmets. Customised items for the queen's dressing table – by Bulgari – were, at best, glimpsed for a few seconds on screen.

There were 26,000 costumes made in total, many of which were stitched by costumiers who had sewn Queen Elizabeth's coronation gown in 1953. Sixty-five of those costumes (at a budget of $194,800) were solely for Elizabeth Taylor, including the gown of pure 24-carat gold that she wore for her spectacular entry into Rome, which alone cost $6,500.

Then there was the *lack* of costumes. 'Acres Of Bare Flesh: Near Nude Girls Frolic In Cleo' ran one tantalising headline. Costume designer Renie commented on the authenticity, 'The climate of the country was terribly warm and it was only natural that the people wear as little as possible.' Vital statistics of the dancers were revealed as 37–24–36.

Rumours emanated from the set that the colour of Taylor's Roman villa changed daily, according to the colour of the cigarettes she was smoking. 'Later I got to see the studio's breakdown on the money waste,' Taylor later told David Kamp. 'They said I ate 12 chickens and 40 pounds of bacon every day for breakfast. *What?*'

The filming just went on. And on. And on. By the time they came to filming the boy originally cast as Cleopatra's baby, 'he looked like Jack Dempsey next to Elizabeth' – cue another casting call.

By the profligate standards of *Cleopatra*, the $22,000 spent on clearing live mines from the Torre Astura beach, where ancient Alexandria had been reconstructed, was miniscule – that is, on top of the $150,000 already paid out for the hire of the beach. Then, despite guarantees to the contrary, NATO decided to use another beach within earshot as a location to test fire their latest artillery, which took away from the period, and added further delays.

Elizabeth Taylor's personal physician was on the budget at a cost of $25,000, plus expenses. Because Cinecitta had no facilities to view the relatively new Todd-AO rushes (the format patented by Taylor's third husband, and the one she insisted was used for *Cleopatra*), they had to be sent all the way back to Hollywood to be processed, then returned to Rome before Mankiewicz could view them.

Other incidental costs included a total of $17,000 to clear the set – of cats. A female cat invaded the set and gave birth to five kittens. She had sneaked under Cleopatra's bed and the new-born kittens howled during a love scene. Then filming was held up for forty-five minutes while another cat was chased off set.

One estimate had the daily costs of *Cleopatra* running at $122,000 per day – that was whether filming took place or not. One element depended on Miss Taylor's menstrual cycle, or on whether the queen and Marc Antony were relaxing together. Like the railway timetables that were so much a part of the world going to war in 1914, *Cleopatra* appeared to be running along the same lines – basically, out of control and unstoppable.

With the benefit of hindsight, and the perspective of half a century, you can read the statistics and you can marvel at the waste, but it is only when you watch the documentaries or see the finished film – knowing what it took to get those scenes on film – that you begin to appreciate the scale of the folly. Hindsight, of course, would caution against using the UK locations and insist on California as a base, where studio executives could be on hand to reign in some of the extravagance. But by now, it was too late.

'Right now,' Mankiewicz ruefully reflected, 'the head of Fox in Hong Kong is taking two hookers to lunch, and it's being charged to my picture!' As *Cleopatra* was the only Fox film in production, *everything* was added to that troubled film's budget. 'If two Fox executives went to lunch in, say, Paris,' the director's son, Tom Mankiewicz, told Michael Troyan, author of *Twentieth Century Fox: A Century of Entertainment*, 'the cost of that meal was charged to *Cleopatra*. This meant that the announced budget was perceived as not only unforgivably profligate, but obscene.'

When filming was finally completed, Mankiewicz was left with 450,000ft of exposed Todd-AO film. If anyone could have found the time to view it all, they would have been in front of the cinema screen for ninety-six hours. The film producer Gilbert Miller visited the *Cleopatra* set in Rome and was offered the sets by visiting producer Walter Wanger for use in a musical. 'Do a musical?' Miller replied. 'Give me a chance and I'll start a new *country*, with those sets as the capital!'

♀

The man with the hands-on management of the film was director and screenwriter Joseph L. Mankiewicz. By the time he came to *Cleopatra*, Mankiewicz was no stranger to turbulent productions and the sensitive handling of temperamental thespians. He was as much admired for his writing as for his directing. Mankiewicz won Oscars for both writing and directing in two successive years, for *A Letter to Three Wives* (1949) and *All About Eve* (1950).

Re-watching *All About Eve* recently, I was struck by just how original it was. 'Written, produced and directed by Joseph L. Mankiewicz.' Just pause and think for a moment: it was Mankiewicz who sat down and created Margo Channing, Eve Harrington and Addison de Witt. Some of cinema's most memorable characters didn't exist until Mankiewicz fashioned them and created immortal, enduring cinematic icons.

Mankiewicz came to 1953's *Julius Caesar* anticipating storms. Hollywood had proved its penchant for costume drama with the success of *Quo Vadis*, but this would be the film capital's first serious stab at Shakespeare. Hollywood, however, was wary (all that *talking*); thus, to ensure its success, the cast was stacked with proven talent – John Gielgud, James Mason, Deborah Kerr, Greer Garson. The maverick casting came with Marlon Brando as Marc Antony.

In his suitcase, along with his trademark torn t-shirt and jeans, Brando was famous for establishing 'The Method' in the movies. While much has been made of how the process brought to the surface elements of the actor's internal conflicts, what cannot be denied was the effortless reality audiences felt when Brando slouched into film history as Stanley Kowalski. Following *A Streetcar Named Desire*, the announcement that the Method man would be 'doing' the Bard sent seismic shocks around the arts world.

In fact, thanks to his own innate genius and Mankiewicz's sensitive direction, Brando turned in a credible performance, mastering the Shakespearian syntax and providing much-needed movie star charisma. So successful was the transition that cynical critics speculated just how the transformation would have worked the other way – the unimaginable sight of John Gielgud storming around in a torn t-shirt and jeans as Stanley Kowalski!

When Brando came to deliver the immortal 'Friends, Romans, countrymen ...' speech, Mankiewicz felt 'a f★★★★★g chill go up my spine ... it was the greatest moment I have ever felt as a director ... it's what made [my] whole career worthwhile'.

As a testament, Brando's performance earned him his third consecutive Oscar nomination. He was to win in 1954 for *On the Waterfront*, and from there, Brando was intended to star in Twentieth Century Fox's turgid Pyramid potboiler, *The Egyptian*.

Disenchanted, Brando split for New York. His instincts were proved right. Despite Fox's promise of '10,965 pyramids! 5,337 dancing girls! One million swaying bullrushes and 802 sacred bulls!', the soporific saga that was *The Egyptian* was swallowed by the desert sands of public indifference.

The first colour film Mankiewicz essayed as writer, producer and director was 1954's *The Barefoot Contessa*, which made full use of the lush European locations. Rarely had Ava Gardner looked more lustrous. The script was as venal about film as Mankiewicz's *All About Eve* had been about the theatrical world. It crackled with his signature dialogue ('What she's got, you couldn't spell – and what you've got, you used to have').

Delighted with his experiences working with Brando on *Julius Caesar*, Joseph L. Mankiewicz was only too happy to take up mogul Sam Goldwyn's suggestion to cast him in MGM's lavish 1955 adaptation of the hit musical *Guys and Dolls*. Mankiewicz and Goldwyn knew that Brando's name in a musical would draw in long-time fans as well as the merely curious, to see if Marlon Brando could carry a tune.

Mankiewicz telegraphed Brando, 'You have never done a musical, neither have I. We never did Shakespeare either. I am confident this would be exciting, gratifying and rewarding experience for both of us.'

For Mankiewicz, the real problem on the set of *Guys and Dolls* was the antipathy between Brando and Frank Sinatra. Approached on set on the first day of shooting by Brando with a query about how to get into his character in a musical, Frank witheringly cast him aside with 'Don't give me any of that Actors Studio shit'. Mankiewicz had his hands full keeping his two principals on the level. It was to prove good practice for *Cleopatra* later on. *Guys and Dolls* went on to become the biggest-grossing American film of 1956 and, following his critical acclaim earlier in the decade, established Joseph L. Mankiewicz as a bankable commodity in 1950s American cinema.

Mankiewicz's final two films of the 1950s were contemporary dramas. *The Quiet American* (1957), adapted from a Graham Greene novel, was the first film to deal with America's growing involvement in Vietnam. *Suddenly Last Summer* (1959) was adapted by Gore Vidal from a Tennessee Williams one-act play. Even by the controversial Williams's standards, the subject was hysterical: rape, homosexuality and cannibalism were hardly typical late-1950s box office fare (*Variety* called it 'possibly the most bizarre film ever made by a major American film company'). *Suddenly Last Summer* was also notable for putting Mankiewicz together with the actress along with whose name his would become inextricably linked in one of the costliest flops in film history – Elizabeth Taylor.

Mankiewicz had high hopes for *Cleopatra*. He came to it on the back of a string of critical and commercial successes. He had established a good working relationship with his film's undoubted star. He had proven himself capable of managing big budgets, and equally able to handle temperamental stars.

The director initially showed no interest in inheriting Mamoulian's directing mantle, telling the studio head, 'Why would I want to make *Cleopatra*? I wouldn't go *see Cleopatra*.' Abandoning the stick, the studio went straight for the carrot. As well as a generous salary, Fox would buy Mankiewicz 's production company for $3 million. 'He was seduced by the opportunity,' the director's son, Chris Mankiewicz, told David

Kamp, 'He never saw a penny from *All About Eve*. Now, for once in his life ... all of a sudden you've got the "F★★k you" money.'

For all the temptation, little did Joe Mankiewicz imagine that *Cleopatra* would match the best-known line from his finest film, 'Fasten your seat belts, it's going to be a bumpy night'. Viewing the runaway success of *Ben-Hur* as he was in pre-production on *Cleopatra*, Mankiewicz was confident that his vision of Ancient Rome could be effectively and strikingly transferred to the screen. A painstaking craftsman, Mankiewicz's original plan was that his version would run for seven hours. His ideal for *Cleopatra* was always to make it into two separate films: Part One would deal with the queen's relationship with Caesar; the second, her affair with Marc Antony. They would then be either released in consecutive years or shown on following nights.

But for many reasons, Fox got twitchy as the production expanded exponentially, the budget soared, and the market for sword-and-sandal epics declined. Twentieth Century Fox wanted a film that could capitalise on the developing scandal. Besides, it was the chemistry between the legendary lovers that would draw the punters in. 'No one,' an executive sniffed, 'was interested in seeing Taylor make love to Rex Harrison.'

The original cut of *Cleopatra* that Mankiewicz showed to his new studio boss, Darryl Zanuck, came in at five hours and twenty minutes. Zanuck ordered further cuts, so on the night of the premiere, Mankiewicz delivered a version which ran to 243 minutes. Subsequent prestige screenings allowed the four-hour film to be neatly divided for a timely intermission at the two-hour stage, allowing for concessionary sales to satisfy cinema managers.

Zanuck was still unhappy, particularly when reports came back that up to 200 customers a day in New York were demanding a refund as they found the epic 'boring'. So, he ordered producer Elmo Williams to trim *Cleopatra* into a manageable roadshow version running at a relatively modest three hours and twelve minutes.

Zanuck knew whereof he spoke. Early in his career he marvelled at how a good editor could 'turn a turkey into a sleeper, just by cutting, editing and rejigging'. In later years, before *Cleopatra* came on his watch, he reflected in Leonard Mosley's biography, 'Unless it is a complete and utter disaster, there is no single film that can't be rescued and turned into a seeable movie, even if it doesn't turn out to be an epic'.

Some films that were poorly received on release went on to be reappraised in hindsight – Michael Cimino's 1980 *Heaven's Gate*, for example. *Cleopatra* has yet to receive that critical revisionism. It didn't even make *Total Film* magazine's 2004 'Top 50 Greatest Epics'. In 1995, there was a meeting to begin a worldwide search for missing scenes in order to restore the film to something approaching Mankiewicz's vision. To date, however, little of the lost material has surfaced.

In fairness, if the studio had adhered to Mankiewicz's original vision for the film, his longer edit would have given *Cleopatra* a greater coherence. A more cohesive script would have fleshed out the characters, giving the film the depth it had lacked. As it stands, the released version limps along, a series of striking spectacles, but lacking the necessary fuller characterisation and plot exposition.

☥

Some might even say there was a curse hanging over the 1963 film of *Cleopatra*. The original producer, Walter Wanger, whose $15,000 investment had snowballed the madness, died in 1968, never getting the chance to make another film. On completion, Mankiewicz joked, 'The next film I make will have one character in a phone booth calling his wife to tell her he'll be home early for dinner.'

Mankiewicz only made three more films – 1967's *The Honey Pot* was flawed but reunited him with a spritely Rex Harrison – but really, only one of them (1972's *Sleuth*) bore testament to his earlier triumphs. His name would always be associated with the perceived failure of *Cleopatra*. As with the film's stars, directors like Mankiewicz, George Stevens and Henry Hathaway found themselves out of step with the radical changes evident in late-1960s cinema.

Right up until his death in 1993, Joseph L. Mankiewicz always treasured the notion of letting the world see *his* version of the film that had so overtaken and, in many ways, ruined his life.

# 13

# *La Dolce Vita*

The scandal that had begun in Rome in 1962 took place beneath the glare of a media that had exploded and grown, snarling in its intensity in pursuit of celebrity prey. Long before camera phones and selfies, celebrities were hounded by sensation-seeking photographers, who were paid on results.

In his engrossing *Dolce Vita Confidential* (2018), Shawn Levy singled out the differences between:

> … the news-gathering cultures of Hollywood, where virtually every media outlet cooperated with the studios, even choosing not to report on the potentially criminal activity of movie stars in exchange for exclusive interviews and privileged access, and Rome, where competition among journalists for scoops was becoming increasingly cut-throat as the economy showed signs of revival and more and more Italians splurged on gossipy publications.

Of the Burton and Taylor affair, Elizabeth Taylor biographer Brenda Maddox called it 'the most public adultery in the world'. And writer Jess Walter later reflected:

> This is where modern celebrity began – the Kardashians and the Lohans – you can trace it to this moment where a kind of Hollywood

decadence reached a peak. It destroyed in one fell swoop the old studio system and brought in its place the kind of celebrity which doesn't distinguish between good and bad.

News of '*le scandale*', which erupted and flashed round the world in record time, had much to do with the Italian location that Burton and Taylor had chosen for their illicit pleasures. In typically boisterous Italian fashion, the nation had bounced back following the Mussolini years. By the beginning of the 1950s, Rome had become the epicentre of style, romance and high living, its sweet life a beacon to a bruised and battered world. And when the film capital came calling with William Wyler's 1953 *Roman Holiday*, it had lent a Hollywood gloss to the eternal city and made a stylish star out of Audrey Hepburn.

Throughout the 1950s, the roving eye of fashion, style and the impossible-to-categorise 'cool' glanced over New York, Paris and London, but it lingered on Rome. In 1945, on the Via Barberini, Brioni opened its doors. In 1952, the tailors hosted the world's first mens' catwalk show. Brioni designed the wardrobe for Gregory Peck in *Roman Holiday* and they dressed Clark Gable, John Wayne and Anthony Quinn.

And all the while, the Roman citizen luxuriated in living in a city that had already become a byword for decadence. Self-indulgence and sybaritic excess were as much taken for granted in Rome as pasta and Parmigiano. Screen goddesses like Gina Lollobrigida, Sophia Loren and Anna Magnani presented a voluptuous new image of the screen siren – earthy, ripe and sensual, they were at odds with the manufactured divas of Hollywood or the prim ladies of Shepperton.

The Roman streets and piazzas bustled with the snazzily dressed. The air was filled with the buzz of poky motor scooters as they cut through the congested streets. At times, the Vespas curled round the Colosseum, like wasps around a picnic; no need for crash helmets in those distant days. The buzzing Vespa scooters faced competition from Ducati and Lambretta. There was no need to worry about the constant fug of cigarette smoke that wound its way down into your lungs with every bracing espresso. Any visitor from the United Kingdom would have been struck by the pervasive odour of garlic – at home, it was only sold in chemists to soften ear wax.

Fashion and cuisine aside, Italy was just spot on with everything by the time *Cleopatra* rolled into town: Olivetti typewriters, fashion, gastronomy, handbags and automobiles such as the people-friendly Fiat 500 or the luxurious models rolling off the production lines of Ferrari, Maserati, Lancia, Alfa Romeo, Lamborghini. On the catwalk, Italian fashion was a byword for style and contemporary elegance. By the 1950s, the Fontana sisters were dressing leading Hollywood stars like Linda Christian, Irene Dunn, Barbara Stanwyck, Myrna Loy and Ava Gardner. In February 1951, Giovanni Giorgini held a fashion show at his Roman villa, which effectively placed Italian fashion and style centre stage on the world market. The reputation of Rome as the centre of global fashion was further enhanced by collections from Emilio Pucci, Simonetta and Fabiani. Then, in 1960, cinematically, Rome went global.

Federico Fellini had been the darling of the critics throughout the 1950s. His quirky and elliptical world views played well in art houses, but it took one film to pinpoint an era as precisely as a specimen on a laboratory slide *La Dolce Vita* shone brilliantly beneath Fellini's lustrous camera. It broke the director out of the art houses and put the Italian for 'the sweet life' onto everyone's lips as they flocked in to tut and disapprove of the high life led by the sybarites who Fellini depicted. *La Dolce Vita was* the high life. It was what the rich did behind closed doors. Soon, anyone who had been intimate, taken a drink on board or was committing adultery found themselves squirming under head-lines as living '*la dolce vita*'. The phrase became a shorthand for sex, and Rome became its home.

However, like the foam on a cappuccino, *La Dolce Vita* faded, and the sweet life was overtaken by the rush to swing. The carnival moved to London. Music and fashion were dictated from recording studios in Abbey Road and along Carnaby Street. One element of Fellini's film, though, remained forever.

Marcello Mastroianni begs a photographer to leave his victim alone, to let the subject have a degree of dignity, but is rebuffed with the timeless photographer's comment that 'It's a great photo'. The name of that fictional photographer was Paparazzo. And that fictional creation from Fellini's film soon became a collective term for the parasitic photographers who have dogged celebrities' footsteps for the ensuing half a century. For much of the 1960s, before the caravan moved on to London and New York, the photographers – Elio Quinto, Marcello Geppetti, Tazio Secchiaroli – and their antics became almost as familiar as the stars whose photos they snatched.

Before paparazzi spread like vermin across the globe, they made their nest in Rome, where they preyed on the louche aristos and playboys. As the rumours emanating from the city's Cinecitta Studios where *Cleopatra* was filming spread, the paparazzi prayed for Elizabeth Taylor and Richard Burton to fall under their lenses.

'They scoot out on their Vespas, they have a remarkable *esprits de corps*,' the film's producer, Walter Wanger, moaned. 'In Rome they are tolerated with amusement and a perverse kind of pride since Fellini saw fit to take notice of their existence … They have been the bane of our experience since we came to Rome.'

The photographers were not bound by any conventions. They knew where the celebrities clustered, and the stars themselves, after years of close protection by the studios in Hollywood, were unprepared for the paparazzi's venal provocation. The guerrilla photographers knew that snaps of the stars raging at them, or illicitly trying to avoid their probing lenses, could generate real income at home and abroad.

The paparazzi taunted and provoked their targets into providing material for their insatiable and intrusive cameras. Suddenly, those above-the-titles names were made human as they tottered out of restaurants, were caught canoodling, or took a swing at the impish photographers.

Elizabeth Taylor remembered:

Photographers dressed up like priests used to come to the door, or they would get inside as workmen or plumbers. Sometimes outside in the garden we were besieged by the paparazzi. They were on the wall climbing up stepladders from the outside. And the servants would come rushing out with brooms and rakes, and the kids turned the hose on those maniacs. And yet we were accused of airing our 'little affair' in public.

There never was a 'curse of *Cleopatra*'. However, there did seem to be a jinx that hung over its home base. Built by Mussolini, the Cinecitta studios were a magnet for the movie-mad Italians. Martin Scorsese began shooting his (Harvey Weinstein-produced) *Gangs of New York* there in 2000. It would not be released for a further two years. The budget spiralled from $84 million to $97 million, and there was on-set friction between stars Daniel Day-Lewis and Leonardo DiCaprio, while Cameron Diaz, who was scheduled for a six-week shoot, ended up at Cinecitta for six *months* ...

# 14

# 'Czar of All the Rushes'

It wasn't just Joseph L. Mankiewicz who suffered before, during and after the debacle of *Cleopatra*. The unmanageable scale of its production almost broke the long-established Hollywood studio that had bankrolled it. From afar, it was now watching helplessly as the film veered out of control, threatening to drag the studio down with it.

Twentieth Century Fox had begun at the birth of the movies, as a nickelodeon novelty in the penny arcades of New York. By 1915, founder William Fox formed the Fox Film Corporation, to make and distribute films. As early as 1912, Fox polled audiences and found an overwhelming demand for moving pictures over vaudeville acts. 'The only explanation I can find,' Fox noted, 'is that motion pictures, perhaps, realize the American idea of speed and activity.'

By 1914, Fox was producing his own films. It was in 1915 that Fox opened his first studio in Hollywood, on the corner of Western Avenue and Sunset Boulevard. Early directors on the Fox lot included the great John Ford and F.W. Murnau, whose 1927 *Sunrise* has often been called the greatest silent film ever made.

Fox was one of the first Hollywood studios to appreciate the benefits of talking pictures (initially called 'noisies') and was quickly aboard the bandwagon in the wake of the Warner Brothers' success with *The Jazz Singer*. Fox's 1935 merger with Twentieth Century, a production company established by ex-Warner Bros whiz kid Darryl F. Zanuck, saw

Twentieth Century Fox established as a major player by the outbreak of war.

By the mid-1950s, Twentieth Century Fox could look back on a glittering constellation of talent. Contract players ran from Shirley Temple to Marilyn Monroe, and distinguished directors from Murnau to Lubitsch had laboured on the Fox lot. The studio had flourished during wartime and seen its audiences return in droves, but while the Free World had vanquished Hitler, Twentieth Century Fox came up against an implacable and unbeatable enemy – television.

In 1946, it was estimated that in Los Angeles, the film capital of the world, there were only 15,000 television sets. What possible threat could such a tiny novelty item, tucked away in a corner of your home like an embarrassing relative, pose to the all-powerful film studios? Hollywood, in fact, reacted to television like the vaudeville theatre owners had responded to the nickelodeon novelty of film, half a century before. Within a few short years, though, the novelty was in danger of destroying the edifice; the walls of the film capital were shaking.

In America, television was the single factor that threatened cinema's cultural and economic stranglehold. Cinema attendances slumped, from 80 million admissions a week to 35 million during the TV boom of the 1950s; a decline of more than 50 per cent within a decade. In a five-year period, between 1946 and 1951, 5,000 cinemas closed down in America.

Hollywood hit back in 1952 with the widescreen revolution. In 1953, Cinerama and 3D were launched. CinemaScope screens were two and a half times as wide as they were tall, along with 3D, Smell-O-Rama was swiftly ditched. Paramount refused to go with CinemaScope's squeezed image and instead offered 70mm Vista Vision (twice the width of the industry standard 35mm).

Those 70mm prints meant new projectors in every cinema and managers balked – it was fast-talking Mike Todd who persuaded a good part of the industry with his 65mm Todd-AO. The man who would become Elizabeth Taylor's third husband modestly patented the new format under his own name. One projector provided a sharper picture than Cinerama – a process which required *three* projectors. It also allowed for six-track stereophonic sound.

All that, combined with the sort of films to fill such a big screen, would surely prise the punters away from their television sets. Fox had been early aboard the biblical bandwagon. Its 1951 production of *David and Bathsheba*, starring Gregory Peck and Susan Hayward, was the surprise No.1 hit at the US box office that year. The success of the epic inspired Fox head Darryl F. Zanuck to marry the studio's new CinemaScope technique to further awesome projects, providing a big-screen sensation that would knock television for six. Audiences were offered 'the new dimensional photographic marvel you can see without glasses! How CinemaScope creates infinite depth and life-like reality to engulf you in the action on the screen.'

As well as biblical spectacle, cinema adaptations of popular stage musicals were a favourite. Hollywood took established Broadway musicals and broadened them out for CinemaScope and Todd-AO.

MGM were the studio most associated with the popular musicals of the 1950s: *Showboat, Brigadoon, Seven Brides for Seven Brothers, Kiss me Kate* and *Guys and Dolls* were all substantial hits for MGM. But Twentieth Century Fox wasn't far behind, with *Oklahoma!, Carousel* and, particularly, *The King and I* ('More than your eyes have ever seen,' the poster boasted. 'More than your heart has ever known!') It became the second most successful film of 1956.

Darryl F. Zanuck had announced the production of *The King and I* in 1954 and had remained as head of production at Fox until 1956, when he set himself up as an independent producer, operating out of France. For over twenty years Zanuck had held sway at Twentieth Century Fox, ruling the studio like a medieval monarch: he was the liege to whom his devoted subjects paid their lief.

Studio heads were tyrannical in their exercise of power. They were only as good as their last picture, but they did show an unerring ability to gauge what their public wanted. They were not intellectuals – on visiting Paris, Zanuck kept the taxi running outside the Louvre, telling his companions, 'All right, we've got twenty minutes to do this joint'. But more by luck than judgement, they kept their kingdoms. 'Give 'em cowboys, tits and gangsters' was Columbia boss Harry Cohn's advice. He kept a bust of Mussolini in his office, though he was more often to be found at the race track. It was Cohn who once inelegantly reflected on the 'culture' of the studio system: 'It's all c★★t and horses.'

The 1965 biopic of the blonde starlet Jean Harlow with Carroll Baker paints a very accurate picture of the studio system and the importance of the casting couch. Sex was the lubricant. Hollywood still drew fledgling and willing actresses, and by all accounts, Zanuck blocked off the hour between four and five in the afternoon to 'interview' recent signings and potential starlets. With his office door locked, Zanuck tested the casting couch technique to its limit.

Zanuck was by no means alone in his predatory tactics. On finally managing to land her contract with Twentieth Century Fox, Marilyn Monroe shrugged, 'Well, that's the last cock I'll have to suck'. Joan Collins was convinced she could have been cinema's most talked-about queen. 'I *know* I would have gotten Cleopatra,' she told *Playboy* in 1984. 'If I had gone along with Skouras' advances. I'm sure I would have.' The Dame amplified the feeling, talking to Piers Morgan in 2021:

> I managed to not fall into the pit of the casting couch. I avoided that many times. I think I lost *Cleopatra*. Both the head of the studio and the CEO of the studio promised it to me if I would be 'nice' to them, and I wouldn't be nice to them.

Such was the demand for screen stardom that Zanuck was rarely short of actresses willing to undergo the indignity of sex for stardom. By 5 p.m., the hapless actress would be secreted out of a side door of Zanuck's office and the monarch would resume the tiring business of ruling his kingdom. Short and pugnacious, Zanuck was genuinely baffled when his wife confronted him over his serial infidelities. 'Why do you get so mad about them? They're just tarts – girls to be f★★★★d and thrown away.'

The writer Philip Dunne knew the mogul well, and commented, 'Like all great executives, he knew when to coddle, when to bully and when to exhort.' Zanuck toted a heavy load: he had up to fifty films a year to keep an eye on, supervising budgets, new contracts, casting, editing, keeping an eye on new technology, what his rivals were up to and the final cut of films on his watch. *Cleopatra* director Joseph

L. Mankiewicz smilingly recalled, 'My nickname for him was "Czar of all the rushes".'

For all his boorish behaviour, grossness and tyrannical behaviour, Zanuck lived and breathed film. Directors marvelled at the mogul's ability to dissect a film, frame by frame, after just one viewing. Others likened his ruthless editing approach to that of Hemingway, stripping his sparse prose to the bone. 'He had the uncanny knack after seeing a film for the first time,' recalled director Richard Fleischer, 'of immediately putting his finger on exactly what was wrong with it.'

It was from France in the late 1950s that Zanuck oversaw such prestigious productions as *The Sun Also Rises* (1957) and *The Longest Day* (1962). Zanuck would choose his own subjects, directors and stars. Fox would put up the bulk of the budget, and their circuit would handle the distribution of Zanuck properties. It was while overseeing his epic, star-studded account of the D-Day landing that Zanuck was invited back by the Fox board to run the studio, which was already reeling from the impact of *Cleopatra*.

Richard Burton was in a Paris studio, filming his cameo for *The Longest Day*, when he informed the mogul first-hand of the madness taking place in Rome during the *Cleopatra* shoot. In far-away Hollywood, Twentieth Century Fox were frankly terrified, as they watched their prestige production go grossly over budget.

As studio head, Skouras had nurtured *Cleopatra* through its extended pre-production and had urged it go ahead when he knew it was far from ready to begin shooting. Yet, like a massive container vessel, which needs to travel miles before it can come to a grinding halt, Skouras knew the film had everything riding on it. Once the filming had relocated to Rome, it was too late to toss the coin, to take a multimillion-dollar hit and cancel the production.

Salt was further rubbed in the wound as the production was at one remove from Fox in Hollywood. The production on which the studio relied for its continued existence was half a world away and careering out of control.

Spyros Skouras had green-lighted the production but remained in ignorance of what he had commissioned. The first rushes he saw were overwhelming – the scale and sumptuous sets – yet, as his biographer, Carlo Curti wrote, 'As he watched the film unfold he knew the masterpiece had arrived too late to save his job. He was watching his own obituary on the screen.'

While still ruling the roost at Fox, Skouras allowed his pet project *Cleopatra* to proceed, but had severe doubts about his rival Zanuck's costly Second World War epic *The Longest Day*. It was a choice: colourful sex in ancient Rome or black and white about some French invasion few Americans knew of. Skouras went for the easiest option and hauled Zanuck back to Hollywood. He threatened to halt production on *The Longest Day* which, more than any actress, had become Zanuck's sole obsession.

Revered now as one of the key Second World War epics, *The Longest Day* had a troubled genesis. But the canny Zanuck balanced his film with established stalwarts (John Wayne, Henry Fonda, Robert Ryan) for the parents, while popular singers (Paul Anka, Fabian, Tommy Sands) could pull in the teenage crowds. With three directors on hand, Zanuck was commanding his own army, navy and air force to accurately convey the scope of the 1944 Normandy landings. In the film's favour, Zanuck was a hands-on producer, on set, barking commands and effectively directing the production. *Cleopatra* was not only out of control, but it was also out of sight.

At the time, though, Zanuck was arguing from a position of weakness, because his last three features (*The Roots of Heaven*, *Crack in the Mirror* and *The Big Gamble*) had not performed well. The Fox board were looking for a scapegoat and the over-confident, cigar-chewing Zanuck was fully aware of it as he entered the New York boardroom. 'You're *it* Dad,' his son Richard told him. 'They think you're on the skids and they'll heap all the shit they can on you.'

None of the Fox board were convinced that the future of their studio lay in a black and white Second World War movie and they were keen to halt its production rather than that of *Cleopatra*. 'I knew,' Zanuck said, 'and they knew, that what was to blame was not me but that godforsaken movie they were making in Rome, which was pouring away the company's money like shit down a sewer.'

Zanuck played his cards with the skill of a practised diplomat when his turn came to save his position. Without mentioning *Cleopatra* once, he instead spoke eloquently and passionately about *The Longest Day*. Fortuitously, one of the board members had been a Second World War general, whose enthusiasm and commitment to the project matched that of Zanuck. Even so, it was by the merest margin of six to five that the Fox board allowed Zanuck to proceed with *The Longest Day*.

In order to guarantee that the studio would properly promote *The Longest Day* and his project would receive priority over *Cleopatra*, Zanuck knew he had to become president of the studio in which he was a major shareholder and which was causing him so much grief. Zanuck ousted Fox chairman, Spyros Skouras in a boardroom coup on 25 July 1962.

Like Dick Rowe, who went down in history as 'the man who turned down the Beatles', Skouras is the man who produced the ruinous *Cleopatra*. But as pop historian Bill Harry pointed out, 'Frankly, instead of being known as the man who turned down The Beatles, which is inaccurate, [Dick Rowe] should have been lauded as the man who signed up the Rolling Stones.' Skouras's biographer made a similar point, 'Spyros Skouras is responsible for *Cleopatra*, the biggest losing film in movie history, but he was also responsible for the biggest winner, *The Sound of Music*.'

Within two hours, Zanuck, in his role as the new president, had issued his first command, 'Stop all production and close down the studios'. One of Zanuck's first actions was laying off 2,000 employees.

Zanuck headed up the Fox board of directors, to which he added the revered director William Wyler. By the early 1960s, Wyler was on a roll. His last two films, *The Big Country* and *Ben-Hur*, had been critical and box-office triumphs. Zanuck obviously hoped that Wyler could bring some of his good luck to Fox.

The director only ever recalled attending two board meetings – at one of which he authorised a further $2 million to be allocated to Zanuck so that *Cleopatra* could be finished. There is a particular irony that the director of *Ben-Hur*, the epic that had become what *Cleopatra* never would be, had a hand in green-lighting further expenditure on the film that was singlehandedly strangling its studio.

Wyler felt he was there because what was needed was 'a film maker, somebody who knew production'. But the veteran director soon found the company of his bean-counting fellow board members – financiers and Wall Street attorneys – less conducive, and resigned.

Determined to alert the world to his epic, Zanuck arranged a spectacular premiere for *The Longest Day* in Paris in September 1962. Three bridges over the Seine were closed to ensure the 2,700 guests were not inconvenienced. As well as socialite Elsa Maxwell and French icon Francoise Sagan, NATO admirals and generals were in attendance, and Edith Piaf sang an amplified version of '*La Marseillaise*' from an illuminated Eiffel Tower.

Against the odds, the black and white epic went on to become a box-office sensation, confirming that Zanuck still possessed the Midas touch. But there was always, and always would be, *Cleopatra*.

In a further irony, William Wyler found himself again involved with the film that would rescue Twentieth Century Fox from its Roman fiasco. 'With *The Longest Day* out of the way,' wrote Axel Madsen in *Willian Wyler: The Authorized Biography* (1974), 'Zanuck bent over the one remaining problem, *Cleopatra* (he and Mankiewicz fought publicly and privately over the cutting of the picture) and gave the go-ahead on *The Sound of Music*, with Ernest Lehman as writer and William Wyler as director.'

It was *The Sound of Music* that saved the studio. Its $8.5 million budget was soon dwarfed by its $115 million domestic box office takings. By the end of 1965, the all-singing, sunshine exploits of the Von Trapp family had helped push the dark days of *Cleopatra* back into history.

In fact, Wyler had become fascinated by filming the first novel of a young schoolmaster called John Fowles, *The Collector*, and he left *The Sound of Music* in the hands of *West Side Story*'s Robert Wise. Wyler's legacy for the film that helped salvage Twentieth Century Fox from the financial doldrums of *Cleopatra* was in suggesting that Maria von Trapp be played by the young actress who had impressed him in the Broadway musical of *My Fair Lady* – Julie Andrews.

☥

Knowing what we know now, studio head Darryl F. Zanuck's first impressions of *Cleopatra* make revealing reading. Called in to help Twentieth Century Fox salvage something from the morass, Zanuck issued a 'Strictly Confidential' memo on 15 October 1962, detailing his first impressions of the film that would all but sink his studio. He confessed himself thoroughly confused by the narrative, and went on:

> The film has been sold to the world as the most expensive film in motion picture history. All potential audiences are going to expect to see an exciting, dramatic and emotional story, loaded with sex. Regrettably, all the battle scenes give the impression of being skimpy, artificial and shot on the back lot.

Zanuck's overriding concern was in getting *Cleopatra* completed, up on the screen and out to the cinemas so that the studio could begin to pull in some much-needed revenue. With all other production suspended, literally everything was relying on *Cleopatra*. The film needed to ride on the coattails of the Burton and Taylor affair to pull in the crowds. Relocated to Paris, Joseph L. Mankiewicz was determined to see his version of *Cleopatra* released as two separate films but Zanuck wanted to get something – anything – out as soon as possible.

Correspondence between the two moguls crackled. Writing to Mankiewicz at the Hotel Lancaster in Paris on 21 October 1962, Zanuck let rip a nine-page letter, contrasting his own production of *The Longest Day* ('I used a total of 23,000 troops at a total cost of $8.5 million') with Mankiewicz's unhappy and infinitely more expensive *Cleopatra*. The new studio head was looking for a scapegoat on which to blame the profligacy. Mankiewicz's was the obvious head on the block. The truth almost certainly lay nearer home – with the studio that had given the go-ahead to a film which was clearly far from ready to go.

In 1961, Twentieth Century Fox had lost $39.8 million. The studio was forced to sell off 260 of its 334 acres in Los Angeles to the Aluminum Company of America for $43 million – coincidentally, just short of the amount that was being spent in far-away Rome. By 1962, Spyros Skouras had had to report Twentieth Century Fox losses of $22.5 million. With so much invested, they were literally banking on *Cleopatra*. It was too late to pull the plug and the film had to be seen.

Going through the Twentieth Century Fox files of the period is a glimpse into a distant epoch. The yellowing pages and faded carbon copies are from a vanished world; an era prior to fax and email, with no texts or tweets to convey immediate urgency. Correspondence was carried by aeroplane or dispatched by cumbersome telexes. From Hollywood, the studio was sending urgent dispatches to remote outposts of its empire like London and Rome. Like Ancient Rome sustaining its empire, Twentieth Century Fox had its distant provinces to maintain. And for the first part of the 1960s, its most important outpost was Rome itself.

# 15

# 'The Cost is Staggering'

The Italian capital had become 'Hollywood on the Tiber' soon after the Marshall Plan poured relief into a scarred and battered Europe in the immediate aftermath of the Second World War. There was an effort to revive the Italian film industry, but profits from Hollywood films screened in Italy were frozen in Italy, so that left the American film studios with only one option – rather than have their assets locked in Italian banks, they would, improbably, start making movies in, of all places, Italy.

It wasn't such an outlandish idea; like the UK, the Italian government offered tax breaks and subsidies if local talent was employed on productions from abroad. In the wake of *Quo Vadis*, Hollywood filmed *The Barefoot Contessa, Ulysses, Helen of Troy* and *Three Coins in the Fountain* in and around the Italian capital. It was mutually satisfying: the studios got lavish productions at bargain rates and the Italians benefitted from the infusion of American lire.

Denis Meikle wrote a fascinating feature for *Cinema Retro* in 2014, 'Rome's Cinecitta studios quickly became an assembly line for an endless stream of Italian epics, which highbrow critics would eventually dub "pepla" from the Greek word "peplum" for tunic.' These epics inevitably featured the musclebound Steve Reeves, beginning with 1958's *Hercules*. The pepla films reached a wider audience when mogul Joseph E. Levine snapped them up, pepped up the soundtracks and dubbed them into English. *Hercules Unchained* was a US box-office smash, which Reeves followed with *Goliath and the Barbarians* and *The Last Days of Pompeii* in quick succession. 'By the end of 1961,' Meikle wrote, '"spectaculars" accounted for almost one-quarter of the 200-odd films produced by the Italian industry during the year.' It was a short-lived phenomenon.

For American visitors, a visit to Rome offered the opportunity to revel in the high life which the Italian capital offered. One of their first ports of call was Alfredo's in Piazza Augusto Imperatore. In a dish Gwyneth Paltrow would recoil from, the restaurant was famous for its fettucine, loaded with butter and parmesan. VIP visitors were served by Alfredo himself, dishing the pasta from a golden fork and spoon which had been 'blessed' by Hollywood's original 'royalty', Douglas Fairbanks and Mary Pickford when they first visited the restaurant in 1927.

By 1957, however, the travel writer H.V. Morton was writing sniffily of the Via Veneto:

This is the American Rome [...] Here you see the 'milords' of the new age, the film stars and the celluloid Caesars, and those executives whose names occupy such a tedious crescendo of type before a film begins.

Morton went on to curl a lip at the ubiquity of the club sandwich, Chicken Maryland, apple pie, hamburgers and American coffee.

The hubris, escalating cost and inexorable catastrophe of *Cleopatra* was not unheard of in the history of Hollywood. 'In 1958,' wrote Axel Madsen:

*Ben-Hur* was the costliest movie ever made. Yet it was not the financial madness of *Cleopatra*. As they go, *Ben-Hur* was not the tightest run movie in film history, but it *was* managed. Ironically, MGM's husbanding was thrown to the winds two years later with the $30 million disaster *Mutiny on the Bounty* that wiped out most of the profits of *Ben-Hur*.

Inextricably linked with *Cleopatra* in film mythology is MGM's 1962 production of the *Bounty* mutiny. The similarities between the two productions are striking but the remake of the 1935 Charles Laughton/ Clark Gable film was beached once and for all by the opportunistic ego-mania of its star, Marlon Brando.

Brando's star was on the wane by the early 1960s. After his initial impact, he had tired of wasting his time frittering his genius on feeble projects like *Desiree, Teahouse of the August Moon* and *Sayonara*. His box-office allure was also in decline. Brando made an inauspicious directorial debut with the western *One-Eyed Jacks* (1960), which set new standards for Hollywood extravagance. According to Peter Manso, Brando's biographer, 'More than a million feet of film had been exposed – six times as much as for the ordinary feature – a new Hollywood record. The budget had gone from $1,600,000 to over $6,000,000.'

Astutely, Brando recognised that a starring role in an epic film could restore his box-office standing. Perhaps something in the rebellious nature of Fletcher Christian struck a chord with the recalcitrant Brando.

Director Carol Reed was hired. Following his successful seagoing screenplays for *The Cruel Sea* and *A Night to Remember*, Eric Ambler was employed to fashion a script, and a full-size 350-ton seagoing replica of HMS *Bounty* was built. The cast included Hugh Griffith, fresh from his Oscar-winning performance in *Ben-Hur*, and Richard Harris, making his Hollywood debut. The ever-reliable Trevor Howard was the marti-net, Captain Bligh. Howard was looking forward to reuniting with his favourite director, who had established him as a major star in *The Third Man*, a decade before.

It was Brando's unprofessionalism which so irked his co-star. Rarely has a star actor suffered such indignities. There were numerous examples of Brando's behaviour. He took to wearing earplugs so he wouldn't have to listen to Howard's lines. Repeatedly, Brando delib-erately fluffed his few lines during Howard's big scenes, waiting for Howard himself to fluff and falter so that Brando could bounce back and reclaim the scene.

Far removed from Hollywood, the Tahiti location for *Mutiny on the Bounty* was running at around $50,000 a day – but that was dependent on Brando's mood. Frequently, whole days would be scrapped due to the star's petulance, which drove Carol Reed to distraction. There was – literally – no communication between the two men.

At Brando's insistence, Reed was replaced by Lewis Milestone. MGM had given Milestone the prestige production as a reward for having brought in the troubled production of Frank Sinatra's *Oceans 11* on time and $100,000 under budget.

Milestone, however, fared little better than his predecessor on the calamitous *Bounty*. While filming, the producer watched the veteran director of *All Quiet on the Western Front* reading a trade paper as a scene progressed. Asked if he wasn't going to direct it, Milestone replied, 'What for? When the picture's finished, I'll watch the whole bloody mess in a theater!'

Tempers rose and costs escalated on the South Pacific location. With little actual filming to accomplish, the cast and crew were at liberty to relax. An apocryphal tale has an MGM telegram from Hollywood to Milestone on location on the island paradise of Tahiti, 'Send details of filming. Cost is staggering,' only to receive the reply, 'So is the cast.'

Like *Cleopatra*, *Mutiny on the Bounty* suspended shooting and switched locations. In January 1961, Tahiti was lashed with monsoons – it rained for seventeen consecutive days, and with only a third of the film shot, the cast and crew relocated to Hollywood for interiors.

Back in Tinseltown, the rumours began about the escalating, out-of-control production, and MGM shares were dropping. By early October 1961, they had plunged ten points in a single day. MGM's production chief, Sol Siegel, even threatened to sue Brando for 'throwing' his performance deliberately to sabotage the film. Siegel was one of the heads that rolled at MGM in April 1963, five months after the film's premiere.

By the time Lewis Milestone wrapped after a draining thirteen-month shoot, *Mutiny on the Bounty* had cost MGM an estimated – and hitherto unheard of – $30 million. On its release in 1962, the film recouped approximately $10 million, with an estimated $10 million abroad. In his exhaustive study of Brando (1994), Peter Manso wrote, 'For all concerned, MGM's remake of *Mutiny* is often linked with

20th Century-Fox's *Cleopatra*, as the one-two punch that irrevocably brought down the Hollywood star system.'

Trevor Howard's official biographer, Vivienne Knight, left little doubt as to where the fault lay in *Trevor Howard: A Gentleman and a Player* (1986):

> *Mutiny On The Bounty* was a star's film, made at the height of studio madness, when the star's demands not only rose to a point above credence, but were met unconditionally by the backers in the belief that one magic name would guarantee box office returns well above the cost of the picture. In this case, the magic name was Marlon Brando.

Lewis Milestone left little doubt about who he felt should shoulder the blame: 'They get what they deserve when they give a ham actor, a petulant child, complete control of an expensive picture.'

Peter Manso quoted producer/director Robert Wise, who had recently triumphed with his film version of *West Side Story* and was to go on and salvage Twentieth Century Fox with *The Sound of Music*, reflecting on the trouble at the time:

> I think the *Mutiny* problems with Brando, plus the problems with Elizabeth Taylor on *Cleopatra*, might well mark the end of the star system as it exists in Hollywood today. The big-star monopoly – the monster that we created ourselves out of fear of television – has now become such an expensive luxury and so loaded with trouble that it's just not worth it.

Of all the principals, only Trevor Howard emerged with any dignity from the *Bounty* fiasco. The experience left him 'with a distaste for star-controlled epics that amounted to nausea'. However, Howard's patrician style was deemed appropriate for Julius Caesar in *Cleopatra*, which had begun filming in earnest as the *Bounty* ploughed through its troubled waters in Tahiti. According to his biographer, Howard turned down the lucrative role of Caesar 'without a second's pause'.

# 16

# Rex Harrison, Rake's Progress

Casting was crucial for *Cleopatra*, and way down the list for the role of Julius Caesar was the man who eventually won the role. For someone who came to epitomise the quintessential English gentleman, Rex Harrison's origins were relatively humble. He was born Reginald Carey Harrison in the Liverpool suburb of Huyton, on 5 March 1908.

By the time of the Armistice in 1918, the young Rex had lost any evidence of a Scouse accent. A heady induction at school introduced him to the stage, and by the time he was a fledgling actor of 22 in rep, Rex had decided that Shakespeare was not for him: 'It's like listening to a lot of people in a pub speaking Welsh!'

Success first came Harrison's way with a starring role in Terence Rattigan's play *French Without Tears*, in 1936. Cinema fame soon followed, with starring roles opposite Vivien Leigh in *Storm in a Teacup* and *St Martin's Lane*, and alongside Wendy Hiller, Deborah Kerr and Robert Newton in Shaw's *Major Barbara*.

It was Harrison's roles in *The Rake's Progress* and Noel Coward's *Blithe Spirit* that cast him in the public eye as a man who rarely departed from his dinner jacket. 'If you weren't the best light comedian in the country,' Coward chided Harrison, 'all you'd be fit for is selling cars in Great Portland Street!'

As playboy Vivian Kenway in Launder and Gilliat's underrated *The Rake's Progress* (1945, retitled *Notorious Gentleman* for American audiences), Harrison was perfectly cast. Although approaching 40, he brought a youthful exuberance to the part, which acted as a reflective valediction to an era which had been brought down by six years of war. Harrison's effortless style cast him as a laconic gadabout, swilling champagne through a haze of cigarette smoke. 'My type's becoming obsolete,' Harrison comments, in character. 'Can't compete with the international situation … The Thirties produced us and the champagne's gone flat and we're going South with the Thirties. Nothing to show for it except cirrhosis of the liver and a lot of wasted time.'

'Sexy Rexy' set female hearts a-fluttering, and international stardom beckoned immediately following the end of the war. The transition should have been seamless. Hollywood always had a soft spot for the romantic Englishman, and by 1947, Leslie Howard was dead, while Ronald Colman, Robert Donat and Errol Flynn were past their prime. Hollywood was Rex Harrison's for the asking.

However, it was not to be a happy introduction. For his role as King Mongkut in *Anna and the King of Siam* (1947), Harrison went to considerable trouble to study and perfect the monarch's guttural speech patterns. He was immediately halted by the director.

'I'm speaking like King Mongkut of Siam,' Harrison explained.

'Out of the question!' John Cromwell snapped. 'We hired Rex Harrison, not a bird imitator!'

*Anna and the King of Siam* was Harrison's first film for Twentieth Century Fox, and the actor was disenchanted when the studio head Darryl F. Zanuck sided with his director rather than his star over the thorny question of the king's accent. Harrison was a keen observer of, but non-participant in, the vicious croquet matches Zanuck regularly hosted. For the mogul, the appeal of the game lay in not only being able to win but also to 'kill' your opponent. 'I learned a lot from being a spectator,' Harrison said later. 'This is where Zanuck got rid of his bile. Think how much there must have been churning around in there, considering how nastily he could behave during his working week!'

Harrison turned down every script the studio offered him for seven long months. 'They were confused by me and didn't know how to cast me. I didn't fit into the American scene of comedy.' Such high-handedness offended the Hollywood establishment, particularly the ruling Queens of Gossip, Hedda Hopper and Louella Parsons.

Harrison's second Hollywood film was far more satisfactory. *The Ghost and Mrs Muir* found him at his debonair best, cast opposite the alluring Gene Tierney in a spectral comedy which found the dream factory at the height of its powers. The film also put Harrison happily in contact for the first time with writer/director Joseph L. Mankiewicz, with whom he would memorably reunite on *Cleopatra*, thirteen years later. Mankiewicz was delighted with Harrison's performance, calling him 'my Stradivarius'.

Despite Harrison's perceived haughtiness, the good reviews and box-office success of *The Ghost and Mrs Muir* were the only language that Hollywood really understood. For Rex Harrison though, the Hollywood which had taken him to its bosom now turned and attacked with the venom of a monster, its teeth bared.

It was while married to his second wife, Lilli Palmer, that Harrison had begun an affair with actress Carole Landis. Landis had begun her Hollywood career as an extra, aged only 18. Such was her, what the gossip columnists called 'high spirits' in the Hollywood of the 1940s, that Landis was soon dubbed 'The Studio Hooker'.

Harrison and Landis were inseparable, but the actress soon realised that Harrison would never leave his wife for her, and on 6 July 1948 she committed suicide. 'Suddenly,' Harrison's biographer, Nicholas Wapshot, noted, 'in death, Carole Landis became a Hollywood heroine, the victim not of a hypocritical film industry but of a married English actor' (*Rex Harrison: A Biography*, 1991).

In the aftermath of Carole's suicide, Harrison was upset that Twentieth Century Fox would not support its star and had flung him so casually to the wolves of the press, who blamed him for the actress's death. Comparisons were made with the infamous Fatty Arbuckle scandal in 1921, which had finished the silent comedian's career, and a month after Carole Landis' funeral, Harrison and his wife left Hollywood for New York, where Harrison was scheduled to appear in a Broadway play.

While previewing in Philadelphia, Harrison let his true feelings about the film capital slip out:

So far as I am concerned, Hollywood is done with. Hollywood and I have no future in common, and I don't know if Hollywood has any future on its own. It's top heavy in its internal and financial economy; it is so egocentric it doesn't know the rest of the world exists. The caste system, based on the hilarious thesis that his salary is the index of a person's worth, is more rigid than anything India ever dreamed of. Hollywood's whole little world is geared to the studio salary list and unless your friends are in your brackets, you can't afford to know them. Me, I've had enough of it.

And Hollywood, patently, had had enough of the lippy, ungrateful English actor. Hedda Hopper wrote, 'Rex Harrison's career is as dead as a mackerel.' In an editorial that was astonishing for its personal viciousness, *The Hollywood Reporter* fulminated:

> In all the years we have been covering the Hollywood front, we don't remember any actor, foreign or domestic, who breached so many rules of good taste in his conduct among his fellow workers as did Mr Rex Harrison. He's washed himself up here, as he will be washed up anywhere he goes should he continue the ingratitude he displayed while he was in Hollywood.

In fact, within four years, Rex Harrison was back in Hollywood. With an irony he would have appreciated, he had been signed to star as Julius Caesar in Howard Hughes' production of Shaw's *Androcles and the Lion*. As a foretaste of what was to come on *Cleopatra*, Harrison was first in, then out, of the troubled 1951 production. By the time filming began, Harrison's schedule meant he had to quit the film.

Harrison's film career throughout the 1950s was desultory – the nadir was his appearance as Saladin in 1954's *King Richard and the Crusaders*. By and large, he kept Hollywood at arm's length during the decade. His energies were devoted elsewhere, in the role he remains most associated with – Professor Henry Higgins in the musical *My Fair Lady*.

Elizabeth Taylor *is* Cleopatra, Queen of the Nile.

ELIZABETH TAYLOR
PETER FINCH
STEPHEN BOYD

# CLEOPATRA

Produced by WALTER WANGER · Directed by ROUBEN MAMOULIAN · Todd-AO · EASTMAN COLOUR

COLOUR CAPTION NUMBER (1)          "CLEOPATRA" OUTDOOR SETS

LARGEST FILM SET EVER CONSTRUCTED IN ENGLAND FOR "CLEOPATRA".

This panoramic shot shows the 8½-acre re-creation of the city of Alexandria, Egypt, as it existed in 50 B.C., ~~nearing completion~~ at the Pinewood Studios, Iver Heath, Bucks, England.

More than 1,500 extras, 350 mounted soldiers and co-stars Elizabeth Taylor (Cleopatra), Peter Finch (Julius Caesar) and Stephen Boyd (Marc Antony) will populate it when it is filmed in Todd-AO and colour for the Twentieth Century-Fox multi-million-dollar production.

The press release with the original cast and director.

The reverse of the press release, showing the construction of the Alexandria set during the ill-fated Pinewood shoot.

Ancient Alexandria, as it looked on completion in Italy.

The set under construction in Italy.

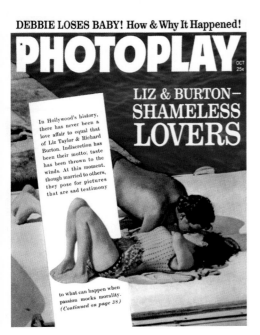

Just a few of the magazines from the period.

The money shot! Cleopatra's entry into Rome.

Taylor with her third husband, Mike Todd.

Caesar (Rex Harrison) embraces his queen. Harrison got the film's best reviews and remained friends with Taylor for the rest of his life.

Costume designer Irene Sharaff adjusts Cleopatra's $6,000 costume, one of the sixty-five she designed for the actress for the film.

Richard Burton in an earlier toga saga, *The Robe*, with co-star Jean Simmons, 1953.

The *other* Cleopatra, the *Carry On …* contribution. Costumes from the Pinewood shoot were used in the 1964 parody.

The original UK quad poster, with Rex Harrison hastily added.

Rare souvenir programme from the Gala premiere in London, 31 July 1963.

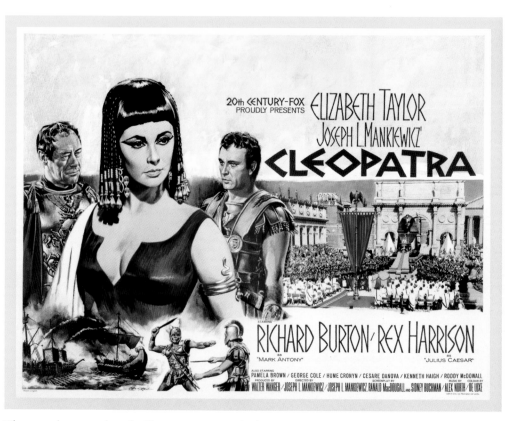

The second poster when the film went on general release.

A newspaper advert for the London showcase: tickets bookable in advance, cheques and postal orders accepted.

MGM's *Mutiny on the Bounty* (1962) was another out-of-hand production that marked the end of the old Hollywood system.

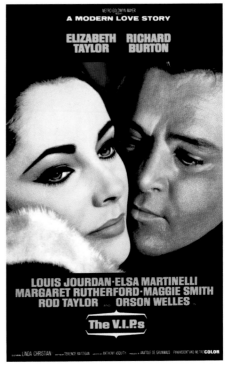

*The V.I.P.s* was a 1963 Burton/Taylor film that was rushed to cash in on the notoriety of *Cleopatra*.

Cleopatra's barge, which was built for the film at a cost of $277,000 ($2 million at today's prices).

The Alexandria set with live extras. The buildings on the horizon are a matte shot.

For many years, lyricist Alan Jay Lerner and composer Frederick Loewe had been determined to transform George Bernard Shaw's play *Pygmalion* into a musical. Their first draft was titled *Lady Liza* and original thoughts for the role of Henry Higgins included Noel Coward, Michael Redgrave and Ray Milland.

Lerner and Loewe had begun work on the adaptation in 1952 but couldn't crack it. They put the project on hold, but persevered, and by 1954, *My Fair Lady* was taking shape. In fact, Gabriel Pascal – the producer of the films of Shaw's *Pygmalion*, *Major Barbara* and *Caesar and Cleopatra* – had first come up with the idea of transforming *Pygmalion* into a musical, and over the years had approached Noel Coward and Cole Porter with an eye to their song-writing skills transforming Shaw's play, but both admitted defeat.

Pascal was convinced that Shaw's 1916 play could be satisfactorily transmuted into a musical. Determined, he approached Rodgers and Hammerstein, who laboured on the project. But even the creators of *State Fair*, *Oklahoma*, *The King and I*, *South Pacific* and *The Sound of Music* were stumped, with lyricist Oscar Hammerstein announcing that adapting *Pygmalion*, 'can't be done'.

Shaw, of course, had been tempted by Hollywood before. In one well-known exchange, Samuel Goldwyn had met the playwright in London, keen to purchase the film rights to his work, but the two could never agree terms, prompting Shaw's familiar response, 'The trouble, Mr Goldwyn, is that you are only interested in art and I am only interested in money!'

The 1938 film of *Pygmalion* was the first talkie adaptation of Shaw, and its success paved the way for others. The film starred Leslie Howard and Wendy Hiller. Even twenty years after it was written, the actress was still capable of shocking audiences with her response to the question, 'Are you walking across the park, Miss Doolittle?'

'Walk! Not bloody likely. I am going in a taxi.'

Playing Higgins, Leslie Howard personified the intellectual, glacial Englishman – while filming the enunciation scene, Hiller gulped that she'd swallowed one of the marbles Howard had placed in her mouth to make her speak better. 'Don't worry,' ad-libbed the actor, 'I've got plenty more!'

And knowing that Rex Harrison had got on well with Shaw during the filming of *Major Barbara* in 1941, the composers approached the actor about casting him as Higgins. In January 1955, Lerner and Loewe, convinced they could transform Shaw's play into a musical, cornered Rex Harrison in a suite at Claridge's to establish just how good his singing was. After a lacklustre performance of 'Molly Malone', Harrison's biographer tactfully noted, 'It was plain he could not sing, or at least not in the conventional sense. He had some grasp of rhythm and a sense of pitch, but what he did could hardly be described as *singing*.' Lerner and Loewe dispatched Harrison to singing tutors, who at least were able to train the actor to 'talk on pitch'.

Determined to stay true to the spirit of Shaw, Rex Harrison insisted that librettist Alan Jay Lerner stick as closely to the language of *Pygmalion* as possible. He was aware just how many noses he could put out of joint by appearing in what many considered to be a Shavian travesty. The conductor Sir Malcolm Sargent called the very idea of *My Fair Lady* 'disgraceful', although T.S. Eliot found time to tell Harrison that, in his opinion, 'Bernard Shaw is much improved by music!'.

In fact, thanks to Lerner and Loewe's inspired music and lyrics and Harrison's assured playing of Higgins, *My Fair Lady* was an immediate triumph from the moment the curtain came down following its Broadway opening on the night of 15 March 1956. It was hailed by theatre historian Mark Steyn as 'a landmark in the theatre, and would eventually be considered by many historians as the most perfect example of the American musical as an art form'.

For all Rex Harrison's years as an inspired comic actor and film star, it was the role of Professor Henry Higgins with which he was indelibly associated until his death, aged 82, in 1990. Of that role, Harrison's biographer, Nicholas Wapshot wrote, 'The role of Higgins gave him more work, in the shape of the film, and work for life, for eventually he was to traipse around the world in a series of revival tours.'

'Twas not always thus – still unconvinced of his singing ability, Harrison was unhappy with the pre-first-night tinkering that director Moss Hart and Lerner and Loewe invested in every rehearsal. While great things were expected of the ingenue Julie Andrews as Eliza, Harrison knew that all eyes would be on him as Higgins. He had to carry the show, and for the first time in a professional career stretching back nearly thirty years, Rex Harrison got stage fright, locking himself in his dressing room and refusing to come out on stage for a preview in New Haven.

Designer Cecil Beaton noted in his diary, 'Everyone except Rex Harrison behaved impeccably. He is beneath contempt and refused to appear at the first night saying he was unprepared and would not go on and make a fool of himself.' Literally at the last minute, Harrison was persuaded on stage. He got through the New Haven preview, and within weeks found himself established as part of the celebrity pantheon following the triumphant reception that Broadway accorded *My Fair Lady*.

The show became a sensation and from his recurring nerves about his lack of a singing voice, Rex Harrison magnificently conquered his inability. Spencer Tracy was with Frank Sinatra as Harrison performed 'I've Grown Accustomed to her Face' and later gleefully told the British actor, 'When you did that last number, you made [Sinatra] cry'.

*My Fair Lady* was the smash of the season. Backstage visitors paying homage to Harrison included Marilyn Monroe, Marlene Dietrich, Charles Laughton, Noel Coward and Cole Porter. Harrison revelled in the adulation and took personal pleasure in slamming his dressing room door in Hedda Hopper's face, making up for her hostility to him during his first visit to Hollywood, a decade before. During a 1980 revival of *My Fair Lady*, one backstage visitor who came to pay his compliments was the unlikely figure of Bob Dylan. (To my delight, this gives me the opportunity to relay a spellbinding piece of trivia: the only two people to win the Nobel Prize for Literature and an Oscar were Bob Dylan and George Bernard Shaw. Dylan's Oscar came for Best Original Song, 'Things Have Changed', while Shaw picked up his for his *Pygmalion* screenplay.)

As Alexander Walker wrote in his Rex Harrison biography, *Fatal Charm* (1992):

Only one theatregoer is on record as coming away unimpressed. 'I thought it was the dullest, lousiest show I have ever seen. Even as Pygmalion without Harrison it was pretty bad; with Rex Harrison it is awful.' The unlikely dissident was P.G. Wodehouse, who one might have expected reveling in the recreation of a period he would have known as a young man.

*My Fair Lady* entered theatrical legend. Tickets were in such demand that one, perhaps apocryphal, story had a woman sitting with an unheard-of empty seat beside her during the Broadway run. On being asked why it was empty, she replied that it had been intended for her husband, but he had died before he could attend. Shamefaced, the inquirer pursued the matter, saying that surely there must have been someone she could have found to accompany her – a friend, or relative? 'Oh no,' the widow chirped. 'They're all at the funeral!'

The Broadway run of *My Fair Lady* entered the record books with an unbeaten run of 2,717 performances, making it the most successful musical in the history of American theatre. It was a record that *My Fair Lady* held until it was overtaken by *Fiddler on the Roof* in 1968.

Rex Harrison stayed in character on Broadway until 28 November 1957. He brought Professor Higgins across the Atlantic to the Theatre Royal, Drury Lane, from 30 April 1958 or a London run of *My Fair Lady*. But after four years growing accustomed to Julie Andrews's face, Harrison finally quit on 28 March 1959, and was out looking for new territories to conquer.

# 17

# Caesar Reigns

Harrison was familiar for playing Henry Higgins, the sort of role an actor would kill for, but he appreciated that, even at the age of 50, he still had a few more years of his professional career left, and didn't want to spend them all beginning every evening asking, 'Why Can't the English?'

In 1960, in the footsteps of Laurence Olivier, Rex Harrison arrived at the Royal Court Theatre in a revival of a little-known Chekhov play, *Platonov*, for a weekly fee of £60, which his biographer estimated was 'hardly enough to pay his dry-cleaning bills'. Among the cast was a young Welsh actress, Rachel Roberts, who went on to become the fourth Mrs Rex Harrison.

By the early 1960s, aged 54, Rex Harrison recognised that he was at a career crossroads. Nicholas Wapshot wrote:

> Three years after the success of *My Fair Lady*, he was being reduced to appearing in small arts theatres in London and poor quality American films. His failure to find good films to act in was less to do with him, although he was growing too old for the better parts, than because the film industry in Britain hardly existed and the American studio system had also collapsed.

To further rub salt in Harrison's wound, as his career declined, that of his partner's was in the ascendant. As the genre of 'kitchen sink' drama flourished, Rachel Roberts's role in *Saturday Night and Sunday Morning* in 1960 was well received, while her performance in 1963's *This Sporting Life* was recognised with an Oscar nomination.

While Rex Harrison was unhappily appearing in a Nigel Dennis play, *August for the People*, his agent Laurie Evans had received a tempting offer for Harrison to appear in a film that would require his presence in Rome. Filming was set to begin on 18 September 1961.

'I will probably be away six months,' Harrison airily told the press. But, as with everything associated with the troubled shoot of *Cleopatra*, nothing was ever that simple, and he found himself committed to the troubled production for over a year.

As well as a substantial salary, the prospect of a role as the best-known Roman emperor would go some way to proving that there was more to Rex Harrison than a professor of linguistics. The prospect of filming in his beloved Rome, the opportunity to flee from a play he felt was doomed and the carrot of a juicy role in what was already the most keenly anticipated film of the decade all tempted Harrison. He was further attracted to *Cleopatra* by the prospect of reuniting with Joseph L. Mankiewicz, who had helped launch his Hollywood career fourteen years before with *The Ghost and Mrs Muir*.

Twentieth Century Fox president, Spyros Skouras, disagreed, however. He recalled the hostility Harrison had aroused in Hollywood on his first visit to the film capital, but of more immediate concern was the fact that, in box-office terms, Rex Harrison was dead in the water. Producer Walter Wanger confided to his diary, 'Skouras threw up his hands and said he'd resign from the company before he'd have Rex Harrison. Rex Harrison couldn't act. He was no good. The press hated him.'

Harrison's ill-chosen film roles during the 1950s had made little money, and with the studio betting the house on *Cleopatra*, Fox executives were determined to only commit to box-office certainties. That explained the studio's willingness to meet Elizabeth Taylor's extravagant million-dollar demand. Taylor also brokered an estimated 5 per cent of the film's gross profits.*

It was the star of *Cleopatra* who had the final say over casting, and with Elizabeth Taylor insisting on Rex as her co-star, on 11 September 1961, Wanger confidently confided in his diary, 'Negotiations finally concluded for Rex Harrison to play Caesar at $10,000 a week, plus expenses, a car and driver and co-star billing'.

The studio and producers' antipathy to Harrison were known by the time he appeared on set. Once in Rome, the auguries for Rex Harrison's involvement in *Cleopatra* were equally unpromising: the responses to his screen tests were discouraging. Even costumier Irene Sharaff commented on Harrison's ability to fill a toga, 'Without the fine tailoring of Savile Row, Rex's figure was not impressive. The Roman costumes with tunics and short sleeves exposed the weak points: narrow shoulders, long thin arms, spindly legs!'

By the time Rex Harrison arrived on the Rome set of *Cleopatra* in September 1961, the production was already infamous. He found that he was not needed for filming for at least a further two months. Instead, he found himself idling his time away in luxury in Rome's Grand Hotel, researching his role. Harrison became quite intrigued by the patrician Caesar:

> I could never quite believe that Caesar, with all the political and military problems that were on his mind at the time, was so absolutely obsessed with Cleopatra. It seems against his character, so I resisted as much as possible the pressure to play it that way.

Immersing himself fully in the role of the ruler of the known world, Harrison reflected nearly thirty years later in *A Damned Serious Business*:

---

* For all the financial catastrophes associated with *Cleopatra*, one estimate had Taylor eventually accruing an estimated $7 million from the film. A clever clause also saw the star profit from the film's release 'in any other format', thus gaining income from VHS, DVD and Blu-Ray sales. No wonder she was later quoted as saying, 'It wasn't a flop for *me*'.

I did a lot of homework on Caesar, and the more I read, the more fascinated I became. I realised that to play such a powerful man, and to suggest being brainy as well as powerful is very hard. I think also it has a lot to do with stillness. There must be nothing tentative in movement or in speech. You have to be totally aware, all the time, of the fact that you *are* a Caesar.

He suffered from a minor form of epilepsy, and he was always terrified that he would have an attack while he was making a public appearance ort speech. No wonder he was terrified. If he had suffered an attack in public, the Romans would have pulled him down into the crowd and torn him limb from limb. A Caesar was not allowed such ordinary, human signs of weakness.

That scrupulous research paid off. Harrison was one of the few to emerge from the farrago with his reputation intact. His Caesar was favourably singled out by the critics.

Harrison was soon joined on location by his lover, Rachel Roberts, and she was found a single room at the Grand Hotel – this was, after all, 1961, and, even in Rome, unmarried couples did not share hotel suites, however grand their name or that of the hotel. Eventually, the couple found a villa on the Appia Antica.

While Harrison was ideally suited for the role of the emperor, his partner was never comfortable with the high life. Rachel Roberts typified the new look of film actresses. Her breakthrough roles were in gritty, realistic dramas. Her politics were forged in the socialist valleys of Wales, while Rex Harrison's brother-in-law was lord chancellor in Harold Macmillan's Conservative government.

Typical of the way the dice rolled on the troubled production, Rex Harrison's first scene as Caesar was the film's most spectacular – the entry of Cleopatra into Rome. That one scene alone was the money shot, with thousands of cheering extras, exotic dancers, elephants, chariots and the golden-gowned queen rolling in atop an enormous sphinx. But director of photography Leon Shamroy was unhappy with the way the light fell, and so the sequence was delayed for six whole months until it could be re-shot.

Poor old Rex Harrison had to utter his first lines of the film in front of an estimated 10,000 Italian extras – nobody was entirely sure how many extras were actually in the scene, as the wily Romans would frequently double up, running back and forward to increase their daily salary. 'Once you start saying I need 10,000 soldiers' outfits,' Tom Mankiewicz told David Kamp, 'this is like an invitation. If you wanted to buy some new dinnerware or a set of glasses for your house, it was the easiest thing to put it on the budget of *Cleopatra*.'

Harrison was also faced with coloured smoke canisters that had to be relit for every scene, an obelisk which, when split open, released hundreds of doves and a 28ft-tall sphinx tugged by dozens of Nubians atop of which sat Cleopatra. There were also hundreds of horses and dozens of elephants.*

So vast was the set constructed in the Roman Cinecitta studio that rockets had to be fired to alert the extras that filming was underway, and another to cue Rex Harrison. It was an unsettling start to an already troubled production.

Caesar's first line before the assembled throng was 'Queen Cleopatra has most graciously had golden medals struck off to commemorate this great occasion for each of our distinguished senators, each medal inscribed with the name of him for whom it is intended'. Try as he might, and professional as he was, Harrison repeatedly stumbled over Joseph L. Mankiewicz's ponderous prose ('I think it was the "of him for whom" which foxed me,' he later admitted).

It was an ominous beginning. Rex Harrison's faltering delivery was not only witnessed by thousands of Italian extras growing increasingly bored, but, even more ignominiously, Harrison's fumbling was in full view of his co-stars; experienced acting colleagues such as Michael Hordern, Kenneth Haigh, Hume Cronyn, Roddy McDowall and Robert Stephens, who stood in their costumes, wilting under the blazing Roman sun, as Caesar repeatedly stumbled over the dialogue.

From behind his camera, director Mankiewicz grew increasingly concerned. This, after all, was Harrison's first day, and already the

---

* Alas, and typical of the problems dogging the production, the animals were circus trained and responded to the music that was their cue to enter – by lying down.

actor seemed to be touched by the jinx that blighted every aspect of the production.

Every Harrison fluff meant a retake; not just going back to the beginning of the scene but the bulky Cinemascope cameras had to be repositioned, while teams of assistant directors spent hours relocating extras, animals and the massive, unwieldy sphinx, which was the Queen of the Nile's chosen method of entry into ancient Rome. Harrison also had to watch with increasing embarrassment as steaming piles of elephant droppings were swept out of sight so that the scene could be shot afresh.

When the light was deemed correct, and the next time Caesar appeared on set, a nervous Mankiewicz announced 'Action', and the ever-professional Rex Harrison sailed through the scene, word perfect.

It was 8 May 1962 that *the* shot was taken. 'The only analogous situation I can think of,' *Cleopatra* star Hume Cronyn commented, 'would be staging a presidential inauguration with Macy's Thanksgiving Day parade.' Perched high on the collosal sphinx, the vertiginous Taylor found no arms on the throne to cling onto. The procession was likened by an onlooker to 'the forward momentum of a 200,000 ton oil tanker'.

☥

In December 1961, Rex Harrison was allowed leave from the set. On his return, he was met by an indignant chauffeur, who had been sacked. In Harrison's absence, producer Walter Wanger had introduced a series of economy measures to try and halt the flow of money that was being spent so profligately in Rome.

As part of the cutbacks, as well as the sacking of Harrison's driver, his luxurious trailer had been sent packing and the star's dressing room was now to be found in a small loft above a sound stage at Cinecitta. He was incandescent with rage – a major film star for nearly a quarter of a century, this was behaviour up with which he would not put! Harrison summoned Wanger to the set, and in a blistering diatribe, lacerated the producer for his penny-pinching ways.

Harrison began building up a full head of steam. Wanger's behaviour was typical of Twentieth Century Fox, which had made Harrison so unwelcome on his initial trip to Hollywood. Unless, raged Rex, his chauffer and trailer were returned immediately, he would not return for filming. At the end of his diatribe, he summoned himself to his full height, stared at the wilting producer, and with an imperious wave worthy of Caesar, announced, 'You are dismissed.' The studio relented to their star's demands, and filming at Cinecitta proceeded.

Harrison was not an easy man. His fellow actors frequently despaired of his imperious attitude. One of the kinder nicknames was 'Tyrannosaurus Rex'; one of the less kind was 'The C★★t'. Harrison off stage was frequently as imperious as he was on stage or in film. Rachel Roberts recalled that when a call went through to the taxi firm the couple used in London, 'they tried to avoid going, as there was never any money in it, and a lot of abuse'.

The next major hiccup came in January 1962, when Richard Burton arrived in Rome to begin filming his role as Marc Antony. Their co-star was not immune to what was happening. 'The much publicised love affair often made work pretty trying for me,' Harrison was to recall years later:

> At the height of it, Elizabeth and Richard kept hitting each other and giving each other black eyes and not turning up at the studio. I was very, very lucky to be in the first half of the picture. Joe [Mankiewicz] hadn't reached his climax of despair at that point.

For all the unwelcome attention that the Burton–Taylor affair brought to the set of *Cleopatra*, Rex Harrison got on well with both his co-stars, although he did resent playing second fiddle. He remained on call while Taylor and Burton were off somewhere on a tryst:

> I had three or four key scenes of Caesar still to play, and they wouldn't call me to the studio to make them because they were keeping me in reserve in Rome, and I hated this. I hated being a stop-gap for Richard and Elizabeth, and being under instructions to wait in case

they – the studio – got into any trouble with their shooting schedule, and then they would call me.

As his biographer Alexander Walker wrote:

> As their romance made the arrangements for filming them more and more erratic, Rex's scenes were kept in reserve. He could be relied on. It would be useful to hold him over 'as cover' in case love stopped play the way rain stops cricket where the other two stars were concerned.

Professionally, Rex Harrison was sublimely happy in the company of both Richard Burton and Elizabeth Taylor. Amidst the spiralling budget, studio shenanigans and movie madness, he was particularly impressed with the professionalism of his queen:

> I loved working with Elizabeth Taylor on the film because she is in every way the consummate film actress and her professionalism on the set and in front of the camera is quite remarkable to see. She was, of course, practically brought up in the studios, and as a result she knows exactly what she's doing with the slightest movement of an eyelash, or curve of a lip. She is always word-perfect, too, something which on *Cleopatra*, with its convoluted words, I found difficult to be. For those of us – including Richard Burton – who had spent our youthful energies on the stage, Elizabeth's film technique is an eye-opener.
>
> A spectacular film like *Cleopatra*, with its combination of huge crowd scenes – for which you have to use something much more like stage technique, make appearances, and even declaim the lines – and intimate two-shot close-ups, is probably the most difficult kind of film to do, and I suppose they'd chosen Richard and myself because we were used to heroic roles in the theatre. Elizabeth, because she was so good in front of the camera, was much more nervous in the stagey scenes, and at one point, when she had to descend a steep flight of steps into the Forum, she had vertigo, and they had a terrible time getting her to go down.

Although they never worked together again, Harrison remained a lifelong friend of Elizabeth's. Notoriously tight-fisted, he gave her an exquisite brooch. In 1977, it sold for $92,500 at a charity auction.

As the Burton and Taylor romance proceeded under the glare of the world's press and the ubiquitous Roman paparazzi, Rex slipped away to Genoa and, on 22 March 1962, married Rachel Roberts. Rachel was a close friend of Sybil, the wife Burton cuckolded to romance his Cleopatra. Rex Harrison had some sympathy with his co-stars and had lent them his villa in Portofino to continue their affair. The move inflamed Roberts's Welsh loyalty, and she complained about lending their house to 'that man and his woman'.

Harrison's role as Caesar occupied – critics would later say, dominated – the first half of *Cleopatra*. The Burton–Taylor scandal was taking minds off the impending Cuban Missile Crisis and the erection of the wall dividing Berlin. Such had been the intensity of interest that it allowed Harrison a degree of laxity. On a trip home from Rome, Harrison went sailing off the Dorset coast. On his return to safe harbour, he found frantic messages relayed from Italy: he was urgently needed on set for a scene and had to return to Rome overnight after being tracked down in Poole.

Such arbitrary summonses did little to delight Harrison, and by June 1962 the actor breathed a sigh of relief when he was scheduled to undertake his concluding scenes for a film which had dominated his life for nine months. Harrison's final scene was – typically, in the hurly-burly chronology of film making – the scene that would open the epic – Caesar's defeat of Pompey's army at the Battle of Pharsalia.

As it entered its third year of production, the studio was understandably frantic over the escalating costs of the film. In desperation, Twentieth Century Fox pulled the plug on the battle, a move that inexplicably sent Rex Harrison into a torrent of dissent. Walter Wanger's diary entry for 4 June 1962 read:

Rex Harrison called. He has heard that the studio is thinking of cutting out the Pharsalia sequence and he believes so strongly that the scene is necessary, he is willing to underwrite the cost of filming it himself. A magnificent gesture!

Harrison's chequebook remained in his pocket. So, with a sigh of relief, Harrison retreated with his bride of three months to his villa in Portofino.

As with every aspect of *Cleopatra*, however, nothing was ever that simple. On viewing what Mankiewicz had shot, after being endlessly chivvied about cutting costs and after being sacked (on 12 October 1962) from his own film, Mankiewicz was recalled.

Fox boss Darryl Zanuck decided that the opening battle scenes at Pharsalia looked *cheap*. This production needed a striking and sweeping opening. So, Mankiewicz was hauled back once again into the director's chair and granted an extra $2 million to beef up the battle.

After he had been off the film for six months, Rex Harrison was summoned back from Italy and filmed his scenes in Almeria in Spain. Although the battle scenes were dramatically reduced, it was still shot on a scale that would otherwise have financed an entire film. Typical of the troubled production were the problems line producer Elmo Williams faced on the Spanish reshoot. Filming could only proceed with permits from the Ministry of Agriculture, the Ministry of Culture and the Madrid chief of police. To ensure a trouble-free shoot, $10,000 had to be delivered to a 'friend' of the police chief under a street lamp at night.

Finally, with locations ranging over Italy, Spain, Egypt and the UK, the unit returned to Pinewood during February and March 1963. Three years after the cameras first rolled, *Cleopatra* was back at the studio where it all began.

According to Rex Harrison:

The immensely long filming of the epic had been something of an endurance test. It had taken from September 1961 to the end of July 1962 at Cinecitta in Rome and on other locations in Italy and in Egypt, with additional shooting in February 1963 in Almeria, Spain, and was finished at Pinewood Studios, England on 2 March 1963.

From Elizabeth Taylor signing the contract in October 1959, three and a half long years later, all concerned must have welcomed Marc Antony's last lines, as penned by Shakespeare, 'The long day's task is done'.

It was finally, after eighteen months, that Rex Harrison quit *Cleopatra*, or so he thought. On viewing a rough cut of the film that had cost his studio millions to date, Darryl F. Zanuck realised that the only way to suck audiences in was to further emphasise the Burton–Taylor romance which had transfixed the world. Writer and director Joe Mankiewicz's original two-film version had long since been dismissed. As it currently stood, *Cleopatra* was equally divided: the first part dealt with Caesar's infatuation with the Egyptian queen, while after the intermission, audiences would watch Cleopatra transfix Marc Antony.

By early 1963, however, it was evident that all the world wanted from *Cleopatra* were the scenes shared by Richard Burton and Elizabeth Taylor. At Zanuck's insistence, Rex Harrison's scenes were trimmed and those of the star-crossed lovers further emphasised. As a result, Harrison's Caesar was marginalised.

In those days of studios having the final say, there was little the actor could do. And Harrison was realist enough to understand that what would draw audiences to the epic were the off-screen antics of his co-stars made visible in the finished film.

He could, though, do something about the advertising campaign for *Cleopatra*. As he was filming his final scenes as Caesar in Spain, shooting the Battle of Pharsalia, Mankiewicz advised Harrison to look out for the 'likeness clause' in his contract. This ensured that Rex Harrison had equal billing on the promotional posters with Elizabeth Taylor and Richard Burton. As the opening date of *Cleopatra* approached, the finished posters were remarkable for the absence of Rex Harrison's face. The huge posters, which were to be fly-posted around the globe, featured only Taylor, reclining on a chaise longue, with a captivated Burton by her side. Of an attentive Julius Caesar, there was no sign.

Harrison was incensed and began legal proceedings against the studio, which seemed singlehandedly out to rupture his career. A hastily redesigned poster found Harrison lurking alongside the lovers ('looking like a Peeping Tom,' as one passer-by observed) or a small portrait of Caesar inserted at the base of the picture. 'It was an ignominious, farcical business,' Harrison admitted. 'Even though I got my "rights" in the end, I disliked the fact that I had literally to fight for a footing in what was a three-handed film, particularly when the other two were friends as well as colleagues.'

Even though the reviews that greeted *Cleopatra* on its release were withering, Rex Harrison was singled out as one of the few reasons to actually go along and see the most talked-about film in cinema history. Harrison was in New York for the lavish premiere. The all-important *Variety* review singled him out, 'Rex Harrison is superb as Caesar. His are the film's most brilliant lines, and something is lost with his assassination.'

So convincing was Harrison's performance that he was nominated for an Oscar as Best Actor, along with Albert Finney (*Tom Jones*), Richard Harris (*This Sporting Life*) and Paul Newman (*Hud*). All lost out to Sidney Poitier, who won the coveted statue for *Lilies of the Field*. It was a further reminder of the changing times: it was the high watermark of the Civil Rights movement, with Poitier becoming the first black actor to ever win an Academy Award.

☥

*Cleopatra* undeniably brought Rex Harrison back to the forefront, but he knew that the memory of the cinema-going public – and that of the film studios – was notoriously short-lived. As his biographer noted, 'Rex needed *My Fair Lady* after *Cleopatra* to consolidate his star status. He did not want to return to having to accept anything that was offered, just to keep the cash rolling in.'

Mogul Jack L. Warner had paid the record sum of $5.5 million for the film rights of *My Fair Lady*. It was to be his swansong at Warner Brothers, the studio he had founded with his brothers in 1918. With such an outlay, Warner, even though he, above all, knew the fickleness of the film industry, wanted a guaranteed certainty when it came to filming *My Fair Lady*. Rather than gamble on the unknown film qualities of Julie Andrews, Warner settled for the lustrous star quality of Audrey Hepburn to play Eliza Doolittle, even if she couldn't sing!

Rex Harrison was the inevitable choice for the film role of Higgins, but on finally witnessing his performance in *Cleopatra*, Warner thought Harrison looked too old. ('Certainly I looked old,' the actor responded.

'I was playing a man in his latter days and an epileptic to boot, not a bounding juvenile.')

Warner was convinced that he had found *his* Higgins in the younger form of Peter O'Toole, who had shot to fame as *Lawrence of Arabia*. O'Toole was the new name on everybody's lips as Warner was casting *My Fair Lady*, and the colourful newcomer had boasted, 'I'm exactly the Professor Higgins type'. Eventually, O'Toole was ruled out when his financial demands were too demanding, and on 25 October 1962, it was announced that Rex Harrison would be playing Professor Henry Higgins in the Warner Brothers production of *My Fair Lady*.

Filming began on 13 August 1963, two months after Cleopatra had opened. Effortlessly, the production of *My Fair Lady* switched from the stage to fill the screen. Audrey Hepburn looked glorious, but sometimes came across as little more than a clothes horse for Cecil Beaton's eye-catching costumes. She did gain some consolation though – for her starring role in *My Fair Lady*, Hepburn picked up a cheque for a cool $1 million, thus becoming the third actress to do so (after Elizabeth Taylor and Sophia Loren). Ironically, Julie Andrews's being passed over for the role of Eliza was her cinematic salvation because she found fame – and an Oscar – playing *Mary Poppins*.

Rex Harrison, who didn't get an Oscar for his role in *Cleopatra*, was nominated and won Best Actor for *My Fair Lady* the following year, as did director George Cukor and producer Jack Warner. *My Fair Lady* swept the board for Warner Bros in the way that Fox had hoped for *Cleopatra*.

For Rex Harrison, the filming of *My Fair Lady* was a welcome respite following his previous cinematic experience. 'After the uncertainties of *Cleopatra*, it was a joy to find a set-up organised almost as in the theatre. We had done something worthwhile, and done it well.'

Rex Harrison took the little gold man home in 1964 for *My Fair Lady*. It was a vindication and gave Harrison the box-office clout he required to keep him in the style to which he had become accustomed. Effortlessly and fluently, Harrison slid into Terence Rattigan's *The Yellow Rolls-Royce*, a slight but nonetheless enjoyable portmanteau film. It was a role that suited him like a pair of Lobb's shoes – the Marquis of Frinton. On finding his wife in flagrante in the eponymous vehicle, he returns the vehicle to the showroom as 'It no longer pleases me'. As Alexander Walker astutely noted, paying tribute to Harrison's commanding presence:

> Five words, but Rex uses them to sum up the stifled cry from the heart of a man who has treated his wife as just another prized possession and now prefers to sacrifice the car rather than suffer the constant reminder of what his neglect has allowed to happen.

With an Oscar on his mantelpiece, Rex Harrison could now command $500,000 a film, and even with the desultory experience of *Cleopatra* recently behind him, he was lured back by Twentieth Century Fox in 1966 for another film that was rapidly eating up the profits generated by *The Sound of Music*.

*Dr Dolittle* was one of those films that had success stamped all over it. Based on the much-loved children's favourite, it came in the wake of successful film musicals like *My Fair Lady*, *The Sound of Music* and *Mary Poppins*. But like so many 'guaranteed hits', before and after (*Star!*, *The Last Tycoon*, *Heaven's Gate*, *Super Mario Brothers*, *John Carter*, *Cats*), *Dr Dolittle* bombed.

Probably the failure came, like *Cleopatra*, with its timing: 1967 is widely recognised as rock 'n' roll's *annus mirabilis*, led by The Beatles' *Sgt Pepper* album and with debut LPs from The Doors, Velvet Underground, Procol Harum, Pink Floyd and the Jimi Hendrix Experience. The audience that should have gone to see Rex Harrison talk to the animals was likely queuing to see *The Graduate*, *In the Heat of the Night* and *Bonnie and Clyde*.

*Dr Dolittle* ended up sucking in $28 million of Fox's money, and its returns barely edged over $6 million.* It was only to be the first in a series of big-budget musical disasters (*Star!*, *Darling Lilli* and even

---

\* It was as if a curse was attached to the tale of the doctor who could talk to the animals. While Eddie Murphy's 1998 take did well at the box office, I cannot remember worse reviews for any film, performance or accent than those that greeted the Robert Downey Jr version in 2019.

*Hello Dolly*) that dogged the studios during the late 1960s. The studios were wrongfooted when audiences flocked to quirky mavericks like *The Graduate* and *Easy Rider*, rather than the multimillion-dollar, star-studded super tankers that the Hollywood studios were churning out, regardless of what audiences wanted.

For the remainder of his life, Sir Rex Harrison (he was knighted in 1990) largely bypassed the cinema, taking his style to the stage. His film roles were largely well-paid cameos in forgettable films like *Ashanti*. However, inevitably, the lure of Henry Higgins was too strong, and in 1979, Rex Harrison returned to the stage in the role with which he would forever be associated. It proved to be a family business; Rex's son, Noel ('Windmills of your Mind') Harrison, appeared as Higgins in touring productions of the musical during the 1970s.

It was not only in the public eye that Harrison was seen as Higgins. While Jack Warner was desperately casting the film back in the early 1960s, he felt Harrison was too old and not enough of a box-office draw, even though, to the entire world, Rex *was* Higgins. Warner was keen to enlist Cary Grant, who he saw as a box-office certainty. The artist formerly known as Archie Leach cabled back a response that has entered cinema history, 'Not only will I not play Higgins, if you don't cast Rex Harrison, I won't go and *see* it!'

# 18

# The Times, They Are A-Changin'

It was Orson Welles, after years of bitter experience, who reflected that all a poet needs is a pen and a painter a brush, but a film maker needs an army. Epic films on the scale of *Cleopatra* and *Mutiny on the Bounty* were not *always* doomed. While *Cleopatra* has become synonymous with failure on a gigantic scale, and the one film cited as the sole reason for its studio's decline and fall, it could so easily have gone the other way.

For William Wyler's biographer, Axel Madsen, '*Ben-Hur* was gigantic, a colossal gamble by Metro-Goldwyn-Mayer to redress the fortunes of a company weakened by years of debilitating proxy fights, hardened arteries and a sorry record.' Wyler slaved over *Ben-Hur* for two years, sixteen hours a day, seven days a week. One of Hollywood's most revered directors, Wyler had proved his abilities with unforgettable, star-studded romances, such as 1939's *Wuthering Heights*. Wyler also took Bette Davis to new heights in *The Little Foxes* and *The Letter*. He was responsible for one of the best pieces of wartime propaganda in *Mrs Miniver*, and the best post-war apologia, *The Best Years of Our Lives*. By the mid-1950s, Wyler had come to appreciate the spectacle that he enjoyed with his western *The Big Country*, and so plumped for an even bigger project for his next film.

Hollywood was convinced that big was definitely best. Svengali Mike Todd, who was to become Elizabeth Taylor's third husband, had seen his lavish, star-studded *Around the World in 80 Days* come in at a budget of $7 million and it had taken $23 million in domestic US rentals alone. Cecil B. De Mille's 1956 *The Ten Commandments* was on its way to making $40 million by the end of the decade.

MGM had already hit pay dirt with Civil War General Lew Wallace's biblical saga *Ben-Hur*, which was first published in 1880 and which MGM had owned since 1923, after its stage success on Broadway (which included a chariot race!).* In 1926, MGM filmed it as a silent epic at a total cost of $4 million. The production included a young William Wyler as a $10-a-day assistant. In 2016, a fourth film version was released.

MGM sensed that *Ben-Hur* could be their mother lode, and in 1957 announced plans to remake the film. *Ben-Hur* was the flagship of the studio's plans to take them from the declining fortunes of the 1950s and on confidently into the new decade. The film was originally budgeted at $7 million, but this soared to over $10 million. Wyle's biographer, Axel Madsen, reported a conversation between the director and producer Sam Zimbalist:

'You know what's going to happen if we make a flop?' the producer asked. 'Metro will go bankrupt and the MGM lot in Culver City will disappear.'

'And once Metro goes under, the others will follow,' Wyler responded, picking up the slack. 'The whole American film industry will vanish.'

'Hollywood will become a desert again.'

'And it will all be the fault of Wyler and Zimbalist!'

*Ben-Hur* eventually came in at around $15 million – the chariot race alone cost $1 million and the cost of dismantling the Roman sets came to a staggering $150,000.

---

* A diversion – Lew Wallace (1827–1905). He became a Union general during the Civil War (1861–65), helping to save Washington from the Confederate Army. In 1865, Wallace sat on a committee investigating the Lincoln assassination. After that, he served as US Ambassador to Turkey and became Governor of New Mexico, where he met Billy the Kid (Wallace was played by Jason Robards in the film of *Pat Garrett and Billy the Kid*). He also found time to write *Ben-Hur*, which was first published in November 1880. It went on to become the bestselling US novel of the nineteenth century.

Immediately following its premiere on 18 November 1959, however, it was apparent that MGM had a smash on their hands. The box-office success was further boosted by the film's eleven Oscar wins, a record that stood until it was equalled by 1997's *Titanic*.

Wyler recognised that scale was a part of the overall success of *Ben-Hur*. Interviewed in 1967, the director emphasised:

> If you have to have a chariot race, you have to have stands of people around it and you have to fill the stands with five or six thousand people, not because you want to, but because you can't have empty stands. We would have much preferred to have a cross-country chariot race; it would have been much cheaper. We could have gone across the hills of Rome and down dirt roads and along beaches, and we could have saved a couple of million dollars.

For many years, 1959's *Ben-Hur* remained the most successful film epic ever made. The all-time box-office champion, 1939's *Gone with the Wind*, took twenty years to achieve a take of $80 million. It was only overtaken in 1965 by the sleeper, *The Sound of Music*. Until the phenomenon of 1972's *The Godfather*, *Ben-Hur* was the fourth most successful film released in North America, following (1) *The Sound of Music*, (2) *Gone with the Wind* and (3) *The Graduate*.

Since 1972, familiar titles such as *Avatar*, *Titanic* and *Star Wars* have dominated the chart. A 2020 survey had *Gone with the Wind* maintaining its No. 1 position, although film historians believe that with a Chinese rerelease, *Avatar* may have overtaken it. There is no dispute that *Gone with the Wind* is the one film that has been *seen* by most people.

Wyler's epic could and should have offered a healthy precedent for *Cleopatra*: an intelligent script, sweeping big-screen spectacle, noteworthy performances, a colourful, extravagant night out. But *Ben-Hur* was everything the lavish *Cleopatra* was not.

After the front-page news across the world, with all the lurid rumours seeping from the set, tales of unrivalled spectacle and interminable production delays, boardroom battles and whole empires crumbling, the world was clamouring for *Cleopatra*. In the immediate post-war climate, the films coming out of Hollywood had been darker, more menacing and less escapist, more concerned with the actuality of life and death. They were tough and gritty: private eyes soaked up hard liquor; scarlet women spat razor-sharp sentences from vermillion lips and staccato shots ricocheted down dark alleys. It was a black and white world, far removed from the frothy escapism Hollywood had offered up before the war.

In Europe, the shock was seismic. A five-year absence from American movies was replaced with the dark genre that the French critics christened 'film noir'.

The films were played out against the shady world of Joe McCarthy and his Communist witch hunts. McCarthy, a senator with the worst record in Congress, took one last stab at redeeming his career. In the unlikely surroundings of the Ohio County Women's Club, in West Virginia in January 1950, he flourished a fake list of 'known Communists' working in government – and America entered one of the darkest periods in its peacetime history.

Friendly witnesses were called before the House Un-American Activities Committee (HUAC) to testify against Communist infiltration. In scenes that were chillingly reminiscent of Stalin's Russia, the very regime to which McCarthy and his stool pigeons were so violently, vehemently opposed, show trials were effectively held, all of which could be witnessed, live on television. Reputations were tarnished, careers destroyed and lives taken by HUAC.

McCarthy was a self-publicist, and movie stars made headlines. So, McCarthy turned his eye west from Washington to Hollywood. It was dispiriting to see the legends turn in their friends, colleagues and comrades to save their own skin. Executives Jack Warner and Walt Disney, director Elia Kazan, actors Ronald Reagan, Gary Cooper and Robert Taylor all 'named names' to avoid being blacklisted.

For a while in the early 1950s, under a nervous newly elected President Eisenhower, McCarthy ran riot, and to many he was seen as a potential leader. But McCarthy shot his bolt when he tried to take on the US Army. That really was a step too far and McCarthy died a broken man in 1957, a man who left his name commemorating an ignoble era.

For Hollywood, emerging from the black-and-white nightmare of film noir, came colour – lurid, blinding colour. Never had anything seemed so vivid, so alive. The massive screens were filled with glaring, bright colours: a 70mm palette of Technicolor.

Location filming was an expensive luxury, but exceptions were made – the Dark Continent for *The African Queen* and *Mogambo*; Spain for *The Pride and the Passion*; Ceylon for *The Bridge on the River Kwai*. Otherwise, for the stars, whole worlds could be created in Hollywood. As the old film capital maxim ran, 'A rock is a rock; a tree is a tree – shoot it in Griffith Park!'

On home turf, the studios could keep a parental eye on their stars. In Hollywood, they also fell under the eagle eye of the all-powerful gossip columnists, Hedda Hopper and Louella Parsons. Of the latter, Sam Goldwyn commented that she was stronger than Samson: 'He needed two columns to bring the house down – Louella can do it with one!'

Like a sandcastle, though, Hollywood was slowly eroding. The lure of television was keeping audiences out of cinemas. With that, the studios' power was also wilting away. A new breed of star was arriving, who had no interest in signing to one studio for a seven-year contract, obliged to humiliate themselves in roles the studio dished out to them.

A new era demanded new stars and, symbolically, the week that Clark Gable quit MGM, after fifteen years as King of Hollywood, was the week that James Dean arrived in town. The birth of rock and roll in the mid-1950s brought newer, less pliable stars to the fore. The crumbling star system, the invasive power of television, the erosion of studio power and the new breed of rebel stars all contributed to the declining power of Hollywood.

The major studios were inextricably bound into 'bigger is better' productions in the early 1960s. Hollywood was convinced that the best card in their hand to combat the cancerous spread of television was the big-budget, all-colour, widescreen spectacle. As the Eisenhower presidency edged over to that of John F. Kennedy, and the 1950s slipped into the 1960s, multimillion-dollar epics were filling the Odeons and ABCs, drive-ins and cavernous cinemas. Among the big-screen titles cinema-goers paid to see before *Cleopatra* was premiered in June 1963 were *The Alamo, Barabbas, Ben-Hur, El Cid, 55 Days at Peking, How the West was Won, The Guns of Navarone, It's a Mad, Mad, Mad, Mad World, Lawrence of Arabia, PT109, The Longest Day, Mutiny on the Bounty, Sodom and Gomorrah, Spartacus* and *Taras Bulba*.

For film-goers, the premise behind the epics of the period was simple: big stars in luxurious locations and the clash and love of individuals, played out against epic, historic backdrops. For all the lavishness of the production values, the stereophonic sound, the Cinerama magic, the pulling power for these epics were the star names above the title.

The stars appreciated their pulling power, which explained Elizabeth Taylor's insistence on, and payment of, her record-breaking million-dollar fee. Charlton Heston was a familiar figure as Moses, El Cid and Ben-Hur. Brando's star was still reckoned to be in the ascendant and therefore capable of pulling paying audiences in to *Mutiny on the Bounty*, which he only accepted after declining, improbably, *Lawrence of Arabia* ('I'll be damned if I'll spend two years of my life out in the desert on some f*****g camel!')

As a lure to ensure crowds, epics such as *The Longest Day, The Guns of Navarone* and *It's a Mad, Mad, Mad, Mad World* came with screen-splitting, all-star casts. As he battled to salvage *Cleopatra*, Darryl Zanuck's *The Longest Day* did the trick – the mogul knew that every time a door opened in his Second World War epic, a star name would appear. So, like rabbits pulled out of a hat, the paying customers were kept on tenterhooks.

None was so keenly anticipated, nor more breathlessly awaited than *Cleopatra*. Ultimately, though, like a doomed condemned aircraft, fundamentally unfit for purpose, the Twentieth Century Fox epic creaked and groaned, and soon, over long hours, sank beneath its own pretensions, avarice and ambition.

# 19

# 'You Must Know Something I Don't'

Finally, the world was ready for the film everyone was waiting for. I remember being dragged along by my parents to the old Dominion cinema, where it ran for a couple of years. The image of the languid Taylor being courted by Burton and Harrison loomed over the top end of Tottenham Court Road. Its use as a cinema is long gone; the Dominion still stands but the whole area has fallen victim to the developers' demolition as Crossrail gouged out large chunks of Charing Cross Road.

On first viewing, it was, as I recall, a curiously dispiriting experience. For my 12-year-old self, *The Alamo* (which, according to my mother's scrupulous diary, I had seen three times by then), *The Guns of Navarone*, *The Great Escape* and *The Longest Day* held far more appeal – many more explosions and much less snogging. From memory, even my parents failed to be captivated. It was probably not sexy enough for my Dad, and certainly too much pseudo-Shakespeare and not enough scandal for my Mum. Sucking noisily on my Kia-Ora, and rustling my Maltesers, I would have enjoyed the battle scenes.

The following year's *Fall of the Roman Empire** was far more up my street – chariot races, big battles, a great final duel in the Forum. Watching it and *Cleopatra* again recently, I was impressed with just how patient audiences were back then. Not just the absence of quick edits or jump cuts, but rather sitting through lengthy expositions on the battle between State and Senate; the army versus divine right; the elaborate rondo around rites of succession; all for small doses of titillation, licentiousness and a little bit of implied incest.

With the benefit of hindsight, the knowledge of the boardroom struggles, the subsequent Burton and Taylor break-ups and with the clear appreciation of just how much money was chewed up by *Cleopatra*, long before the video reacquaintance and frame-by-frame DVD and Blu-Ray rereleases, it was weird finally seeing the film once again with an audience. A screening at the National Film Theatre, nearly forty years after its release, was packed. It was a horribly bleached print, but the only 70mm one available in the UK. It was impressive to see it finally fill the screen for the first time since 1963, but the problem was, it looked like our TV when it's on the blink. Bleached and stripped of all its luminous glory, this *Cleopatra* was literally a pale shadow of its former self.

I was lucky enough to be working as film editor on *Vox* magazine during the 1990s, when the studios lavished money on cleaning up classic films for cinema showings. So, I got to see *Lawrence of Arabia*, *The Godfather*, *My Fair Lady* and *Spartacus* as they were intended to be seen – on a cinema screen, with an audience.

In the wake of reviewing *Spartacus* at the cinema, *Cleopatra* seemed even more limp than I remembered from all those years ago. The first hour is undeniably powerful, a worthy addition to Hollywood toga sagas, but that is largely due to Rex Harrison's languid, yet charismatic Caesar. Harrison dominates the first half of the epic and following his assassination, it becomes a much emptier film.

---

*      As a point of interest, Sophia Loren became only the second actress after Taylor to ask for and receive a million-dollar salary for this film. Alas, after a run of spectacular spectacles – *King of Kings*, *El Cid*, *55 Days At Peking* – the box-office failure of this Roman epic was the one which sadly ended the career of fascinating maverick producer Samuel Bronston.

Harrison brings a gravitas to Caesar. He is imperious, conveying a ruler's haughty allure, but the performance also lends Caesar a humanity. His is a very practical demi-god. Surrounded by a phalanx of the best in British supporting actors, Harrison nonetheless dominates. His Caesar is magisterial and all-powerful, truly a ruler of all he surveys; not just the character, but Harrison's performance. *Cleopatra* is a flatter film without his presence. All audiences should beware the Ides of March – it means no more Rex Harrison in this movie.

Taylor's queen is undeniably sensual; she was at the peak of her on-screen allure. Her Cleopatra is inveigling and seductive, but Her Majesty is petulant and her imperiousness is kittenish. Where there should be a commanding presence at the centre of the sprawl, there is instead a vacuum. It is a black hole matched by Taylor's lustrous, luminous eyes, but any regality is marred by that voice – the very worst kind of whiny, mid-Atlantic, Anglo-American squawk. In silence, she is beguiling, mesmerising. In short, over a long film, only rarely does she suggest queenly majesty; what comes across is shrewish, short temper.

As Harrison's biographer, Alexander Walker, wrote:

> Rex's wonderful voice made Caesar into a figure who was both colloquial and commanding. He did not seem to read his lines. But to live them in every step, look or gesture. Beside him, Elizabeth sounded girlishly shrill and flat rather than sharp and feline.

Her Cleopatra would have been a disappointment to the actress's long-term fans. Leaving aside the hyperbole surrounding *Cleopatra*, Taylor was coming to the role on the back of a series of stellar performances, not least *Giant, Cat on a Hot Tin Roof, Suddenly Last Summer* and *Butterfield 8*.

Burton is no better. His Antony is an embarrassment – a roaring, raging bull, incongruous and sulky. He harumphs, sulks and expresses emotion in a kind of Bardic speed test. The kindest comment is that it is a stage performance, which is magnified by film. Realistically, it is a hyperbolic, inflated performance, roaring and raging through the sets, doing everything but chewing the scenery to gain attention.

Like Joe Mankiewicz, Elizabeth was upset by how the original vision had been gutted. Of Burton's performance, she later reflected, 'They cut the film so that all you see is him drunk and shouting all the time, and you never know what in his character led up to that. He just looks like a drunken sot.'

A full half a century on, a DVD review was interesting (the fiftieth-anniversary Blu-Ray version restored the film to its opening night length of 246 minutes). Beginning with a black screen as Alex North's sinuous overture played, you could imagine shuffling into the 10-bob seats and opening up the Quality Street. Even on our television, the colours were luminous. The uncredited narrator was Ben Wright, who also supplied voices for *101 Dalmatians*. The first thing that struck me – again – was how on God's green earth did anyone ever imagine that the wonders of ancient Alexandria could be recreated in *Buckinghamshire*?

What makes it all worthwhile is Harrison's imperious Caesar, not an easy emperor, but his blithe spirit sweeps all before him until his untimely assassination. His entrance to Alexandria is a masterclass. Harrison strolls through the waterfront market as if sauntering through the food hall of Harrod's. In fairness, it should also be pointed out that Burton's performance in Part I is quite resigned, exerting a subdued power.

Kia-Ora and Maltesers in hand you are braced for Part II, in which, while requiring wheat for Rome, we know Antony gets his oats. The problem with the film is that it is not bad, just leaden. It lies there like a bloated whale. It plods where it should soar, limps where a sprint is required. *Cleopatra* is full of spectacle – the lush interiors, Antony's confrontation with Octavian's army, the lavish costumes, the Battle of Actium, the entry into Rome are all moments that provide a spectacle. But, ultimately, *Cleopatra* is just somehow not spectacular.

It is tantalising to try to imagine the impact of the film back then. It was a very different world. A 1962 letter from Jim Parson in Wimbledon welcomed the opportunity for late-night film screenings: 'Right now, the capital is a pretty dull place. When I compare the night life of London with other capitals, I wonder why people bother to come here at all.' So much was awaiting the most keenly anticipated film of all time.

Imagine, then, it is the early summer of 1963. The Beatles are a promising pop group, touring to promote their third single 'From Me to You'. There is a breathing space of mere months before 'She Loves You' unleashes Beatlemania.

In the White House, President Kennedy is safely installed, eyeing his second term and the campaigning for the 1964 election that must begin soon after his return from Dallas in November 1963. A century after the Civil War, to highlight the nation's embedded racism, Martin Luther King organises a march on Washington in August.

At 10 Downing Street, Harold Macmillan is receiving first word of the scandal concerning War Minister John Profumo. By year's end, Macmillan will be gone and Kennedy will be the victim of an assassin's bullet. All this was the background against which *Cleopatra* opened.

The 10 April 1963 issue of *Life* featured Burton and Taylor on the cover as it promised the inside track on 'The Most Talked About Movie Ever Made'. The ten-page special declared that the film 'may astonish everyone by having more appeal for egg-heads than for gossip-loving lunkheads'. Leafing through the pages, I was struck by the cigarette adverts; the car advertisements making no mention of any environmental concerns; RCA's $199.95 Cordon Bleu automatic-threading cassette, recording and playing back in true stereo; and the tantalising 'When you wear a TV set on your wrist you can <u>still</u> be writing with your 1963 gift: the Shaeffer Lifetime fountain pen'.

What did audiences expect when they paid their 12s 6d? Unrivalled licentiousness? Unprecedented carnality? What Fox had paid over $1 million for, what had sundered two marriages and what the world was waiting for came twenty minutes into the film when, unglamorously unfurled, Elizabeth Taylor's Cleopatra emerges, unrolled from a carpet!

Indoors, the film is static. Poor old Joe Mankiewicz is hamstrung by the hassles over *le scandale* and having to do rewrites when he finishes shooting every day. Fuelled by Benzedrine to write after a day's shooting, other chemicals are applied when he returns to the director's chair. Understandably, with all else raging around him, his eye is off the ball.

There had been deep intakes of breath when Mankiewicz was announced to succeed Mamoulian on the troubled production. He was known as a literate scriptwriter, and on the plus side, Taylor respected Mankiewicz. As well as her hefty million-dollar salary, her insistence on using the Todd-AO process and a location outside the USA, Taylor also had director approval. It was a short list: one was George Stevens (who had steered her to maturity in *A Place in the Sun* and, later, *Giant*), but Stevens was experiencing his own headaches with his own troubled production of *The Greatest Story Ever Told*. Embroiled in that production, Stevens passed. That left just one other name that would meet with the star's approval.

True, Mankiewicz had got on well with Taylor on *Suddenly Last Summer*. He had led Bette Davis to screen glory as Margot Channing, coerced great performances out of the notoriously truculent Marlon Brando, and yet ...

The writer/director also wanted his film to be on a par, if not with Shakespeare, then at least edging up alongside George Bernard Shaw. But his script is leaden. Burton's remark on the queen's golden entry – 'Rome has seen nothing like this since Romulus and Remus' – is one of the few lines anyone recalls.

In fairness, Mankiewicz was wearing three hats – producer, director and scriptwriter. He inherited a production which, at best, could be described as 'troubled'. It should be remembered that the *Cleopatra* Mankiewicz had in mind was *two* films. While he was writing – in longhand – with little or no opportunity to redraft, much of the film had to be shot chronologically. That added further costs to the already inflated budget as sets and actors stood idle while Mankiewicz tried to fuse plot, narrative and literate dialogue between orchestrating elaborate action scenes, coaxing actors and battling studio executives.

Mankiewicz knew he was taking hold of a poisoned chalice when he undertook the project. In a magazine interview prior to the film's opening, he wryly remarked, 'I feel like whoever directed *Our American*

*Cousin* at Ford's Theater the night Lincoln was shot'. No wonder when Mankiewicz was filmed – on live TV – at the New York world premiere and congratulated on his 'wonderful achievement', he smiled and remarked, 'You must know something I don't'.

The problem with *Cleopatra* – just *one* of the problems with the film – is that it is static. It doesn't move. It lies flat on the screen. There is no drama, no development and, curiously, no passion. The scenes between Harrison's Caesar and Cleopatra do spark, but all too soon he is gone and you are left with two limp protagonists – all too obviously, their on-screen passion was translated and lost in off-screen ardour. The scenes between Burton and Taylor lack any residue of the all-engulfing romance that was spellbinding the gossip-hungry world. As Antony and Cleopatra, it is as if the two had just bumped into each other for the first time on location at Cinecitta, in a queue for a cappuccino from the catering truck.

There is always something reassuring in seeing all the Brit Pack out in force – as with every Hollywood epic of the period, the cast is populated with drama school graduates from London. One of the few surviving cast members is the teenage Francesca Annis, already well into a burgeoning drama career. Aged just 16, she was cast as Elizabeth Taylor's handmaiden. Talking to Rachel Corcoran in 2020, Francesca had nothing but fond memories of her time with Taylor in Italy: 'I learned a lot from her about not being intimidated by the system, which held me in very good stead. Working with Elizabeth made me feel I could be my own person. Elizabeth showed me that work is just a part of your life.'

The actress paid fulsome praise following Elizabeth's death in 2011, when she wrote a glowing obituary for *The Daily Telegraph*:

Many people describe how, when meeting Elizabeth Taylor for the first time, they expected her to be special, given all they had heard about her and seen of her – but that still she took their breath away. And when I met her on the set in Rome, that is how it was for me.

It was partly how she looked. I remember her eyes so clearly. They really were violet, and she had these very dark eyelashes. But she was a completely natural beauty: extremely glamorous on the red carpet, but it was no great shock to see her without her make-up.

Early on, we went on location to Ischia in the Gulf of Naples, and she asked the production team where I would be staying. I assumed I'd be with the rest of the crew at one end of the island, whereas she was going to be in a five-star hotel at the other end. And she said: 'There is absolutely no question of Francesca staying down with the unit. She's too young. She must come up and be with me and the family.'

That was typical of her. And so I stayed with her and her children, who she was careful to protect from the limelight. I'd be there when she was playing naturally with them in the swimming pool. I wonder now if her concern for me had something in common with the care she showed many times afterwards for those who had been – like her – child stars. I wasn't one, of course, but I was still young and she was very protective.

When I was cast in my next film, *The Eyes of Annie Jones*, I arrived on set on the first day to find my dressing room full of flowers – irises, a nod to the character I'd played in *Cleopatra* – and a hand-written good luck card from Elizabeth. On set, she didn't stand apart. What I remember most is her laughing a lot. She didn't mind if silly behaviour was going on around her – pieces of orange being thrown about, that sort of thing. She had a silly side.

For British audiences who paid to see the film during its initial run, many of the supporting cast were familiar from the UK's two black-and-white television channels, doing the rounds of *Dr Finlay's Casebook*, *Compact*, *Armchair Theatre* and *No Hiding Place*: Robert Stephens, Finlay Currie, Gwen Watford, Michael Hordern (in an uncomfortable-looking blonde wig), Desmond Llewellyn (soon to be Q), Douglas Wilmer (about to be TVs best-ever Sherlock Holmes), George Cole (*Minder*, many years hence), John Alderton, Jeremy Kemp and Ronald Allen, with *Please Sir*, *Z Cars* and *Crossroads* on the horizon. They all perform manfully.

Kenneth Haigh was an intriguing piece of casting; as Brutus, he delivers the fatal blow to Caesar. Haigh was *the* angry young man from the original stage production of *Look Back in Anger*. In *Cleopatra*, he shares time with the cinematic Jimmy Porter and Richard Burton. Haigh's next film after *Cleopatra* was equally memorable – he played the facile advertising executive patronising George Harrison in *A Hard Day's Night*. But seek in vain for his name on the credits. Producer Walter Shenson told journalist Roy Carr, 'He was a Shakespearean actor and, like a lot of established people back then, he didn't want to be associated with The Beatles.'

In *Cleopatra,* there is the usual sight of those venerable thespians standing around in Roman uniforms or twirling their togas, having to deliver whole, indigestible yards of dialogue. (I was reminded of Harrison Ford's remark to George Lucas on *Star Wars*, 'You can type this shit, George, but you can't *say* it.') The opening Battle of Pharsalia is striking, yet even the set-piece battle scenes lack the visceral thrill of *Spartacus* or *Fall of the Roman Empire*. The first hour does convey spectacle, passion and politics; everything, in fact, you expect from an epic. Ancient Alexandria is brought alive before your very eyes – another cinematic wonder. The cohorts march, the Roman senators plot and centurions hail Caesar. But then there is still the best part of another three hours to go.

Mankiewicz's script suggests the uneasy alliance between politics and passion in Ancient Rome. But it is only suggested; like so much of *Cleopatra*, it is not investigated with any thoroughness. There is little happening beneath the togas. There is a lot about the divinity of Caesars, which is hardly gripping. In Kubrick's spellbinding *Spartacus*, Charles Laughton's scheming Senator Graccus and John Gavin's aspirational Caesar got across political complexity without diminishing any of that film's undeniable spectacle. *The Fall of the Roman Empire* successfully dealt with inheritance and succession, and *Ben-Hur,* for all its many flaws, at least conveyed the motivating power of Christianity as something to occupy the principals and keep the audience quiet before the chariot race.

Richard Fleischer's underrated 1961 *Barabbas* also hinted at what *Cleopatra* could have been. A literate script, a genuine eclipse of the sun and a powerful performance from Anthony Quinn as the thief spared from crucifixion. The scenes of ancient Jerusalem suggest a majesty, while the agony of the sulphur mines is convincingly conveyed. The stoning of Silvana Mangano is powerfully shot. The problem, of course, watching any of those sword-and-sandal sagas today is they have to stand comparison with *Monty Python's Life of Brian*.

There is no subtlety or duality in *Cleopatra*. What you see is what you get: Taylor trouncing and pouting; Burton roaring and raging ('Why do you not lie at the deepest hole of the sea, bloodless and bloated and at peace with honourable death?')

Somehow, nothing is handled appropriately in *Cleopatra*. The queen's son by Caesar is all too soon forgotten in a film when one of the themes of the film is succession. The Shakespearian power of the throne ('uneasy lies the head that wears the crown') is a powerful, motivating force for film drama. But that is all too quickly marginalised here.

Of course, staunch defenders say that all the film's manifold flaws can be explained away by how Twentieth Century Fox, eager for a quick buck, tore the film away from Mankiewicz's original magnificent dual vision, and the *Cleopatra* we see today is a pale substitute. Critics may well have a point in discussing the studio's hijacking and butchery of, say, *The Magnificent Ambersons*. But *Cleopatra* is flawed from the start. Again, in fairness to Mankiewicz, the film he inherited was being pulled in different directions by a studio in far-off Los Angeles while he persevered under trying circumstances in Rome.

There is little or nothing to suggest that *Cleopatra* has anything to say – *Quo Vadis*, *The Robe*, *Barabbas*, *Ben-Hur*, *King of Kings*, even *Demetrius and the Gladiators* – all were inspired by Christianity, the Christian message and Christian steadfastness in the face of hostility. In particular, Nick Ray's *King of Kings* endeavoured to convey the humanity of Christ. Jeffrey Hunter's Jesus was fallible, keening, a young Messiah – it was often referred to as '*I was a Teenage Jesus*'.

Set in the years before Christ, *Cleopatra* obviously lacks that engaging Christian element. But Mankiewicz was keen to depict the melding of empires, the struggle for succession, the founding of a dynasty and the manifest destiny of monarchy.

And yet, seeing *Cleopatra* at the National Film Theatre (now BFI Southbank) within weeks of 1992's *Gladiator* was intriguing. William

Nicholson's script deftly captured all those elements. It tips its helmet to Bronston's 1964 *Roman Empire* epic. And Ridley Scott could do spectacle. There is a jaw-dropping moment in that film when Russell Crowe first enters the full-size Colosseum, packed to capacity with meticulously costumed Roman extras, and for one brief shining moment, after a gap of 2,000 years, you are able to marvel at the scale of the Roman games.

Except, of course, even the naivest late-twentieth-century cinema-goer knew that those crowds are all conjured at the flick of a computer switch, and the scale of *that* Roman Empire was generated by a computer. From the 1980s onwards, crowds of thousands, entire cities, whole worlds could be created from within a computer. Even death had no dominion; when Oliver Reed died before he completed his role in *Gladiator*, unfinished scenes were shot using a stand-in wearing a 3D CGI mask.

With *Cleopatra*, what you saw was what you got – there really were thousands and thousands of Italian extras, all meticulously costumed and coiffured, roaring their approval at Elizabeth Taylor's stately arrival. The queen's barge was built to sail; it was even rumoured that when all the ships were assembled for the film's sea battles, it became one of the world's largest navies. Fatally flawed and fundamentally feeble it may have been, but they really don't make them like *Cleopatra* anymore!

And yet, seeing the restored *Lawrence of Arabia* a year after the reviewing of *Cleopatra* at the National Film Theatre, one was left marvelling at how right David Lean had got it. If the meticulous director wanted 10,000 Arabs cantering across the desert on camels, you hired 10,000 Arabic people, plus the relevant number of camels, and shouted 'Action!'. You also made sure there was someone to sweep the desert clean after each take.

There is little of that jaw-dropping cinema magic in *Cleopatra*. There is in *Lawrence*, like *Ben-Hur*, a character to identify with. Those polished scripts have a focal point. There is someone to fascinate, and whose progress you can willingly follow. As she appears in the finished film, Cleopatra rendered by Elizabeth Taylor is too much of a whinger; there is not enough depth or ambiguity for her to be an enigma. She is, in Oscar Wilde's withering words, 'a Sphinx without a secret!'

# 20

# Finally, The World is Ready

The world premiere of *Cleopatra* was held on 12 June 1963, at the Rivoli Theatre, New York. The cheque the cinema presented to Fox executives for $1.275 million for advance bookings made news in itself. In a bid to claw back the millions seeping from the film, Fox demanded that cinemas guarantee a minimum run. The Rivoli committed to seventy-five weeks (though, in the event, *Cleopatra* only played for sixty-four). The studio also insisted on 70 per cent of advance ticket sales.

A crowd of 10,000 crammed Broadway that premiere night. They were there to glimpse the stars. Among those attending were Frank Sinatra, Henry Fonda, Nat King Cole, Anne Bancroft, Paul Anka, Joan Fontaine, Leonard Bernstein and singing cowboy Gene Autry, who sagely told Hedda Hopper on exiting, 'A great spectacle – but that's the last of the big spenders'. Of the stars, only Rex Harrison (who used the opportunity to plug his upcoming role in *My Fair Lady*), with his new wife Rachel Roberts, attended. Harrison was wheeled out for all the big events – disappointment registers on the faces of the onlookers caught by the newsreels, who were expecting the lovers, but Burton was filming *Becket* in England and Taylor was loyally by his side.

To her credit, Elizabeth also avoided the American premieres out of loyalty to Mankiewicz. She was furious at the cuts the studio made in interviews underlining just how chaotic the production had been before

Mankiewicz came on board. Like the director, the star originally envis-aged *Cleopatra* as a game of two halves and was furious at its butchering.

The Los Angeles premiere found Jack Lemmon, Rosalind Russell, Gene Kelly, Lucille Ball, Zsa Zsa Gabor, Donald O'Connor, Rita Moreno, June Allyson, Jane Fonda and the second Mr Elizabeth Taylor, Michael Wilding. A contemporary newsreel makes for extraordinary viewing. The fans began queueing at 3 a.m. for a glimpse of the legends made mortal. Squeals and screams greeted each arrival. The look on the fans' faces is a mixture of ecstasy and envy. The scene recalls the tragic events John Schlesinger conjured up in *The Day of the Locust*, where the fans literally tear their idols apart.

The UK premiere of *Cleopatra* was held at the Dominion, Tottenham Court Road, on 31 July 1963, one of the few London cinemas able to screen Todd-AO films. *South Pacific* had enjoyed a record-breaking 231-week (four and a half years) run at the cinema. In diligent pursuit, I reviewed *South Pacific* and came away reeling from its turgid plot and eye-watering colour filters – 'garish' doesn't begin to describe it – and what was with Mitzi Gaynor?

## London, July 1963: A Snapshot

I had forgotten that, on general release, north London got films a week before they crossed the Thames. So, if you wanted to see your favourite star first, you had to go to Finchley (Glenn Ford in *All This and Money Too*), rather than Forest Hill (Henry Fonda in *Spencer's Mountain*).

*Hamilton* was preceded at the Victoria Palace Theatre by the long-running *Black and White Minstrel Show*. Sophie Tucker ('The last of the red-hot Mommas') was at the Talk of the Town ('Floorshows, superb three-course dinner, dancing to two famous orchestras, all for 55/-'). Rex Harrison could have popped along to the Blue Angel to see his son Noel in cabaret.

The *Daily Mirror*, on the day *Cleopatra* opened, featured the front pages 'Spy Philby In Russia' and 'Protect Me, Pleads Christine' (Keeler).

Also 'Ward Awaits Verdict'. Stephen Ward, the Profumo scapegoat, had overdosed the night before and died on 3 August 1963.

Immediately preceding *Cleopatra* in London cinemas was the Samuel Bronston epic, *55 Days at Peking*. Quickly cashing in on *Cleo*, the Carlton Haymarket was reshowing *The Robe* ('Richard Burton In His Greatest Role To Date'). Other films showing in the capital the week *Cleopatra* opened were Dirk Bogarde in his final surgical role, *Doctor in Distress*; Frank Sinatra in *Come Blow Your Horn*; *West Side Story* in its '2nd great year' and *Marilyn*, a documentary 'personally narrated by Rock Hudson', which implausibly suggested that Mr Hudson would attend every screening during the film's London run.

Among those who'd paid for their 2-guinea seats that July night at the Dominion premiere were the infamous Mandy Rice-Davies,* who commented mischievously afterwards, 'I liked it [...] spoilt only by the fact I knew what was coming. You see, I'd read the book.' Other luminaries included original *Cleopatra* star Stephen Boyd, as well as Yul Brynner, Robert Mitchum, Anna Neagle, Richard Attenborough, Noel Coward, the Duke and Duchess of Bedford, Billy Butlin and Sean Connery. Normally, the 007 star's attendance would have provoked near riots, but the second Bond film, *From Russia With Love*, was still three months away from its UK opening.

Kate Landis, of NW3, loyally wrote to *Photoplay*, the month before the film opened, 'I know the film cost millions to make. But I'm sure it will make even more millions at the box-office. Everyone will want to see it. I don't think Fox need worry.'

In protest, Burton and Taylor stayed away, even though the premiere was effectively only at the other end of Oxford Street. London was undergoing a heatwave ('82 in the shade') and that evening, they repaired to the rooftop bar of the Dorchester. Seats in their name at the Dominion were taken by their private secretaries, Dick Hanley and

---

\*    In his diaries, Noël Coward was scathing: 'I think I hate "Mandy Rhys Cardboard" (or "Mandy Rice Pudding") the most. ... *Who* I should like to know invited her to The Film Premyeer [*sic*] of *Cleo* and to the party afterwards? She was wearing a dress that she had made herself – and it *looked* like it. What is England coming to?'

John Ley, much to the disappointment of the crowd of 2,000, who had gathered outside the cinema, eager for a glimpse.

Once the film opened to the general public there were two performances, at 2 p.m. and 7 p.m. This elevated the film to a pseudo-theatrical event. Seat prices were 30*s*, 25*s* and 20*s* for the dress circle and 15*s* and 10*s* for the stalls.

Reeling out of the cinema, you could visit one of only three Indian restaurants listed in *What's on in London* magazine (the Asia Grill, Gulistan or Light Of India). Men about town could saunter along to the Georgian Club on St James's where 'our gorgeous young ladies will serve you with drinks, dine and twist with you'. Club Concorde on Oxford Street was less welcoming: 'No beatnik-ish togs. The management bar girls in jeans and insist on lounge suits and ties for the chaps.' The Café Royale was offering a Playgoers Dinner for 25*s*. Or you could visit Raymond's Revuebar International Striptease Spectacular featuring Lou Lou Santiago, Nana Pilon and Miss Côte d'Azur.

Six months later, *Cleopatra* was still doing 'steady' business at the Dominion, according to *Variety*. The 1,712-seat cinema hosted London's second most successful film in the week of 4 February 1964, only beaten by the 'mighty' performance of the film Richard Burton had narrated, Stanley Baker's *Zulu*.

☥

Twentieth Century Fox could only live off the scandal of *Cleopatra* for so long. There had to come a time when the most expensive, most talked-about, most keenly anticipated motion picture of all time would bring in the crowds. Worryingly, within ten days of the film's US opening, Fox shares had plummeted $35.50 to $28.50.

On his appointment, Zanuck had scythed through the studio. In June 1961, Fox had twenty-nine producers, forty-one writers and 2,154 salaried employees. Within a year, it was down to fifteen producers, nine writers and 606 staff, supervising a mere nine films.

Before the crowds could flock and fill the Coliseum of their local cinema, the critics had to have their say. Today, in the twenty-first century, with a nervous studio, a major project like *Cleopatra* might conceivably bypass the hard-hitting critics. The studio could hype it over the first hurdle of that crucial opening weekend and puff it up with online enthusiasm. Audiences today could be pulled in by the sheer scale of the cinematic event; the drawing power of its stars; the sheer hype to get the punters in before the first damning critical notices appear.

With *Cleopatra*, though, even when the disparaging notices did appear, it didn't harm the initial box-office takings. It went on to become the highest-grossing film of the year. However, it had to go a long way to recoup the eye-watering costs of its troubled, two-year production.

Despite their inherent qualities, 'event movies' of the 1970s, such as *The Godfather, Jaws, The Exorcist* and *Star Wars*, effectively bypassed the critics. Word-of-mouth enthusiasm guaranteed crowds, and by the time the reviews appeared, the movies had taken on a life of their own.

But that all lay a decade after *Cleopatra*. The 1963 film had to make money from audiences paying admission at the box office. If it was perceived as a box-office hit, then the studio could begin to reclaim some of its production costs, but also heist the price for later television screenings. *Cleopatra* had to hit the ground running, make its mark at the box office during its cinematic run, or it was doomed. There was no safety net of satellite television screenings, home video, laser discs, DVD, Blu-Ray or paid streaming.

To make a film such as *Cleopatra* a real event for the ticket-buying public, it would be shown on its initial run as a Road Show presentation. Premiered in London, the film would then run at one cinema in key cities such as, in the UK, Birmingham and Manchester. Once the prestige bookings dipped, the title would be leaked out into the suburbs. The thinking was that something of this scale and size could not even be attempted by TV. On a good day, with a following wind, one of 'The Big Films' of the period could enjoy a theatrical run of up to two years, or if you were determined to wash that man right out of your hair, four years.

Curiosity alone drew in initial audiences. At the time, British television was restricted to a meagre two channels, broadcasting within an extremely limited timeframe in black and white. Cinematically, *Cleopatra* suggested unprecedented drama, colour, sex and spectacle.

Once inside the cinema during the film's initial run, audiences would be immediately struck by the foyer, specially decorated in the style of the film they were about to see. Like at opera and theatre productions, souvenir brochures of the film could be bought at the cinema. Audiences would be greeted by admission music while they were shown to their seats. During the intermission, specially composed music would be played, just as it would to accompany them to the exit at the conclusion of their three-hour diversion.

The big films of the period were all launched in this fashion: because of their epic scope and subsequent length, only two screenings could be accommodated every day. To make the film more of an event, tickets could be reserved in advance. Fill in a form in a newspaper, post it with a cheque (or postal order) for the time and performance you wished to see, and wait for the tickets to be returned to you by the Royal Mail.

Magazines played a major role. UK *Photoplay* ran a holiday competition ('the most glamorous holiday of your life in the land of *Cleopatra* flying BOAC jet liner'). The winner was Colin Forster of Margate, who listed the correct reasons for seeing the epic film as Script (1), Top Stars (2), Exciting Fight Sequences (3), Breath-taking Locations (4), Cast Of Thousands (5), Background Music (6), Fabulous Costumes (7), Great Story From History (8).

Pre-opening publicity helped, from whatever source (or sauce) – one magazine ran 'What's Cooking With The Stars?' and revealed Liz Taylor's favourite dish was chicken steamed in wine. It was the early days of merchandising, but big films of the period were frequently tied in with marketing, and *Cleopatra* was no exception. Egyptian chess sets, furniture, hairstyles, bathing suits, jewellery, 'feast like a Queen' food and 'Did Cleopatra use Buto', the fashionable hair-removing cream? Much was made of the fashions featured, and the make-up: Revlon's 'Sphinx Eyes' left few in any doubt whom their new 1963 line was based on.*

In February 1962, presumably in anticipation of the film's release (it was actually a year early), *Life* magazine ran a three-page special on 'The Cleopatra Look':

---

\* In one of the many ironies associated with the film, the model chosen for the Revlon TV campaign was Suzy Parker, at one time shortlisted for the title role in the film.

The Cleopatra look has already shown up in the collections of top fashion designers in Paris, Italy and the US. Guaranteed to stop traffic in chic supper clubs or crowded supermarkets, the new look heralds fashion's return to making women look the way they were made to look – like the queens they are.

A 3s 6d Panther paperback tie-in was a boost, but producer Walter Wanger's score-settling *My Life with Cleopatra* and the Fox publicists' *The Cleopatra Papers* did the film few favours when they were published soon after its release. Both titles revealed the behind-the-scenes extravagance and made for uncomfortable – if gripping – reading. Billy Wilder recounted the tale that, when finished, *Cleopatra* was screened for rival studio head Jack Warner, who commented afterwards, 'If every person who's in the picture comes to see it, they're gonna break even.'

*Cleopatra* needed a critical thumbs-up to entice audiences in to cinemas. The all-important weekly magazine *Time* was encouraging: 'Physically, Cleopatra is as magnificent as money and the tremendous Todd-AO screen can make it. The De Luxe Color is perfection'. But then the sting in the tail:

Sad to say, however, the deep-revolving, witty Mankiewicz fails most where most he hoped to succeed. As drama and as cinema, Cleopatra is raddled with flaws. It lacks style both in image and in action. Never for an instant does it whirl along on wings of epic elan; generally it just bumps from scene to ponderous scene on the square wheels of exposition.

One of the few champions was the esteemed Bosley Crowther of the *New York Times*, who called *Cleopatra* 'a surpassing entertainment, one of the great epic films of our day [...] brilliant, moving, satisfying'. But his was a voice in the wilderness. Rarely has one review attracted such opprobrium, and Crowther was forced to defend his review over the coming weeks. The media reported, 'A small weekly paper of dissent, *The Village Voice* gleefully ran a banner headline on its front page "The Fall Of Bosley Crowther".'

The esteemed critic Andrew Sarris, on that 'weekly paper of dissent', was withering. Sarris found fault in Crowther's sycophancy, picking out:

… pungent moments to relieve the soul-destroying tedium of little people lost on big sets in the most expensive session of hide-and-seek ever to masquerade as a movie […] For the first time in anyone's memory, Mr. Crowther's review was literally undercut on the same page by a news story, which emphasized the mixed reactions to 'Cleo' and neutralized Crowther's enthusiasm for a film suddenly transformed into a critical scandal […] As far as the influential freeloading audience was concerned, Sphinx rhymed with Stinx, and not even the *New York Times* could say differently.

But, as with so many elements associated with the film, by the time the critics were let loose, their knives were sharpened. Philip Oakes, writing in the *Sunday Telegraph,* was more considered, but witheringly caught the general mood:

Seeing *Cleopatra* at long last is rather like watching the birth of an elephant. In each case the interest is clinical rather than aesthetic. In each case the gestation period runs into years. And in each case the end product is big, costly and clumsy. All things considered, I prefer the elephant.

The *Daily Telegraph* review was headlined 'Cleopatra Disappoints … Elizabeth Taylor Is No Siren Of The Nile'. It diplomatically began:

Whatever else may be said about *Cleopatra* it seems certain that it will not go down in history as the greatest film ever made. There were many expressions of disappointment. Perhaps we had expected too much. Perhaps the huge expenditure of money [does] not necessarily produce an artistic triumph.

Another critic, David Susskind, harshly found Taylor 'overweight, overbosomed, overpaid and undertalented. She set the acting profession back a decade.' John Coleman, in the *New Statesman*, was equally withering: 'Miss Taylor is monotony in a slit skirt, a pre-Christian Elizabeth Arden with sequined eyelids and occasions constantly too large for her.'

Crucially, the showbiz bible *Variety* was initially impressed, 'a supercolossal eye-filler … a giant panorama … Elizabeth Taylor grows as the story progresses to become the mature queen who matches the star's own voluptuous assurance.' Even their critic admitted, however, 'Ironically some of the weakest moments in the film are the love scenes between Liz and Dickie.'

That is where critics and public alike were united: the lack of the passion between the two lovers, which had so spellbound the world during production but never transferred to the screen. *Newsweek* called it 'the world's longest coming attraction for something that will never come'. Judith Crist, in the *New York Herald Tribune*, picked up the same point:

> I might note at the outset that an even greater disappointment awaits those whose interest has been titillated almost exclusively by the Taylor–Burton real-life parallel to their Cleopatra–Antony romance. [An] hour and 15 minutes elapse before their first embrace and that, beyond much love talk and soulful ogling, their physical encounters are scarcely five degrees warmer than the Caesar–Cleopatra liaison – and that's a cool one. Perhaps the sexy bits ended up on the cutting room floor.

Reeling from the barrage of negative criticism, to his credit, Joseph L. Mankiewicz broke cover within weeks of the film's opening. Made legendary by Martin Luther King's 'I have a dream' speech, the March on Washington on 28 August 1963 marked the high watermark of the Civil Rights movement. There was a television debate on the rights of black people in America at that time and Hollywood was well represented – Marlon Brando, Charlton Heston, Harry Belafonte – and the only behind-the-camera face taking part was that of the committed liberal, Joseph L. Mankiewicz.

# 21

# 'Infamy, infamy ...'

It would be disingenuous, and inaccurate, to say that *Cleopatra* was the film which singlehandedly destroyed the studio system. In its wake, the Hollywood studios blindly persisted in investing millions of dollars in a single film, gambling everything on the single roll of a dice.

However, *Cleopatra* was Hollywood at its worst – here was arrogance, unparalleled and unchecked. This was the studio, starstruck by Burton and Taylor, determined to proceed without a finished script, willing to pour untold millions into a film, the style of which was already edging up to its sell-by date. Like the rabbit mesmerised by the headlights of the car coming to kill it, Twentieth Century Fox could not – *would* not – believe that the film could fail to recoup its costs. The hurricane of publicity that engulfed *Cleopatra* from its inception would surely be enough to attract an audience that would hurl the film into profit, even leaving aside its spiralling budget and out-of-control expenses.

They got it horribly wrong. Yes, *Cleopatra* did eventually recoup the studio's investment, but over decades, not the necessary weeks in time to save Fox. However, Hollywood being Hollywood, it did not learn from the debacle. From when the filming of *Cleopatra* began to its premiere, more had moved on than mere calendar time. The world had left *Cleopatra* marooned high and dry. Yet still the studios would not countenance budgeting ten films at $4 million or forty at $1 million – they would rather go the Vegas route and roll everything on one $44 million project, and hope and pray that it would come off.

Even as *Cleopatra* lumbered towards completion, Twentieth Century Fox was clearly struggling. The films it released while the behemoth ate up time and dollars did little to suggest it was learning any lessons. *Cleopatra* was intended for a 1962 release, which it missed by a year; the studio's other releases of the period all performed badly, too. All of them:[*]

*The 300 Spartans*: 'Ralph Richardson does his best … but no one is going to list this portrayal as one of the great achievements of his career'.

*Hemingway's Adventures of a Young Man*: '… a disquieting tendency to oscillate between flashes of artistry and truth and interludes of mechanics and melodramatics'.

*The Inspector, The Condemned of Altona, Nine Hours to Rama.*

*State Fair*: 'There's something crass and antiseptic about the atmosphere […] none of four young stars comes off especially well'.

*Satan Never Sleeps.*

*Sodom and Gomorrah*: '… has many of the faults of the Biblical epic'.

*Tender is the Night, It Happened in Athens.*

*Mr Hobbs Takes a Vacation*: '… misfires chiefly in the situation development department'.

Pat Boone ('a surly singing idol') in *The Yellow Canary*: '…limp and fuzzy in character definition'.

*Five Weeks in a Balloon*: 'The inclusion of Fabian shows how desperate the movie is to attract attention' (the fact that 'Chester the "Human" Chimp' got equal billing was surely indicative of just how low expectations were).

Here was a major studio squandering millions of dollars on releases, few of which should ever have got off the drawing board and all of which received poor reviews and under-performed on release.

The studio's biggest star, Marilyn Monroe, was notoriously unreliable, and her final film for Fox (*Something's Got to Give*) was cancelled,

---

[*]   All reviews cited are from contemporary issues of *Variety* magazine.

with the studio sacking her in June 1962. Two months later, Marilyn Monroe was dead. Not much wonder the studio was banking everything on *Cleopatra*.

Twentieth Century Fox could have learned a lesson from one of Darryl Zanuck's innovations while running the studio. This was an International Classics division, picking up low-budget foreign films. An early success was 1963's *Zorba the Greek,* which recouped its $800,000 budget on the New York run alone and Henry Fielding's *Tom Jones*, starring Albert Finney as the title character, who became an unexpected box-office hero.

In the wake of *Cleopatra*, young audiences instead flocked to *A Hard Day's Night*, *The Graduate*, *Easy Rider*, *Midnight Cowboy*, *The Wild Bunch*, *Butch Cassidy and the Sundance Kid*, *Bonnie and Clyde* and *Woodstock*. All were, by Hollywood standards, relatively cheap to produce – their budgets combined were less than that of *Cleopatra*.

Equally significantly, few relied on established box-office stars – The Beatles' film was primarily designed to sell soundtrack LPs; *Easy Rider* relied as much on its soundtrack as its cinematic virtues; *Woodstock* was sold to the hippies who never made the original festival. Paul Newman was balanced by the unknown Robert Redford in *Butch Cassidy* and Warren Beatty by newcomer Faye Dunaway in *Bonnie and Clyde*. *The Graduate*'s Dustin Hoffman was an unknown quantity, as was his *Midnight Cowboy* co-star, Jon Voight.

Long before its release, *Cleopatra* was already notorious. Such was the anticipation in the Taylor–Burton film, that in the climactic party scene of *The Pink Panther*, released soon after *Cleopatra* premiered, an Elizabeth Taylor lookalike admonishes Peter Sellers's bumbling Inspector Clouseau, 'Take your hands off my asp!' In 1963's *Take Her, She's Mine*, Sandra Dee appeared as Cleopatra in a fancy dress scene. The oddball *What a Way to Go* (1964) had Gene Kelly's egotistical actor 'Pinky' overwhelming all competition in an unnamed biblical epic, causing one extra to marvel, 'And to think they wanted to put that Welshman in the part!'

Following their filming *Becket* together, as a favour, Richard Burton obliged Peter O'Toole with a cameo in 1965's *What's New Pussycat*. 'Don't you know me from somewhere?' Burton asks.

'Give me regards to whatshername,' O'Toole chirpily responds.

*Cleopatra* had become synonymous with waste and extravagance. In 1964, the bleak and underrated Kenneth More drama *The Comedy Man* dwelt on the downside of acting. 'We're not making *Cleopatra* here!' smirks the oleaginous agent played by Dennis Price. Kenneth More actually met his wife, Angela Douglas, after she had finished filming *Cleopatra* as part of 'the rep company'. More later wrote, 'This involved about 25 actors and actresses who were each paid a flat £50 a week and expenses, and they had to be ready to play any small part at short notice – if they wanted another gladiator or a maidservant or slave or whatever.' Angela Douglas recalled meeting with casting director Stuart Lyons and being selected as one of twelve actors who were asked to live in Rome for four months and 'play small parts if and when they cropped up in a script that was continually changing'.

That ultra-hep cat Lord Buckley riffed on it with his 'Hipsters, flipsters and finger-poppin' daddies, knock me your lobes, I came here to lay Caesar out, Not to hip you to him'. His Lordship singled out 'this Cleo was an early day Elizabeth Taylor – this chick had more curves than the Santa Fe Railroad making the Grand Canyon'.

In pop music, Sante and the Evergreens were quick off the mark with 1960's 'Time Machine' ('Thought she lived in 44BC/ Cleopatra is the chick for me'). John Leyton chipped in with 1962's 'Down the River Nile'. In 1964, at the beginning of their recording career together, Sonny and Cher went out as 'Caesar and Cleo'.

The film would go on to provide endless fodder for news, film and celebrity magazines. In 1964, Alfred E. Neuman's *Mad* magazine joined the list with two pages of 'Cleavagepatra' – 'spectacular displays of emotion, jealousy, rage, temperament and rudeness', a '20th Century Farce' production, 'the spectacle that took 10 years to make, 28 banks to finance and left us hopelessly in the red for 40 million bucks to start out with!' The two-page mock poster ended with a credit: '20th Century Farce gratefully acknowledges the cooperation of Charlton Heston for giving us his permission to use Israel for some of the film sequences'.

In recent years, there has been a vague vogue for sword-and-sandal epics, led by Ridley Scott's *Gladiator* – though all of his subsequent period epics (*Kingdom of Heaven, Robin Hood, Exodus: Gods and Kings*) failed to match Russell Crowe's Roman. There was Wolfgang Petersen's *Troy*, Paul W.S. Anderson's *Pompeii* and Timur Bekmambetov's remake of *Ben-Hur*. Like many, Oliver Stone's *Alexander* left me wanting – in his search for authenticity, the director had the Greeks and Macedonians speaking with similar regional accents. Thus, Colin Farrell's Alexander and his cohorts came across like the cast of *Father Ted*.

Hot on the heels of the *other* Cleopatra, the *Carry On* team jumped on the bandwagon. *Carry On Cleo* was filmed during the summer of 1964 and in the cinemas not long after the Taylor and Burton film went on general release. Producer Peter Rogers admitted, 'In our film, unlike the other production, all expense will be spared. And the nearest we shall get to Egypt will be the corn.'

The 'other' *Cleopatra* was originally intended to have been the sultry Fenella Fielding, but she had to decline due to contractual commitments. To fill her shoes, the spritely Amanda Barrie stepped in. The actress admitted to *Film Review* that she did have one thing in common with her predecessor: 'We have the same size feet. In fact, I'm wearing Liz Taylor's shoes from *Cleopatra* in our film. They're size 3½ or 4.'

The supporting cast featured a future Sherlock's mum (Wanda Ventham) and the ubiquitous character actor Victor Maddern (his daughter once approached Michael Caine, identifying herself and reminding him that his first film role was opposite Victor Maddern. Caine apparently responded, 'Darling, *everybody's* first film was opposite Victor Maddern.')

The plot thickens: a Talking Pictures TV viewer heard that Victor Maddern bought the *Cleopatra* sets and rented them out to the *Carry On* crowd.

Aficionados of the genre rate *Carry On Cleo* highly. The tenth in the series, its high esteem is primarily because it contains the best-known line in all the thirty-odd productions. Pursued by assassins, Julius Caesar (Kenneth Williams) turns to the camera and screams, 'Infamy! Infamy! They've all got it in for me!' (Denis Norden later admitted that it was a line he and partner Frank Muir donated to the *Carry On* script.)

Otherwise, it is production-line loo humour. Sid James yuk-yuks his way through as romantic lead Marc Antony; Williams confesses to feeling queer; a statuesque handmaiden comes from – where else? – Bristol. Crumpet obviously finds a home. Reference is made to a senator's small majority and Charles Hawtrey is introduced as 'a truly great sage', 'Yes, and I know my onions'.

Long-time *Carry On* scriptwriter Talbot Rothwell is credited with this, although generously acknowledges, 'From an original idea by William Shakespeare'. A later credit does admit that 'certain liberties have been taken with *Cleopatra*'. The film's budget would have delighted Twentieth Century Fox executives at a modest £194,000. Like Alexander weeping that there were no more worlds left to conquer, those same executives must have shed tears.

Legend has it that *Carry On Cleo* was shot on the sets built for the Fox epic at Pinewood, and when I saw it, there was one fleeting scene that was obviously shot on the abandoned sets at Pinewood. But the UK filming had been abandoned in 1961 and the sets could not have stood idle for three years. Perhaps some elements were dismantled and stored. Certainly, some of the costumes were used, and quite possibly some of the interiors, so in later years, 'The Pinewood Cleopatra' did finally find a home in a finished film.

# 22

# 'I Should Have Known Better'

Even though it went on to become the biggest success at the box office during 1963, with more than $57 million worth of tickets sold, the fact that Twentieth Century Fox had hurled an estimated $44 million at the production meant that it would still struggle to make a profit. *Cleopatra* had to do much better than that because of the way film studios calculated final profits (further investment came in publicity, promotion and duplicating copies of the film). Those returns only covered a fraction of the cost of the production. By 1964, the trade papers were reporting 'Cleo Breaking Even', diplomatically noting the production was 'plagued by a plethora of stumbling blocks during its production'.

By the time *Cleopatra* opened in cinemas during the middle of 1963, the world had changed dramatically from when filming had begun all those years ago. The contraceptive pill was introduced in the UK in 1961, and even if only available to married women, it brought with it a sexual lassitude that had been markedly missing from when Burton and Taylor began their affair.

The era of sexual enlightenment had been heralded by the publication in 1960 of *Lady Chatterley's Lover*, but it was the spiralling Profumo affair that hogged the headlines during the early part of 1963. The risqué goings-on and the saucy activities of high people in low places held the British public spellbound. Rarely had sex been so closely linked to scandal. The Profumo affair undeniably hastened the end of fourteen years of Conservative government. Prime Minister Macmillan suddenly seemed fustian and wholly out of step with a nation that was finally, belatedly, coming out of the shadow cast by the Second World War and austerity.

Sex was intended to help sell *Cleopatra*, and it brought controversy in its wake. When it opened in Manila, censors cut six scenes, including Taylor's nude bath. *Photoplay* magazine reported, 'Evidently 20th Century Fox hopes these scenes will help recover the staggering £11,000,000 spent on the picture.' In Franco's Spain, thirty minutes of footage were removed ('No Bosom Angles For Cleo In Spain,' boomed *Variety*). The *Cleopatra* trailer hinted at what audiences might expect, when the queen is 'said to employ her special talents, which are said to be considerable'; 'My breasts are filled with life and love,' breathed Taylor, and the posters emphasised the actress's legendary cleavage. Meanwhile, the trailer and posters hyped, 'The picture the world has been waiting for.' They spoke of 'the spectacle of spectacles'.

However, in the UK, the soundtrack to that whole year was provided by The Beatles, not the film's score. Composer Alex North (1910–91) came to *Cleopatra* trailing clouds of soundtrack glory – his jazz score for *A Streetcar Named Desire* was as revolutionary as Brando's performance. The long-forgotten *Unchained* (1955) gave the world 'Unchained Melody'. Immediately prior to *Cleopatra*, North contributed soundtracks to *The Misfits* and *Spartacus*.* The *Cleopatra* soundtrack briefly reached No. 2 on the US LP charts in June 1963.

At the beginning of 1963, the name of The Beatles was little known outside cellars in Liverpool and Hamburg. At year's end, everyone from milkmen to government ministers knew who they were. One of the UK's most perceptive critics, the late Alexander Walker, in his biography of Elizabeth Taylor (*Elizabeth*, 1990), wrote about one of the Burtons' later departures:

---

\* North was reunited with Stanley Kubrick for the soundtrack to *2001: A Space Odyssey* (1968), but true to form, the mercurial Kubrick decided to ditch North's commission and go with the existing classical pieces.

At Los Angeles airport where they were embarking for a holiday at the Casa Kimberley in Puerto Vallerta, an over-familiar sound made their hearts sink: the sound of squealing, like hundreds of pigs being simultaneously slaughtered in an abattoir. The fans had caught up with them. But they were wrong. The crowd wasn't there for them, but for the incoming Beatles ... For the high-decibel welcome accorded the Beatles was the sound of a generational change – a tumultuous reception by youth and for youth – that boded ill for the fortunes of the ageing Burtons. But off they flew to their own kingdom by the sea, leaving the Beatles to possess the future.

Elizabeth was always conciliatory towards her fans. She had been in the public eye for so long that there was no other space for her to inhabit. Filming *Reflections in a Golden Eye*, her co-star Marlon Brando pitied the 'misguided people' waiting for a glimpse of him. As Sam Kashner and Nancy Schoenberger wrote in *Furious Love* (2010), 'Elizabeth was far less gloomy about the whole thing. She saw her fans as a part of the job; she didn't live for their approval – hardly! – but she didn't pity them either. It could be worse, she told Brando, "We could be The Beatles".'

Even in the cinema, the allure of the Burton–Taylor star machine was not guaranteed. Soon after *Cleopatra* opened, the second of the James Bond films, *From Russia with Love* opened. Along with The Beatles, James Bond came to signify the blossoming birth of Swinging London – indeed, in one of those strange coincidences, the release of The Beatles' debut single 'Love Me Do' on 5 October 1962 was followed within twenty-four hours by the premiere of the first Bond film, *Dr No*. That same week also saw the first issue of the weekly magazine *New Society*, which was launched to reflect the changes the country was undergoing. If you could carbon date the birth of the Swinging Sixties, the first week of October 1962 is perhaps the best of any date to choose.

As *Cleopatra* proceeded around the world during the summer of 1963, the world had moved on since it began filming: not just The Beatles, Profumo and 007, but events on the world stage. In Dallas, as the clocks struck midday on 22 November, the end of an era was signalled when a fusillade took the life of President John F. Kennedy.

Even knowing what we know now of Kennedy's sexual peccadillos, political chicanery and personal unreliability, there is no denying the impact of his assassination. That day in Dallas really did mark the end of an era. It undermined confidence and took away the final certainty; if a gunman (gunmen?) could murder the President of the United States, how could anyone in the Free World guarantee their safety?

The star power of the Burtons remained considerable. Between the premiere of *Cleopatra* and the opening of the cash-in *The V.I.P.s* was probably the apex of their popularity. From their Dorchester eyrie, the couple would descend and be made mortal. Burton enjoyed watching the Welsh rugby team play whenever he got the opportunity; Elizabeth made her regal progress around town. Their fame brought back some of the lustre of the golden age of Hollywood.

☥

As it proceeded in stately cinematic progress across the world, *Cleopatra* came to epitomise the swansong of an era. No more would audiences be beguiled and enticed by the promise of big-screen entertainment with stars who were out of the reach of their audience. Not when The Beatles, Rolling Stones, Searchers and the myriad beat groups who swarmed in their wake could be witnessed performing in the flesh for a few mere shillings on stage at your local Odeon or ABC.

It was to be a further four or five years before Hollywood appreciated that successful films didn't necessarily need big names above the title to pull in the crowds. Younger audiences were attracted by subject matter, rock soundtracks and a new generation of stars. The zeitgeist soon had a hand in box office takings.

By the time the most talked-about film in the history of cinema reached the screen, Elizabeth Taylor (31) and Richard Burton (38) seemed part of an era that was vanishing when seen alongside the emergence of newcomers like Sarah Miles, Samantha Eggar and Julie Christie, or Tom Courtenay, Alan Bates and Albert Finney. Interestingly, *Photoplay*, the UK's leading film magazine, by 1963 was putting pop acts like Billy Fury, The Beatles and Jet Harris and Tony

Meehan on its cover. Because of the length of her incredible screen career and her well-publicised private life, Taylor seemed so much older than she actually was. By the time *Cleopatra* opened, she had been a film star for nearly twenty years.

There was, however, no denying the actress's incandescent 'star power'. Taylor could eclipse the poor films that followed. Had she lived, one senses that Monroe would have struggled with the shifting sands of celebrity. As a woman who projected an aura of sexual confidence, had surfed a lifetime of celebrity, and was financially secure, you sense Elizabeth Taylor could handle anything the future could hurl her way.

The same year that *Cleopatra* finally opened, *Billy Liar* was premiered. John Schlesinger's film remains the most acute cinematic take on the changing Britain. With its appreciation of the power of pop music and popular culture (bingo, radio, TV), *Billy Liar* is bang on. And in its working class hero, unforgettably played by Tom Courtenay, a new breed took centre screen.

If anything, Courtenay was eclipsed by his co-star. *Billy Liar* was the film that saw Julie Christie make a stunning impact following a couple of desultory roles. Christie came to symbolise the sexually liberated, independent woman of the 1960s. Leaving Billy marooned on the station platform, it was Christie's decision to ride the milk train to London in which the direction of cinema during 1963 lay, not in the bloated artifice of *Cleopatra*.

Pinned up alongside the freewheeling Julie Christie, Elizabeth Taylor seemed to represent an altogether different, more distant era. Next to the flawed introversion of Tom Courtenay, Richard Burton seemed to characterise a roistering type of actor – Errol Flynn, Peter Finch – much loved in the 1950s, but by 1963, on his way to becoming as antiquated to contemporary cinema audiences as Ramon Navaro and Clara Bow.

The London train that Julie Christie boarded in *Billy Liar* offered so much liberation, and the floodgates soon opened. The Swinging Sixties may not have swung much for anyone further than 100 yards either side of the Kings Road, or unless your surname was Beatle or Rolling Stone, but it was a time of enormous change. In 1963, the Crystals' 'Then He Kissed Me' hinged on the boy in question nervously meeting Mum and

Dad. Precisely a decade later, the Rolling Stones sang of a 'starf★★★★r' 'giving head to Steve McQueen'. *Plus ça change* ...

☥

*Cleopatra* did not destroy Hollywood, but in its grandiose aspirations, orgiastic absorption of capital and the studio's abasement before the whims of its stars, lay the seeds for the destruction of the film's capital and its single-minded belief in the studio and the star system. The binding contracts were no longer an enticement; as the power of the agents grew, loyalty to an individual studio was a thing of the past.

The film may have given the studios pause, but after *Cleopatra* the blockbusters still came. Studio profligacy did not end with that one film. The moguls persisted in throwing enough money into a movie to ensure its success.

After a near forty-year run, where sound film had enjoyed an unequalled scale of success, where it had become the premiere entertainment medium, its time had now come. There would still be audiences for films, but with the explosion in pop music, embodied by The Beatles and the developing folk poetry of Bob Dylan, and with the increasing quality and quantity of television, by the time it came to open, the time of *Cleopatra* and its stars had perhaps already gone.

In equal measure, it was Elizabeth Taylor's acceptance of her seven-figure salary that held Hollywood to ransom. By agreeing to pay her $1 million, Twentieth Century Fox – and then all the studios – laid themselves open effectively to blackmail.

In fairness to Taylor, she only pitched so high because she was convinced the studio would never pay such an exorbitant fee. Who was more foolish, the studio to offer or Taylor to accept? In a sense, it didn't matter if *Cleopatra* was a hit or not. In agreeing to her demands, Hollywood effectively capitulated. It laid them wide open for further, larger, more fatuous demands and pay cheques. Ellis Amburn, one of Taylor's more perceptive biographers, concluded his chapter on *Cleopatra*, 'It was Elizabeth Taylor who'd effectively demolished the old studio system and unmanned its moguls' (*Elizabeth Taylor*, 2000).

It would be misleading to say that *Cleopatra* emphatically killed off the star-led, big-budget studio spectacle of the old Hollywood. While *Cleopatra* was lumbering towards completion, George Stevens was cuing up *The Greatest Story Ever Told*. This proved to be as disastrous to United Artists as *Cleopatra* was to its rival across the street at Twentieth Century Fox.

It certainly boasted an all-star cast – Charlton Heston, John Wayne, Sidney Poitier. Stevens even tried coaxing his protégé from *A Place in the Sun*, Elizabeth Taylor, into the cast as Mary Magdalene. Finally coming in at $21.5 million, even a decade later, Stevens's cumbersome biblical epic had only recouped $7 million of its budget.

In an irony so typical of the time, following Zanuck's decision to sell off the studio backlot, Stevens's epic was the only film production occupying space at the Twentieth Century Fox studio. Some sets for *Cleopatra* were prepared on the Fox backlot, following the cancellation of the London shoot, but were discarded when the Stevens production ate up all available space and the *Cleopatra* production switched to Italy.

As Michael Troyan noted in his history of Twentieth Century Fox (2017), the big-budget epics had not salvaged the studio:

> CinemaScope turned out to be only temporary life support for the studio system. In fact, it worsened the problem because these widescreen pictures required bigger budgets and costly location work that led to fewer pictures being made and less need of the Fox lots, whose real estate value was going up.

Troyan's exhaustive book reveals the scale of those Fox backlots – among others, the Algerian Street, the Chicago Street, Midwestern Street, Old French Street and Square, Old New York Street and Tombstone Street. The Algerian Street was built for a 1929 John Ford film, *The Black Watch*, and later saw service in *David and Bathsheba*, *The Robe*, *The Egyptian*, *The Left Hand of God* (China), *The Barbarian and the Geisha* (Japan) and *The Wizard of Baghdad*. In the end, the real estate realised $56 million for the beleaguered studio.

You would have thought – hoped! – that the studio would have learned from its profligate mistakes. Yet it was Twentieth Century Fox that poured $28 million into the unloved *Dr Dolittle*; it was Twentieth Century Fox that pumped $14 million into *Star!*, a disastrous biopic of Gertrude Lawrence starring Julie Andrews. And it was, after all, Twentieth Century Fox that poured $24 million into the screen version of *Hello Dolly*, a bloated, lifeless whale beached in the era of *Easy Rider* and *The Graduate*.

'Historically, the only event more disruptive to the industry's eco-system than an unexpected flop is an unexpected smash,' wrote film historian Mark Harris. 'Caught off guard by the sudden arrival of more revenue than they thought their movies could ever bring in, the major studios resorted to three old habits: imitation, frenzied speculation and panic.'

☥

*Cleopatra* promised, on its initial release, exotic, sensual allure and escapism in a manner not seen since the vintage days of the classic 'old Hollywood'. What it delivered was a stillborn anachronism, a film desperately clinging to a past which, by the time the first frames flickered through the projector before a paying audience, was already dwindling.

When *Cleopatra* was on release, the circus was already on its way out of town. Its vanity, avarice and bloated sense of its own grandeur showed that Hollywood was wildly out of step with its viewers. The films struggled to reach an audience. From being a British novelty during 1963, by February 1964 when they landed in America for the first time, The Beatles had blown the dust off the tomb into which the Burton and Taylor *Cleopatra* was sealed.

Ironically, one of the film's few supporters from that new breed was Andy Warhol. He adored the 'look' of *Cleopatra* – he called it 'the most influential film of the 1960s'. In 1962, Warhol painted Taylor in costume as 'Silver Liz', which sold at auction for $665,700 in 2001.

And now, the film is only of interest to film historians and scholars, who tantalisingly speculate on what might have been. Like the archeologists of the 1923 expedition that uncovered the tomb of Tutankhamen, they sift through the sands for missing fragments of film, desperate to unearth something that might lend confirmation to Mankiewicz's vision of the film which not only destroyed him but took the old Hollywood with him.

Then there is, as with any catastrophe, the speculation: what if the studio had stuck with its original, modest Joan Collins vehicle? What if, once the costs began spiralling, they had closed it down when filming in England was abandoned? What if the studio had the courage to adhere to Mankiewicz's two-part, six-hour vision?

☥

Soon after the film's opening, Taylor seethed at Fox's mutilation of Mankiewicz's original vision. 'They cut out the heart, the essence, the motivations, the very core and tacked on all those battle scenes.' Many, many years later, the Burtons screened their films for their inquisitive children. Watching *Cleopatra* for the first time since 1963, Elizabeth reflected, 'You know, it's really not that bad after all.'

When *Cleopatra* began filming, Rome epitomised the *dolce vita*, the apogee of feminine beauty was Elizabeth Taylor, and roistering Richard Burton represented stalwart masculine values. When, after all the draining years and escalating costs, *Cleopatra* finally did open, Britain had begun swinging, with vivacious Jean Shrimpton as its symbol and four Liverpool lads pinned on every teenage girl's wall.

*Cleopatra* is an ostentatious symbol of a disappearing world. In its sprawling vacuity the studios sowed the seeds of their own destruction. They had only themselves to blame. It is bloated and artificial, needlessly sprawling and a magnificent, vain-glorious symbol of greed, vanity and hubris. Unwatched and largely unlamented, *Cleopatra* stands titanic, like one of the ancient wonders so many strived for it to be, but ultimately, a faded symbol of an old world.

The film has not worn well; age has withered it and few speak fondly of it. Clive James got a little bit moist-eyed:

*Cleopatra* was the real last blast of the trumpet for the blockbusters. There was never such extravagance again, mainly because no star can any longer charge the earth as Elizabeth Taylor did. Sometimes one misses the madness.

David Kamp's excellent 2011 *Vanity Fair* piece was comprehensive, but as with so much to do with the production of that feted film, it was the chaos surrounding its creation that still appeals – and appalls.

Never one to see a bandwagon without jumping on it, Kim Kardashian wore one of Elizabeth Taylor's gowns from the film for a 2011 *Harper's Bazaar* cover shoot. Taylor's own immortality was ensured in the saleroom, and soon after her death Christie's held an auction of her jewellery, fine art and dresses which raised an astonishing $156.8 million for her AIDS charities.

*Cleopatra* was a film, in Joseph L. Mankiewicz's famous phrase, 'conceived in a state of emergency, shot in confusion and wound up in a blind panic'. It is legendary for the three Is – inflation, infidelity and on into infamy.

# Afterword: *The V.I.P.s*

As a footnote, the film the Burtons rushed straight into immediately following the epic that had brought them together is of some interest. Made to cash in on the furore surrounding *Cleopatra*, *The V.I.P.s* was shooting at MGM's Borehamwood Studios while *Cleopatra* was being edited in America. The film revealed just how astute Elizabeth had become. The bulk of her career found her contracted to MGM. Finally freed from them, she formed Taylor Productions, thus capitalising on her fame and leasing herself at favorable terms to her old studio.

*The V.I.P.s* is a guilty pleasure; the story is functional and workmanlike, a welcome trot through familiar *Grand Hotel* territory – viz, motley crew hurled together for dramatic impact, in this case, a selection of Very Important Persons who are fogbound at Heathrow. In truth, it is a glossier, colourful update on 1954's *Out of the Clouds*.

Terence Rattigan's smooth, Rolls-Royce script was fashioned out of a liaison between one of *Cleopatra*'s original stars, Peter Finch, and Vivien Leigh. The fogbound lovers gave Rattigan the idea for what became *The V.I.P.s*, which MGM commissioned for a comfy $100,000.

There is a picture of Rattigan emerging from the premiere of *Look Back in Anger* in 1956, smart and suave in evening dress but looking absolutely shell-shocked. With the praise poured on the ground-breaking John Osborne play, and the savage criticism heaped on

Rattigan, it was as if Rattigan's salad days were numbered. Ironically, following Rattigan's death in 1977, his became the theatrical star in the ascendant, while Osborne's reputation has withered. Recent years have seen triumphant London revivals of Rattigan's plays, including *Flare Path*, *Love in Idleness*, *The Winslow Boy* and *The Deep Blue Sea*.

Rattigan's biographer Geoffrey Wansell astutely noted:

> *The V.I.P.s* was due to be released in the autumn to coincide with *Cleopatra*, MGM having calculated that while there was an audience who – after all the publicity – actually wanted to see Elizabeth Taylor and Richard Burton in a film together, some might find the four hours of *Cleopatra* too long.

The film is dated in a thoroughly engaging kind of way. This is how we mere mortals were allowed a glimpse into the VIP lounge of the jet set; the condition we all aspired to. Burton blithely inquires of Louis Jourdan if he'll join them on the yacht for Ischia and Capri. This was what went on behind the closed doors of The V.I.P.s while civilians like us lined up in snaking queues below. A world of Givenchy and heaving bosoms; cocktails and covert assignations. A glimpse of a time long ago when you could drive straight up to Heathrow's departure terminal without parking miles away.

Michael Hordern flusters on form as the Airport Director, facing twenty-seven flights and 3,000 passengers delayed in one morning – presumably pre-Covid; that would be an hour's worth of trade today.

The all-star cast shine: Rod Taylor is the blunt Aussie businessman; Orson Welles is the tyrannical movie mogul; Margaret Rutherford, the lovable British eccentric; Maggie Smith, the loyal secretary, a long way from *Downton Abbey*. Louis Jourdan is suitably dashing and amoral in his gigolo character. Then there's the bloke who played the verger in *Dad's Army*. The doctor is the chap who was a regular on *Last of the Summer Wine*. There's the Scottish chef out of *Crossroads*. Mention should also be made of David Frost's only dramatic appearance, as a snide reporter with a hairstyle that seems to have its own ambitions for a separate film career.

But all eyes are on the Burtons. 'I can't open [a magazine] without finding you,' Burton's Paul Andros remarks to his screen wife in one of the lines that could not help but find resonance with the film's audience.

The film was modestly budgeted at barely over $3 million – less than a tenth of the cost of *Cleopatra*. In fact, they work much better together in well-cut civilian clothes. Burton is dyspeptic but suggests power and wealth. He reins in his performance as Andros (the name intended to suggest millionaire tycoons like Niarchos or Onassis). Taylor is gloriously, extravagantly beautiful, captured at the zenith of her on-screen allure. Ironically, in a profile of *The V.I.P.s*, Sam Kashner wrote, 'Oddly, their [Rod Taylor, Maggie Smith] love affair is more touching than the Sturm & Drang of the Taylor-Burton relationship.'

While they were filming *The V.I.P.s* during 1963, '*le scandale*' was breaking all around them, and Rattigan's script cleverly parallels the real and fictional. For much of the year, Burton and Taylor were photographed endlessly arriving and departing from VIP lounges. The film suggests what went on behind those closed doors. Their whole affair recalled Auden's lines, 'Private faces in public places/ Are wiser and nicer/ Than public faces in private places'.

Because its ambitions were dramatically less, *The V.I.P.s* succeeds on its own modest level – like Anthony Asquith's subsequent *The Yellow Rolls-Royce* (another Rattigan script), *The V.I.P.s* is a smoothly efficient portmanteau film. It is a wilful throwback to former MGM glories. There remains something comforting in seeing the stars of the time (Burton and Taylor) battle with the up-and-coming (Rod Taylor and Maggie Smith) and supported by the ever-dependable (Orson Welles, Margaret Rutherford and Michael Hordern).

And for all the diva glamour of Taylor, it was Margaret Rutherford's finely balanced 'Duchess of Brighton' that picked up the plaudits. On her first flight to Miami ('My army') and summoning a haughty stewardess as 'conductress' or fussing that she hadn't brought her seat belt with her, Rutherford's is a nicely condensed cameo in a film groaning with them.

As the film neared release, Rutherford admitted, 'I always dreamed of playing Cleopatra, but now I fear Miss Taylor has beaten me to it.' Against a formidable trio – Diane Cilento, Dame Edith Evans and Joyce Redman in *Tom Jones* – as well as Lilia Skala in *Lilies of the Field*, in a field remarkable for the absence of American names, the 71-year-old Rutherford was the surprise winner for that year's Oscar for Best Supporting Actress.

Rod Taylor recalled alcohol-fuelled days on set, but time was always found for afternoon tea with Margaret Rutherford playing mother. On-set visitors apparently included the Kray twins, who Burton was keen to supply security for him and his paramour while in London.

That *The V.I.P.s* cashed in on the Burton–Taylor scandal is no surprise. Its London opening (4 September 1963) was barely a month after the other Burton–Taylor film.

In its first week, *The V.I.P.s* broke box-office records in London and New York. The reviews were generally favourable. The *Hollywood Reporter*:

> The love stories seem unreal anyway. Placed next to Miss Rutherford's unassailable reality, they almost fade away altogether. Tickets for *The V.I.P.s* will be bought because of Miss Taylor and Burton. But because of Miss Rutherford's salvage job on the otherwise tepid creation, spectators will leave the theatre as her fans, eager for another Rutherford picture. MGM would do well to capitalize on this as fast and as frequently as possible. Miss Taylor needs something stronger than this to display her talents, and so does Burton.

*Variety*:

> This has suspense, conflict, romance, comedy and drama. Its main fault is that some of the characters and the by-plots are not developed enough.

In a sense, the reviews hardly mattered (except to Margaret Rutherford's agent) because at the time, Elizabeth Taylor and Richard Burton were undeniably the most famous couple in the world. They coasted on their notoriety; one estimate of the seven films they appeared in together between 1963 and 1967 was a worldwide gross of $200 million. Most were lamentable, with the audiences drawn by their infamy rather than the films themselves. They were 'the Burtons', a brand as identifiable as Dior or Chanel. They occupied a realm that was far beyond mere fame.

Try as Burton might to adhere to his roots, the last time the entire Jenkins clan was together was in London in 1967. Burton was distanced from reality and cocooned in that septic tank of celebrity. Old friends like Robert Hardy found it impossible to reach him. Elizabeth had been famous before she was a teenager; she was a legend in her twenties and her legend grew throughout her life. The couple's entourage grew demonstrably and effectively became their bodyguards.

'This is how they lived, on the world stage,' wrote Sam Kashner and Nancy Schoenberger. 'The private marriage of Richard and Elizabeth was increasingly held hostage to the public marriage of "Liz and Dick". Theirs was the first reality show, a marriage with an audience.'

The voice of the new generation that came in on the coattails of *Cleopatra* recognised the fact. On his breakthrough second album, *Freewheelin'*, released early in 1963, Bob Dylan fantasised about 'makin' love to Elizabeth Taylor; catch hell from Richard Burton!' The Dylan fanzine *Isis* revealed that the stage facade for his 1969 appearance at the Isle of Wight festival was from the *Cleopatra* set, which one of the promoters had somehow picked up at Pinewood.

Taylor rarely spoke of the film on its completion. By 1963, her world, and that of her fifth husband, was reeling and rocking. In 1998, however, she broke cover and spoke to David Kamp in a revealing *Vanity Fair* profile: 'It was probably the most chaotic period of my life. What with "*le scandale*", the Vatican banning, people making threats on my life, falling madly in love... It was years of my life.'

It would be unfair and misleading to lay the blame for the decline of the entire Hollywood studio system solely at the door of *Cleopatra*. But undeniably at the time, in tandem with *Mutiny on the Bounty*, the writing was on the wall. With one film spinning out of control in far-away

Rome, Hollywood lost its confidence. *Cleopatra* delivered a body-blow from which the old studio system never fully recovered. In its wake, in cinema, nothing was ever quite the same again.

By the early years of the twenty-first century, the game had changed demonstrably. It used to be 'Twentieth Century Fox [or United Artists or MGM] presents ...'. But with the studio system in tatters and the escalating cost of production, it was frequently a joint presentation – 2013's *World War Z* had no fewer than six production companies. By the beginning of 2020, Twentieth Century Fox itself was rebooted as '20th Century Studios'.

Even the way films were seen had altered irrevocably. Yes, some of the big showcase cinemas (in London, the Odeon and the Empire in Leicester Square) did survive. However, with streaming to phones, tablets and home televisions, the days of the 'event film' were gone.

The global pandemic of 2020 delivered the final knockout; with audiences denied access to cinemas, even blockbusters were heading straight to streaming. It is dispiriting to think that the bulk of the films prepared in the twenty-first century are designed to be seen on computer screens, tablets and other small handheld gadgets. Inevitably, any spectacle is diminished.

Of course, when reflecting on the 1963 film, hindsight is a wonderful thing. With the finished film of *Cleopatra* finally premiering and eventually easing into profit, and with Burton and Taylor hurtling into a stratosphere reserved for the beyond famous, no one could have known what lay ahead. Now the Internet supplies a steady stream of on-set gossip immediately online, with studio insiders texting and twittering on a twenty-four-hour cycle, and camera phones virtually rendering the paparazzi redundant, none of which the once all-powerful studios have control over. Salacious gossip concerning the stars is still hot copy, but equally so are the budgets which go into the CGI spectacles that pass for epics.

Yes, there are still stars, but looking at the 2020 list is a dispiriting experience: four out of the top five most successful actors (Samuel L. Jackson, Robert Downey Jr, Chris Pratt and Tom Holland) owed their box office durability to the *Avengers* and *Spider-Man* franchises.

In the late 1960s, low-budget independent films that were lacking star names, nipped around the lumbering star-bound ocean liners of the 'old' Hollywood like nifty speedboats. Later on, *Titanic* went on to become the world's most successful film, going for the big splash rather than the pulling power of the above-the-title stars. James Cameron's aquatic disaster looked like going the same way as *Cleopatra*. The initial budget was $120million, which soon shot to $200 million, and it was only Fox's partnership with rival Paramount that saw *Titanic* completed and soar to box-office glory.

Cameron's *Avatar* managed to overtake it without any visible stars. And then, thanks to a 2021 re-release in China, the world's biggest cinema market during the Covid era, *Avatar* regained its pole position. James Cameron's fantasy became, once again, the most financially successful film released in the entire 100-odd-year history of cinema.

Then the comic book franchises came, relying on special effects and cartoon characters rather than established stars. *Avengers Endgame* trounced them all on its 2019 release. It did have star power, yet it was the cumulative magnetising of the Marvel superheroes that saw it trounce the opposition. It is the comic book characters from the DC galaxy, or Marvel Comic Universe which have dominated cinema screens. As the Marvel Universe grew ever larger (thirty-two films and twenty-one TV series, as of May 2023), the universe began to show signs of sagging. You sensed the weariness in June 2021 as Josh Stephenson patiently explained to *Metro* readers that 'the Loki who stars in *Loki* is not the Loki we saw murdered at the beginning of *Avengers: Endgame*. Instead, Loki's Loki is the Loki from 2011's *Avengers Assemble*'. Meanwhile, DC's costly decision to write off the $100 million *Batgirl* must have set alarm bells ringing.

What a century of cinema it has been, developing from a novelty circus sideshow to become the twentieth century's best-loved and most affecting art form. As the technology soared ahead, the stars lubricated the industry and benefitted from it. Or in some cases – Marie Provost, John Gilbert, Marilyn Monroe – fell victim to it.

I have lived long enough to remember marvelling at films like *Cleopatra* in cinemas, now long demolished. I have stood beneath the

Hollywood sign and reflected that, alongside rock and roll, the movies from there have played such a formative role in my life.

Even now, I appreciate that one 1963 film was not responsible for effectively sealing the fate of those huge studios, but there is no denying that Hollywood has lost its stranglehold. The stars have shrunk. The names that made the headlines are gone on the celebrity wind – earlier Burton–Taylor biographers, Sam Kashner and Nancy Schoenberger, mentioned their project to a college graduate, 'I never knew Elizabeth Taylor was married to Tim Burton!'

With cinema itself being side-lined in the twenty-first century, inevitably the new stars could never match the single-minded intensity that was lavished on the Burtons. And for all their triumphs, I do find their names inextricably linked to that one turbulent production and its agonising progress from rainy Buckinghamshire to the Roman *dolce vita*. That sweep, that hubris, remains remarkable, emblematic of a cinematic world and gone with the wind.

However, in reflecting on just what *Cleopatra* cost Hollywood, above and beyond its $44 million budget, one cannot help but recall Winston Churchill, reflecting on the 1942 victory at El Alamein, 'It is not the beginning of the end, but it is, perhaps, the end of the beginning.'

# Bibliography

## Biographies and Autobiographies

Amburn, Ellis, *Elizabeth Taylor* (Robson, 2000).

Blake, Mark*, Bring It On Home, Peter Grant, Led Zeppelin & Beyond, The Story Of Rock's Greatest Manager* (Constable, 2018).

Bosworth, Patricia, *Montgomery Clift* (Harcourt, 1978).

Bragg, Melvyn, *Rich: The Life of Richard Burton* (Hodder & Stoughton, 1988).

Cottrell, John, & Fergus Cashin, *Richard Burton* (Coronet, 1971).

Crawford, Michael, *Parcel Arrived Safely Tied with String* (Arrow, 2000).

Crowe, Cameron, *Conversations with Wilder* (Faber, 1999).

Curti, Carlos, *Skouras* (Holloway House, 1967).

Davies, Russell (Editor), *The Kenneth Williams Diaries* (Harper Collins, 1994).

Edwards, Anne, *Vivien Leigh* (Coronet, 1978).

Faulkner, Trader, *Peter Finch: A Biography* (Angus & Robertson, 1979).

Ferris, Paul, *Richard Burton* (NEL, 1981).

Fisher, Eddie, *Been There, Done That* (Arrow, 2000).

French, John, *Robert Shaw: The Price Of Success* (Nick Hern, 1993).

Harrison, Rex, *A Damned Serious Business* (Bantam Press, 1990).

Heymann, C. David, *Liz* (Heinemann, 1995).

Jenkins, Graham, *Richard Burton: My Brother* (Michael Joseph, 1988).

Junor, Penny, *Burton: The Man Behind the Myth* (Sidgwick & Jackson, 1985).

Kashner, Sam, & Nancy Schoenberger, *Furious Love* (Harper Collins 2010).

Kelley, Kitty, *Elizabeth Taylor: The Last Star* (Michael Joseph, 1981).

Knight, Vivienne, *Trevor Howard: A Gentleman and A Player* (Muller, Blond & White, 1986).

Madsen, Axel, *William Wyler: The Authorized Biography* (W.H. Allen, 1974).

Manso, Peter, *Brando* (Weidenfeld & Nicholson, 1994).

More, Kenneth, *More or Less* (Hodder & Stoughton, 1978).

Morley, Sheridan, *John Gielgud* (Sceptre, 2001).

Mosley, Leonard, *Zanuck* (Granada, 1984).

Spoto, Donald, *Marilyn Monroe: The Biography* (Arrow, 1994).

Taylor, Elizabeth, *An Informal Memoir* (Harper & Row, 1965).

Walker, Alexander, *Elizabeth* (Weidenfeld & Nicholson, 1990).

Walker, Alexander, *Fatal Charm: The Life of Rex Harrison* (Orion, 1992).

Wansell, Geoffrey, *Terence Rattigan: A Biography* (Macmillan, 1997)

Wapshot, Nicholas, *Rex Harrison: A Biography* (Chatto & Windus, 1991).

## Film History

Bodsky, Jack, & Nathan Weiss, *The Cleopatra Papers* (Simon & Schuster, 1963).

Drazin, Charles, *The Finest Hours: British Cinema of the 1940s* (Andre Deutsch, 1998).

Fraser, George MacDonald, *The Hollywood History of the World* (Michael Joseph, 1988).

Harris, Mark, *Scenes from a Revolution: The Birth of the New Hollywood* (Canongate, 2009).

Hay, Peter, *MGM: When the Lion Roars* (Turner Publishing, 1991).

Kashner, Sam, & Jennifer Macnair, *The Bad and the Beautiful* (Little Brown, 2002).

Katz, Ephraim, *The Film Encyclopaedia* (2nd edition, Harper Collins, 1994).

Levy, Shawn, *Dolce Vita Confidential* (Weidenfeld & Nicholson, 2018).

McFarlane, Brian, *The Autobiography Of British Cinema* (Methuen, 1997).

Morley, Sheridan, *Tales from the Hollywood Raj* (Coronet, 1985).

Munn, Mike, *The Stories Behind the Scenes of the Great Film Epics* (Argus, 1982).

O'Brien, Margaret, & Allen Eyles (eds), *Enter the Dream House: Memories of Cinemas in South London from the Twenties to the Sixties* (BFI, 1993).

Rees, Nigel, *Cassell's Movie Quotations* (Cassell, 2000).

Salamon, Julie, *The Devil's Candy: The Bonfire of the Vanities Goes to Hollywood* (Cape, 1992).

Troyan, Michael, *Twentieth Century Fox: A Century of Entertainment* (Lyons Press, 2017).

Walker, John (ed.), *Halliwell's Who's Who in the Movies* (Harper Collins, 1999).

Wanger, Walter, & Joe Hyams, *My Life with Cleopatra* (Bantam, 1963).

Wayne, Jane Ellen, *The Golden Girls of MGM* (Robson, 2002).

Whiley, Mason, & Damien Bona, *Inside Oscar* (Columbus Books, 1986).

Young, Caroline, *Roman Holiday: The Secret Life of Hollywood in Rome* (The History Press, 2020).

Zierold, Norman, *The Moguls* (Avon, 1969).

# Acknowledgements

Along the way and over the years, many people have helped bring this book to where we are now: James Alexander, Colin Davies (the gate-keeper), Sheldon Hall, Brian Hannan, David Kamp, Mark Lewisohn, Lee and Dave at *Cinema Retro* magazine, and Barbara Hall, research archivist at the Margaret Herrick Library, in the Academy of Motion Picture Arts and Sciences.

I would particularly like to thank Andrew Batt. On reading through a first draft, his eagle eye lighted on many errors which, had they appeared in print, would have caused me considerable professional embarrassment. Andrew supplied the images that so enhance the text from his own collection. He also alerted me to Elizabeth's hard-to-find 1965 autobiography, *An Informal Memoir*.

Old friends David Taylor, film enthusiast par excellence, Mark Seaman, and Lawrence Morphet were ceaseless in their enthusiasm and encouragement over many, many years. Alannah Hopkin put me in touch with Duncan Sprott, who kindly corrected some of my historical howlers.

Gill Paul was very encouraging, and her engaging 2013 novel, *The Affair*, centres around the filming of *Cleopatra* in Rome and captures some of the madness of the production. And to Lottie, with thanks for buying me time to write.

As ever, my devoted wife Sue Parr provided support when it was most needed, not least when sitting through repeated screenings of *Cleopatra*.

I am only sorry that my parents Eric and Paddy did not live to see this book. It would have gone some way to repay those visits with me to long-gone Granadas in Sydenham, Crystal Palace and Brixton; the Astoria, Charing Cross Road; the Metropole, Victoria; the Dominion, Tottenham Court Road; the ABCs in Brixton and Forest Hill; and Odeons in East Dulwich, Peckham and Camberwell.

The website moon-city-garbage.agency has a fascinating selection of photos of the *Cleopatra* sets under construction at Pinewood. They give a clear indication of the scale – and the waste.

For details of my career to date and forthcoming books and events, please go to www.patrickhumphries.co.uk.

In conclusion, it is worth quoting Hollywood star Lina Lamont's touching eulogy from *Singin' in the Rain*, 'If we bring a little joy into your humdrum lives, it makes us feel as though our hard work ain't been in vain for nothin'.'

In the end, at the end, all and any errors are my own.

Patrick Humphries,
South-East London,
January 2023

# Index

Note: *italicised* page numbers indicate illustrations, and the suffix 'n' indicates a note.

*55 Days at Peking* 185, 187n, 199

Amburn, Ellis 217
Andrews, Julie 18, 89, 149, 162–4, 176–7, 219
Annis, Francesca *114*, 192–3
Arbuckle, Fatty 26, 159
*Around the World in 80 Days* 44–6, 180–1
*Avatar* 20, 182, 228
*Avengers* franchise 228–9

Bacall, Lauren 83–4
Baker, Stanley 70, 120
Bara, Theda 26, 56, *113*
*Barabbas* 67, 185, 194–5
*The Barefoot Contessa* 133, 152
Barrie, Amanda 54, 210
*Batgirl* (never released) 14, 229
Baxter, Keith 70–1
The Beatles 55, 75, 122, 124, 148, 178, 190, 208, 213–17, 219
Beaton, Cecil 163, 177
*Becket* 119, 121, 197, 208
*Ben-Hur* 12, 16, 20–1, 67, 134–5, 148, 153, 180–2, 185, 194–6, 210
Bergman, Ingrid 103

Berkeley, Ron 92–3
*The Big Country* 148, 180
*Billy Liar* 56, 75, 216
*The Birth of a Nation* 25–6
*Bitter Victory* 89
Blackman, Honor 83–4
Bogarde, Dirk 76, 199
Bogart, Humphrey 39, 45, 83, 84
*The Bonfire of the Vanities* 17–19
*Bonnie and Clyde* 178, 208
*Boom* 50
Bosworth, Patricia 41–2
Boyd, Stephen 13, 67–8, 71, 76
Brando, Marlon 50, 70, 75–6, 132–4, 154–6, 185, 191, 205, 214
*Brief Encounter* 125
Bronston, Samuel 187n, 196, 199
Brown, David 21, 73
Brynner, Yul 70, 199
Burton (*née* Williams), Sibyl 82, 84, 89–91, 94–7, 99–101, 118–20, 173
Burton, Philip 80–1, 121–2
Burton, Richard 10, 49, 50, 75–91, *109*, 125, 197, 215, 225–6
  alcohol issues 78, 84, 87, 89–90, 92, 96, 119, 123, 125–6

*Cleopatra* 13–16, 19, 77, 79, 90–102, 122–3, 125–6, 171–2, 175, 188–9, 192, 195, 205
film actor 12, 19, 76–9, 83–6, 89, 97, 119–21, 124–6, 146, 199–200, 208, 216, 222–5
marriage to Sybil Williams 82–3, 89–91, 94–7, 99–101, 118–20
marriages to Elizabeth Taylor 92–102, 117–26, 213–14, 222–6
Oxford University 78, 81–2, 121
RAF 81–2
stage actor 12, 76–9, 82–3, 87–91, 96–7, *114*, 120–2, 126
*Butterfield 8* 66, 70, 188
Byrne, Gabriel 78

*Caesar & Cleopatra* 57, *112*, 161
Caine, Michael 210
Calvert, Phylis 83
*Camelot* (play) 89–91
*Candy* 124
Capote, Truman 66
*Carry On Cleo* 210–11
*Casablanca* 39, 64, 103
*Cat on a Hot Tin Roof* (film) 47, 66, 188
*Cats* (film) 18–19, 178
Cazalet, Victor 33–4
Chaplin, Charlie 26–7
Chayevsky, Paddy 67
Christie, Julie 215–16
Churchill, Winston 33–5, 105, 229
Cinecitta 129–31, 141, 152, 169
CinemaScope 84–5, 127–8, 143–4, 170, 218
Clement, Dick 124
*Cleopatra* (1917 film) 11, 59, *113*
*Cleopatra* (1934 film) 57, 80, *112*
*Cleopatra* (1963 film) 11–22, 52–74, 92–102, 129–32, 134–6, 147–8, 150, 173–6
casting 56, 68–71, 74–6, 90, 130, 145, 156–8, 166–7, 193–4
Cleopatra's entry into Rome *116*, 117–18, 123, 130, 168–70, 189, 191, 196

costs 14, 18–20, 71–3, 99, 129–31, 147–8, 150–1, 170, 173–4, 191, 212
extras 62–3, 72n, *116*, 118, 128, 169–70, 196
premieres and screenings 17–18, *109*, 135, 176, 189–90, 192, 197–200, 213
reviews and reception 118, 176, 200–5
takings 20–1, 201, 212
Clift, Montgomery 40–2, 49, *110*
Cohn, Art 46
Cohn, Harry 144–5
Colbert, Claudette 54, 57, *112*
Cole, George 16, 193
Collins, Joan 11–12, 69, 145
Colman, Ronald 28, 45, 158
Connery, Sean 70, 199
Courtenay, Tom 215–16
Coward, Noel 45, 70, 157, 161, 163, 199
Cronyn, Hume 16, 169–70
Crowther, Bosley 203–4
Currie, Finlay 128–9, 193

*David and Bathsheba* 127, 144, 218
Davis, Bette 29, 35, 180, 191
de Havilland, Olivia 84
Dean, James 27, 39, 43, 49, *111*, 184
*Demetrius and the Gladiators* 127, 195
DeMille, Cecil B. 24, 57, 80, 127, 181
Dietrich, Marlene 29, 45, 163
*Doctor Faustus* (film) 77
*Dr Dolittle* 178, 219
Dylan, Bob 55, 163, 217, 226

*Easy Rider* 179, 208, 219
Edward VIII 103–6
*The Egyptian* 133, 218
Eisenhower, Dwight D. 55, 183–4
Eisenstein, Sergei 28
*El Cid* 20, 185, 187n
Eliot, T.S. 90, 162
Elizabeth II 106, 130

Fairbanks, Douglas 26, 153
*Fall of the Roman Empire* 187, 194

*Father of the Bride* 39
Fellini, Federico 103, 139–40
Finch, Peter 13, 64, 66–7, 71, 76, 216, 222
Finney, Albert 176, 208, 215
Fisher, Eddie 12, 15, 47–8, 69–70, 94–5, 97, 99–100, 120
Fleischer, Richard 146, 194–5
*The Flintstones* 51
Flynn, Errol 29, 158, 216
Fonda, Henry 147, 197, 198
Ford, John 29, 58, 142, 218
Fox, William 142
*From Russia with Love* 199, 214
Frost, David 223

Gable, Clark 29, 39, 138, 154, 184
*Gangs of New York* 141
Garbo, Greta 29, 34, 46, 57, 84
Gardener, Helen 56
Gardner, Ava 133, 139
Garson, Greer 66, 132
Genn, Leo 70, 128–9
*The Ghost and Mrs Muir* 159, 166
*Giant* 41, 43, *111*, 188, 191
Gibbon, Edward 129
Gielgud, John 45, 70, 76, 88n, 121–2, 124, 132–3
*Gladiator* 195–6, 209
*The Godfather* 182, 187, 201
Goldwyn, Samuel 28, 133, 161, 184
*Gone with the Wind* 18, 26, 29–30, 34, 182
Grade, Lew 64
*The Graduate* 178, 182, 208, 219
Grant, Cary 29, 179
*The Greatest Story Ever Told* 191, 218
*Green Grow the Rushes* 83–4
Griffith, David Wark 25–6
Guinness, Alec 86, 124
*Guys and Dolls* (film) 133–4, 144

Haigh, Kenneth 97, 169, 193–4
*Hamlet* (play) 87–8, 96–7, *114*, 120–1, 125

*A Hard Day's Night* 194, 208
Harlow, Jean 29, 145
Harris, Richard 154, 176
Harrison, Rex 13, 53–4, 70, 98, *115*, 136, 157–79, 187–9, 192, 197
Hart, Moss 91, 162
Hayward, Susan 68, 144
*Heaven's Gate* 18, 136, 178
Hecht, Ben 28, 67
*Hello Dolly* (film) 178–9, 219
*Henry V* (film and play) 57, 83, 88
Hepburn, Audrey 69, 138, 176–7
Heston, Charlton 12–13, 16, 67, 185, 205, 209, 218
Heymann, C. David 102
Hilton, Nicky 41–2, 128
Hitchcock, Alfred 34, 41, 58, 103
Hopper, Hedda 158, 160, 163, 184, 197
Hordern, Michael 169, 193, 223–4
*How the West was Won* 20, 185
Howard, Leslie 158, 161
Howard, Trevor 154, 156
Hudson, Rock 43, 49, 76, 199

Jackson, Michael 50
James, Clive 220–1
*The Jazz Singer* 28, 142
John, Elton 50
Jolson, Al 28
*Julius Caesar* (film) 75–6, 132–3
Junor, Penny 81, 89

Kamp, David 93, 130, 134–5, 169, 221, 226
Kardashian, Kim 221
Kashner, Sam 214, 224, 226, 229
Keaton, Buster 26, 45
Kelly, Gene 198, 208
Kelly, Grace 107
Kennedy, Jacqueline 15
Kennedy, John F. 55, 75, 184–5, 190, 214–15
Kerr, Deborah 66, 128, 132, 157
*The King and I* 144, 161
King, Martin Luther Jr 30, 190, 205

*King of Kings* 20, 187n, 195
Kubrick, Stanley 64, 194, 213n

*La Dolce Vita* 56, 139
*Land of the Pharaohs* 69
Lane, Jackie 68–9
*Lassie Come Home* 35
Laughton, Charles 154, 163, 194
Lawford, Peter 55
*Lawrence of Arabia* 20, 177, 185, 187, 196
Lean, David 196
Leigh, Vivien 46, 54, 57, *112*, 157, 222
Lerner, Alan Jay 89, 91, 161–2
Levathes, Peter 101–2
Levine, Joseph E. 152–3
Levy, Shawn 103, 137
*Lilies of the Field* 176, 225
*Little Women* 39
Lloyd George, David 104
Loewe, Frederick 161–2
Lollobrigida, Gina 72, 138
*The Longest Day* 20, 97, 146–50, 185–6
*Look Back in Anger* (film and play) 76, 89, 193–4, 222
Loren, Sophia 54, 128, 138, 177, 187n
Lyons, Stuart 209

MacLaine, Shirley 13–14, 66, 143
McCarthy, Joe 183–4
McDowall, Roddy 17, 21, 35, 49, 169
McFarlane, Brian 83–4, 127–8
Maddern, Victor 210
Madsen, Axel 149, 153, 180–1
*Major Barbara* 157, 161–2
Mamoulian, Rouben 13, 62–4, 66, 73
Mankiewicz, Joseph L. 17, 46–7, 75–6, 134–6, 145–6, 149–50, 159, 166, 191–2, 197–8, 203, 205, 220–1
   *Cleopatra*, directs 13, 17, *116*, 118, 130–1, 169–71, 174–5, 190–2
   *Cleopatra*, writes script 67, 118, 169, 190–1
Mankiewicz, Tom 131, 169
Manso, Peter 154–6
Margaret, Princess 106–7

Marsh, Jean 93
*Marty* 67
*Mary Poppins* 177–8
Mason, James 70, 86, 132
Mastroianni, Marcello 139–40
Mature, Victor 85
Maugham, Somerset 27–8
Meikle, Denis 152
Melies, Georges 56
Metro-Goldwyn-Mayer (MGM) 12, 70, 119, 127–8, 133, 144, 153–5, 180–2, 184, 222–5
   and Elizabeth Taylor 35–7, 39–42, 47, 49, 222–5
*Midnight Cowboy* 21, 208
Milestone, Lewis 155–6
Miller, Gilbert 132
*The Mirror Crack'd* 50
*The Misfits* 13, 213
Mitchell, Margaret 29
Monroe, Marilyn 13, 70, 143, 145, 163, 207–8, 229
More, Kenneth 209
Morgan, Piers 145
Mosley, Leonard 120, 135–6
*Mrs Miniver* 35, 180
*Mutiny on the Bounty* 18, 153–4, 185, 226–7
*My Cousin Rachel* 84, 89
*My Fair Lady* (film and play) *115*, 149, 160–4, 176–7, 179, 187

*National Velvet* 35–6, 39
Newman, Paul 176, 208
Nielsen, Leslie 70
Norman, Barry 73
North, Alex 189, 213
Novak, Kim 13–14, 50, 69

*Oklahoma!* (film) 44, 144
Olivier, Laurence 57, 70, 76, 78, 85, 124, 126, 165
Osborne, John 76, 222–3
O'Sullivan, Richard 16, 70
O'Toole, Peter 76, 123, 177, 208

paparazzi 12, 19, 56, 95, 100–1, 103, 137–41
Paramount 40, 69, 143, 228
Parkinson, Michael 125
Parsons, Louella 47, 85, 158, 184
Pascal, Gabriel 57, 161
Peck, Gregory 138, 144
Philip, Prince 71
Piaf, Edith 149
Pickford, Mary 26, 153
Pinewood Studios 13–14, 60–4, 66–8, 70–1, 73–4, 174, 211
*The Pink Panther* 208
*A Place in the Sun* 40–1, *110*, 191, 218
Podesta, Rosanna 13–14
Poitier, Sidney 176, 218
Porter, Cole 84, 161, 163
Presley, Elvis 27, 39, 55, 69
Profumo affair 107–8, 190, 198–9, 212–13
*Pygmalion* (film and play) 161–3

*The Quiet American* 134
Quinn, Anthony 138, 194
*Quo Vadis* *112*, 127–8, 132, 152, 195

*The Rains of Ranchipur* 78, 86
*Raintree County* 41–2, 45, 66
Rattigan, Terence 83, 119, 157, 177, 222–4
Reagan, Ronald 64, 183
Redgrave, Michael 70, 76, 161
Reed, Carol 154, 155
Reeves, Steve 152–3
*Reflections in a Golden Eye* 50, 214
Reynolds, Debbie 12, 47–8, 66, 94
Richardson, Ralph 70, 76, 124, 207
*Robbing Cleopatra's Tomb* 56
*The Robe* 84–5, 92, 127, 195, 199, 218
Roberts, Rachel 165–6, 168, 171, 173, 197
Rodgers & Hammerstein 18, 161
Rolling Stones 148, 215, 217
*Roman Holiday* 138
Rossellini, Roberto 103

Rothwell, Talbot 211
Rutherford, Margaret 223–5

Salamon, Julie 17–18, 24–5
*The Sandpiper* 121
Schlesinger, John 198, 216
Schoenberger, Nancy 214, 226, 229
Scott, Ridley 196, 209–10
Selznick, David O. 28, 34
Shamroy, Leon 17, 168
Shaw, George Bernard 57, 157, 160–3
*The Sheik* 57
Siegel, Sol 155
Simmons, Jean 69, 84
Sinatra, Frank 45, 47, 134, 155, 163, 197, 199
Sinclair, Andrew 49
Skouras, Spyros 11, 69, 72, 85, 122, 145–8, 151, 166
Smith, Maggie 54, 223–4
*Sodom and Gomorrah* 185, 207
*Something's Got to Give* 13, 207–8
*The Sound of Music* (film) 18, 148–9, 156, 161, 178, 182
*South Pacific* 161, 198
*Spartacus* 20, 185, 187, 194, 213
Sprott, Duncan 53
*The Spy Who Came in From the Cold* 120–1
Stanwyck, Barbara 29, 139
*Star!* 178, 219
*Star Wars* 182, 194, 201
Starr, Ringo 124
Stevens, George 40–1, 136, 191, 218
Stone, Oliver 210
*A Streetcar Named Desire* 132, 213
*Suddenly Last Summer* 66, 134, 188, 191

*The Taming of the Shrew* (film) 50
Taylor, Elizabeth 8–16, 19, 49, 68, 77–8, *109–10*, *112*, *114*, *116*, 192–3, 202, 213–14, 216
    AIDS activism 50, 221
    *Cleopatra*, demands over 60, 130–1, 167

*Cleopatra*, fee for 11, 22, 61–2, 69–70, *113*, 166–7, 185, 217
*Cleopatra,* performance in 172, 188, 192, 195–6, 204–5
early life and parents 32–9, 44, 49
films 34–7, 39–43, 49–51, 55, 77, *110*, *112*, 119–21, 128, 134, 188, 216, 222–6
health 13, 61–2, 65–6, 71–3, 97–8, 130–1
marriage to Eddie Fisher 12, 48, 69–70, 94–5, 97, 99–100, 120
marriage to Michael Wilding 42–3, 46
marriage to Mike Todd 43–8, 72
marriage to Nicky Hilton 42, 128
marriages to Richard Burton 92–102, 117–26, 213–14, 222–6
Technicolor 30–1, 44, 184
television 30–1, 44, 55, 58, 143–4, 156, 184, 193, 201, 217
Temple, Shirley 38, 143
*The Ten Commandments* 127, 181
Thomas, Dylan 88–90, 124–5
*Titanic* 20, 182, 228
Todd-AO 30, 44–5, 63, 130–1, 143–4, 191, 198, 203
Todd, Mike 43–7, 72, 93, 130–1, 143, 180
*Tom Jones* 176, 208, 225
Tracy, Spencer 27, 39, 163
Troyan, Michael 131, 218
Twentieth Century Fox 13, 72, 84–6, 131, 133, 142–8, 150–1, 178, 200, 206–8, 218–19, 227–8
  *Cleopatra* 11–12, 14, 18, 21, 57, 59, 68–9, 70, 73, 75, 101–2, *113*, 118–19, 122–3, 134–5, 146–8, 166–7, 173–4, 197, 200, 206
  Rex Harrison 158–9, 166, 171, 173, 178
*The Sound of Music* 18, 149, 156
*Unchained* 213
*Under Milk Wood* (film and radio drama) 49, 88, 125
Ustinov, Peter 127–8

Valentino, Rudolph 26–7, 57
*The V.I.P.s* 50, 119–21, 215, 222–5

Walker, Alexander 163–4, 172, 178, 188, 213–14
Wallace, Lew 181
Walter, Jess 137–8
Wanger, Walter 11, 57–9, 69, 96, 132, 136
  and *Cleopatra* 14, 20, 58–9, 68, 71, 73, 90–1, 101, *113*, 122, 129, 136, 140, 166–7, 170, 173, 203
Wapshot, Nicholas 159, 162, 165
Warhol, Andy 219
Warner Bros 14, 69, 142, 176
Warner, Jack L. 176–7, 179, 183, 203
Wayne, John 40, 57, 138, 147, 218
Welles, Orson 70, 180, 223, 224
*West Side Story* 156, 199
*What's New Pussycat?* 121, 208
*Who's Afraid of Virginia Woolf?* (film) 35, 50, 121, 126
Wilcoxon, Henry 57
Wilde, Oscar 27, 67, 78, 196
Wilding, Michael 42–3, 46, 57n, 198
Williams, Elmo 135, 174
Williams, Emlyn 82
Williams, Kenneth 89, 210–11
Wilson, Woodrow 26
*Wuthering Heights* (film) 29, 180
Wyler, William 16, 138, 148–9, 180–2

*The Yellow Rolls-Royce* 177–8, 224

Zanuck, Darryl F. 84, 86, 97, 122, 135–6, 142–50, 158, 174–5, 185, 200, 208, 218
Zimbalist, Sam 181
*Zorba the Greek* 208
*Zulu* 120, 200